The Splendor of Marriage

The SPLENDOR *of*
Marriage

ST. JOHN PAUL II'S VISION OF
Love, Marriage, Family,
&
the Culture of Life

RICHARD A. SPINELLO

Angelico Press

First published in the USA
by Angelico Press 2018
Copyright © Richard A. Spinello 2018

For information, address:
Angelico Press, Ltd.
169 Monitor St.
Brooklyn, NY 11222
www.angelicopress.com

ISBN 978-1-62138-389-5 pbk
ISBN 978-1-62138-390-1 cloth
ISBN 978-1-62138-391-8 ebook

Book and cover design
by Michael Schrauzer
Cover Image:
Raphael, *Wedding of the Virgin* (detail)
Source: Wikimedia Commons

For the Padrevitas
Anna, Gloria, and Rose

The truth about creation and the truth about God as the Creator is the first step the human mind takes towards God. This first step seems very difficult to many people today due to certain cognitive assumptions that have developed in the modern understanding of the world. This understanding is devoid of transcendence.... The discovery of the Creator is not only the belief in the First Cause, which is Esse Subsistens. *It is also — and first and foremost — the discovery of love. To create means not only to reveal power, omnipotence that surpasses all, but also it means: to give being, existence, and goodness, therefore to love.*

Pope Saint John Paul II
Spiritual Diaries

CONTENTS

PREFACE

The final battle between the Lord and the reign of Satan will be about marriage and the family. Don't be afraid because anyone who works for the sanctity of marriage and the family will always be fought and opposed in every way, because this is the decisive issue.

—Sister Lucia

WHEN CARDINAL CARLO CAFFARA WAS charged in 1981 with starting Pope John Paul II's Pontifical Institute for Studies on Marriage and Family, he wrote to Sister Lucia dos Santos of Fatima. Sister Lucia was one of the three children who saw the visions of Our Lady at Fatima, and she lived in seclusion in Portugal. Cardinal Caffara was only seeking her prayers, and yet she wrote back to him a long letter. The letter included this frightening prophecy: the last confrontation between God and Satan would be over marriage, the most ancient sacrament. A fleeting glance at the latest cultural chaos is enough to confirm that this prophecy is now being fulfilled. We seem to have been suddenly thrust into a titanic struggle for the dignity of marriage and the dignity of the human person.

The Catholic Church has always resisted the siren call of social mores and fashionable trends when it theologizes about marriage. It has continued to uphold a model of marriage centered on procreation and the education of children. However, there is a widespread conviction that those teachings are an irrelevant relic. Marital permanence and heterosexual marriage are lovely ideas whose time has come and gone. People prefer a nonjudgmental approach to sexual morality, and a willingness to adapt the institution of marriage to the latest social trends. Unfortunately, Catholics are not immune from these tendencies. At a well-known Catholic university, a group of scholars recently gathered to discuss Pope Francis's exhortation *Amoris Laetitia*. Rather than affirm the Church's teachings, they expressed their hope that the Catholic Church would finally get beyond its obsession with the sixth and ninth commandments. What's needed in this historical moment, they proclaimed, is more flexibility and pastoral sensitivity rather than insistence on ancient dogmas.

Saint John Paul II may not have known about Sister Lucia's vision. But from his first days as a priest and teacher he spoke about the sacredness of marriage, which is the pillar of civilization. Although many popes have stepped forward to defend Church doctrine on monogamous and indissoluble marriage, none have done so as imaginatively and extensively as Saint John Paul II. In inspired documents such as *Letter to Families*, the Pope directs our attention to the causes of today's marriage crisis, which are rooted in a rejection of human nature and the whole natural order. This rejection leads to confusion about basic notions of personhood, sexual identity, and freedom. The Pope tangles with the high priests of modern philosophy who seek to re-write the "truth about man" (RH 1). In a distinct and original voice, John Paul II resolves this confusion and defends a proper understanding of marriage consistent with natural law and the Gospel. He also turns to Scripture in order to recapture the Creator's divine plan for marriage expressed so transparently in the words of Genesis. By retrieving man's original experience, we can gain that sense of immediacy and freshness that is sometimes lost when these teachings become dogmatic formulations.

The need for this retrieval has certainly taken on new immediacy since the Pope's death in 2005. In *Familiaris Consortio* John Paul II implied that the traditional Christian understanding of marriage was being slowly hijacked by "appealing ideas and solutions" that were incompatible with the dignity of the human person (FC 4). Unfortunately, even more revolutionary proposals about marriage have been set forth since that papal letter was written in 1981. The dilution of doctrines such as marital permanence entices many Catholics, including some bishops and cardinals. Same-sex marriage has also become an "appealing" idea, even though it ignores how sexual reciprocity and procreation are central to any reasonable definition of marriage. Similarly, transgender ideology dismisses human bodily identity and sexual difference willed by the Creator. And the metaphysical poverty of the cognitive elites filters their gnostic views of marriage and sexuality. Thus, the epic confrontation disclosed by Sister Lucia continues to intensify.

Those who dare to enter onto the battlefield will need weapons. And some of the most potent weapons are the refined writings of Saint John Paul II. The simple aim of this book is to make those writings more accessible and to highlight his account of the Church's vision for marriage, love, life, and family. That vision must not be allowed to lie dormant or to be dissolved into the darkness of postmodern relativity.

ACKNOWLEDGMENTS

I AM MOST GRATEFUL FOR THE SUPPORTIVE ENVIronment for research and writing at Boston College. A special thanks to Ezabel Lynch for helping me to acquire some of the research material used in preparing this book. I also owe a debt of gratitude to my colleagues and students at St. John's Seminary in Boston with whom I have discussed some of the ideas in this book. And my thanks to the priests and parishioners at St. Mary of the Assumption parish in Dedham, Massachusetts, where Pope John Paul II is held in the highest esteem. I am especially grateful for the prayerful support of friends and family, particularly Edith Fiore and Mary Burton. A special word of thanks to our pastor, Father Wayne Belschner, and his assistant, Father Mark Storey, for their moral and spiritual support.

My deepest gratitude goes to the editors at Angelico for their professionalism and editorial skills. I am particularly grateful to John Riess for his confidence in this project. I am also indebted to my wife, Susan, for reading and editing the first draft of this book. Her constant encouragement has been an immeasurable benefit to me during the solitary hours spent writing four books on the late Holy Father's works. She first introduced me to the writings of John Paul II, and her passion for this subject matter matches my own.

Richard A. Spinello
Totus Tuus
December 12, 2017
Feast of Our Lady of Guadalupe

ABBREVIATIONS

ENCYCLICALS OF JOHN PAUL II:

DV	*Dominum et Vivificantem*
EV	*Evangelium Vitae*
FR	*Fides et Ratio*
RH	*Redemptor Hominis*
VS	*Veritatis Splendor*

In all cases the editions used have been published by Pauline Books and Media and use the official Vatican English translation. See the bibliography for full citations.

OTHER WRITINGS OF JOHN PAUL II/KAROL WOJTYŁA:

AV	*The Anthropological Vision of* Humanae Vitae
CTH	*Crossing the Threshold of Hope*
FC	*Familiaris Consortio**
GM	*Gift and Mystery*
LF	*Letter to Families**
LR	*Love and Responsibility*
LW	*Letter to Women**
JS	*The Jeweler's Shop*
MD	*Mulieris Dignitatem**
MI	*Memory and Identity*
PC	*Person and Community*
RF	*Radiation of Fatherhood*
RW	*Rise, Let Us Be on Our Way*
SC	*Sign of Contradiction*
TB	*Man and Woman He Created Them: A Theology of the Body*
JPSW	*Pope John Paul II Speaks on Women*

*References are to paragraph numbers in this book. For all other works references are to page numbers.

DOCUMENTS OF VATICAN II

GS   *Gaudium et Spes*

LG   *Lumen Gentium*

Unless otherwise noted, the translations used are my own based on the Latin texts found in Norman Tanner (ed.), *Decrees of the Ecumenical Councils*, vol. 2.

OTHER PAPAL WRITINGS/VATICAN DOCUMENTS

ADS   *Arcanum Divinae Sapientiae* (Pope Leo XIII)

CC   *Casti Connubii* (Pope Pius IX)

DOV *Donum Vitae* (Congregation for the Doctrine of the Faith)

HV   *Humanae Vitae* (Pope Paul VI)

ONE

The Pope of the Family

I N THE DIM LIGHT OF DAWN, WORKERS WERE MAK-
ing last minute preparations in Vatican Square for an unprecedented
event. On this Divine Mercy Sunday, April 27, 2014, two Popes were
to be canonized: Pope John XXIII and Pope John Paul II. Churches in
Rome had remained open the night before the canonization ceremony for
mass and prayer vigils. Pilgrims clutching umbrellas were already making
their way into the square. They came from everywhere but most especially
from Poland, John Paul II's beloved homeland. During his own papacy
John Paul II had made the canonization ceremony a common event in
the "eternal city." He canonized 482 saints in 51 ceremonies.

Fortunately, despite the low-hanging clouds, the spring rains held off
as the ceremony finally got under way. The Swiss Guard in their blue and
gold uniforms overlooked rows of bishops and cardinals. Behind invited
guests and dignitaries a massive crowd extended from Vatican Square
down the Via della Conciliazone to the Tiber River. At a simple mass
presided over by Pope Francis, his two distinguished predecessors were
declared the newest saints of the Catholic Church as a light wind rippled
through the square. Pope Francis presented heroic portraits of both men,
who lived through some of the darkest days of the last century. In Poland,
church bells pealed when their native son was proclaimed a saint. As the
crowds melted away after the canonization mass, the skies opened up.
The countless pilgrims who had come to honor these two Popes didn't
seem to care. They departed Rome with fond memories after witnessing
this latest chapter in the Church's long papal history.

During the days leading up to this memorable event, various articles
and essays appeared about the greatly admired Pope John Paul II. Some

commentators talked about his formidable personal talents, his farsightedness, and his geopolitical deftness. Others reminded their readers of his pivotal role in the downfall of the Soviet Union. Catholics focused on his renewal of Marian piety, his promotion of the Divine Mercy devotion, his World Youth Day initiative, and his tireless ecumenical efforts. John Paul II sowed the seeds of renewal in the Catholic Church through his call for a new evangelization. He fought tirelessly to defend the life of every human person, especially the most vulnerable. His papal encyclicals and letters reaffirmed Catholic theology and quietly dispelled any lingering rumors of impending doctrinal changes. All of these important accomplishments during his twenty-seven year papacy merit high praise.

There is another important legacy, however, that deserves close attention. Saint John Paul II left the Church an inspired body of teachings about love, marriage, and family that goes well beyond his ground-breaking work on theology of the body. With his simple eloquence, Pope Francis reminded people of this particular legacy during his homily at the canonization mass. "In his service to the People of God," said the Pope, "Saint John Paul II was the pope of the family."[1] When Pope Francis made this statement there was sustained and prolonged applause. Everyone present seemed to realize that this was a most fitting title for the Church's newest saint. Pope Francis also called upon Saint John Paul II to guide the Church as it sought to heal the wounds inflicted on the embattled institution of marriage.

Beyond any doubt, this Pope of the Family can inspire us from his place in the heavenly kingdom. But he can also guide the Church through his superior theological reflections, which have undoubtedly elevated Catholic doctrine on marriage and family. Above all, the Pope's exposition on spousal love and marriage proposes a radical alternative to the sexual revolution still sweeping over the barren cultural landscape. In this brief chapter we shed some light on that alternative by reviewing the Pope's vital contribution to the Church's understanding of marriage and family. But we begin with an overview of the reflections offered by his predecessors, which serve as a suitable springboard for examining the Pope's writings.

---

1 Pope Francis, "Holy Mass and Rite of Canonization of Blesseds John XXIII and John Paul II" (homily, St. Peter's Square, Rome, Italy, April 27, 2014), accessed March 22, 2016, http://w2.vatican.va/content/francesco/en/homilies/2014/documents/papa-francesco_20140427_omelia-canonizzazioni.html.

Marriage and the Magisterium

John Paul II was certainly not alone in taking a stand against a cultural climate increasingly hostile to the tradition of marriage. Other modern popes have consistently reinforced Church teaching on marriage and family life, often with sharp spiritual insight. Earlier threats to the institution of marriage included attacks on its sacramental value along with claims that the marital act could be detached from its procreative purpose. These issues were addressed in three major encyclicals and a number of papal allocutions. In 1880, Pope Leo XIII dealt with the first threat. He authored an encyclical called *Arcanum Divinae Sapientiae*, which saw a dual purpose in marriage: propagation of the human race and an enhancing of each spouse's life through "their great mutual love" (ADS 10). Marriage is not just a civil contract, explained Pope Leo, because it has God for its Author. Moreover, Christ Himself "raised marriage to the dignity of a sacrament,...and gave power to attain holiness in the married state" (ADS 9). Therefore, liberal civil divorce laws could never supersede the divine law of exclusivity and indissolubility.

The drive for artificial birth control use accelerated in the early decades of the twentieth century, only to be met with valiant resistance by the papacy. In his noted encyclical, *Casti Connubii*, Pope Pius XI argued that the primary end of marriage was "procreation and the education of children" (CC 9). The Pope explained that the fostering of conjugal love and fidelity was a secondary end or "blessing" of marriage. But Pope Pius XI also argued that marriage should be looked at "not in the restricted sense as instituted for the proper conception and education of the child, but more widely as a communion, companionship, and association of life as a whole" (CC 48). Like *Arcanum*, *Casti Connubii* offered a forceful defense of the perpetual bond of a married couple that cannot be dissolved by man or state. Both encyclicals also struck a more "personalist" tone that underscored how marriage enriches a person's life and enhances his or her dignity.

Pope Pius XII was preoccupied with the savagery of World War II and the political turbulence of post-war Europe, but he was not silent on these matters. In a moving allocution to Italian obstetricians he, too, insisted that contraception interfered with the integrity of the marital act.[2] Also, in the encyclical *Humani Generis* he underscored the obligation of Catholics to give religious assent to *all* Church teachings, including those on sexual morality.

Finally, Pope Paul VI's encyclical, *Humanae Vitae*, issued in 1968, was a graciously written statement about the dangers of uncoupling the unitive and procreative dimensions of the marital act. According to Paul VI, it remains the Church's "constant teaching" that every marital act must be oriented to the procreation of new human life (HV 14). A contraceptive sexual act can never be an act that expresses conjugal love. Contraception threatens marriage because it can "open wide the way for marital infidelity" (HV 12). This affirmation of the prohibition against direct human intervention in procreation established a critical threshold for Catholic morality, especially as the Church grappled with new reproductive technologies such as in vitro fertilization and human cloning.

Pope Paul VI's teaching on marriage was not confined to the issue of contraception. He called attention to the "most serious role of parenthood," a mission that sets marital union apart from other human bonds such as friendship (HV 1). Yet the Pope never referred to children as the "primary end" of marriage. Instead he presented a more integrated vision: "Husband and wife, through that mutual gift of themselves, which is specific and excusive to them alone, develop that communion of persons, in which they perfect each other, so that they may cooperate with God in the generation and rearing of new lives" (HV 8).[3]

All of these encyclicals and papal pronouncements outline a coherent theology of marriage that is further elaborated in the Catechism and in Canon Law. These doctrines were also reaffirmed by the Second Vatican Council, most especially in the document *Gaudium et Spes*. *Humanae Vitae* closely echoes the key sections of *Gaudium et Spes* that deal with marriage. Those sections condemn both abortion and contraception, and confirm that true conjugal love must "preserve the full sense of mutual self-giving and of human procreation" (GS 51). The Council Fathers go on to say that married couples "cannot rightly follow ways judged wrongful by

2   Pope Pius XII, "Allocutio Conventui Unionis Italicae inter Obstetrices," *Acta Apostolicae Sedis,* 43 (1951): 835–39.

3   See also Germain Grisez, *Living a Christian Life* (Quincy, IL: Franciscan Press, 1993), 566. This translation of *Humanae Vitae* has been amended by Grisez.

the Magisterium in its interpreting of divine law" (GS 51). That statement is followed by references to the condemnation of contraception expressed in the writings of Pope Pius XI and by Pope Pius XII.[4]

In addition, *Gaudium et Spes* directs our attention to the personalist dimension of marriage, which is "an intimate partnership of married life and love" (GS 48). This vision of marriage goes beyond juridical terms and stresses that marriage is a covenant rather than a contract. While marriage is most important for its role in the continuation of the human race, it also has an enduring impact on the personal development and eternal destiny of each member of the family. None of this new language, however, contradicts papal teaching about the permanence of the marital bond. The Council Fathers explicitly assert that "this sacred bond...does not depend on human decision" (GS 48). That bond is unbreakable and indissoluble: it is formed not only by the spouses but by God Himself, for "it is God who is the author of marriage" (GS 48). Finally, *Gaudium et Spes* wisely reminds Catholics that the graces of matrimony extend for the life of the marriage: "By virtue of this sacrament, as spouses fulfill their conjugal and family obligation, they are penetrated with the spirit of Christ, which suffuses their whole lives with faith, hope, and charity" (GS 48).

John Paul II's Contribution

John Paul II's extensive reflections on marriage amplify and enrich the disciplined work of the Council and the wisdom of popes like Pius XI. He more fully unveils the mystery of sexual love, which gives marriage and family its indelible shape. Moreover, John Paul II doesn't treat these matters in an isolated encyclical or a brief pastoral letter or two. Rather, these themes permeate his papal and pre-papal writings. The prolific vitality of this Pope on the themes of marriage and family is without precedent in papal history. His theology of marriage is reinforced by the rational arguments of philosophy and even the suggestive imagery of literature. The challenge, therefore, is to integrate these copious reflections, which are scattered across so many different documents, letters, and books, into a single, unified perspective.

4 John Finnis, "On Retranslating *Humanae Vitae*," in *Religion and Public Reasons*, ed. John Finnis (Oxford: Oxford University Press, 2011), 345–46.

Consider just *some* of the works in the Pope's ample treasury of writings about marriage and the family. Before he was Pope, Karol Wojtyła wrote a famous play on marriage (which was later made into a movie) called *The Jeweler's Shop*. Another play called the *Radiation of Fatherhood* deals with the parallel themes of parenthood and fatherhood. One of his crowning philosophical achievements is a book called *Love and Responsibility*, which delves into the qualities proper to love. In addition, there are numerous philosophical essays dealing with the themes of marriage and family life such as "The Anthropological Vision of *Humanae Vitae*." As Pope, he dedicated 133 Wednesday audience talks to the theology of the body, which have been collected in a popular book called *Man and Woman He Created Them: A Theology of the Body*. These talks seek to comprehend the predetermined duality of man and woman in creation as well as the language of the body. After the 1980 Synod on the Family, he composed a stirring apostolic exhortation on marriage and family life called *Familiaris Consortio*. In 1994 he issued another remarkably rich reflection on these topics called *Letter to Families*. His apostolic letter, *Mulieris Dignitatem* (1988), specifically addresses feminine gifts that contribute so much to family and culture. That was followed up by the "Letter to Women," issued in 1995 as a support for those attending the United Nation's Beijing Conference, which focused on issues such as contraception and population control.

If we read and ponder these different works, what emerges is a consistent vision of love, marriage, family, and the culture of life. The Pope's robust declarations represent an original and persuasive response to the shallow sexual morality proposed by the champions of the global sexual revolution. In his mind, the defense of marriage and family is a defense of the person, who needs this intimate communion in order to flourish. This conviction explains his insistent focus on marriage and family in a world that had many other serious problems such as poverty, political oppression, and war. The Pope clearly saw the immense confusion resulting from the sexual revolution that has led people to affirm everything from genderless marriage to serial cohabitation. At the same time, the negotiable marriage contract has slowly displaced permanent vows that rescue us from our self-centered desires and emotional whims.

At the heart of the problems that plague marriage and family life lies a deep intellectual crisis that the Pope once described as a general "crisis of meaning" (FR 81). Society is hopelessly confused because it has broken away from the truth about God and "the full truth about man" (LF 20). In *Letter to Families* the Pope laments this severe "crisis of truth," that amounts to a "crisis of concepts" (LF 13). People do not understand familiar words such as "love," "freedom," "sincere gift," and even "person," since those words no longer "convey their essential meaning" (LF 13). When we lose the meaning of words like "love" and "self-giving" we cannot understand what marriage or family is all about. "Contemporary man remains to a great extent a being unknown to himself," writes the Pope, "consequently the family too remains an unknown reality" (LF 19).

With this in mind, let us review seven key themes articulated in the Pope's writings on marriage and family that will shape the discussion of this book. Since John Paul II was convinced that we will never understand marriage unless we understand ourselves, he constructs an "anthropology of the Gospel" as the foundation for a credible theology of marriage (TB 545). A human being is a person, a natural unity of body and soul capable of self-determination and self-giving. This person is a social being who flourishes only by being immersed in communion and community. When a man and woman give themselves totally to each other they form a personal communion that is the basis of a lifelong, fulfilling marriage. Marriage, therefore, is rooted in human nature. To understand that nature correctly, however, we must fathom that the masculine or feminine body, as informed by the soul, *is* the person. If we misconceive the body as sub-personal, we cannot begin to appreciate the nature of total marital self-giving that is expressed in the conjugal act. Thus, the Pope's anthropology is centered on the ideas of person, gift, and communion, and loudly echoes the teachings found in Sacred Scripture.

Only a person, who is made in God's image and likeness, is capable of love and self-giving. However, man's hedonistic tendencies have muddled the meaning of romantic love. Just as people are confused about what it means to be a person, they are confused about love. Few twentieth-century philosophers have given much thought to this issue, but Karol Wojtyła remedies this glaring deficiency in *Love and Responsibility*. Here he provides a comprehensive account of love and its implications for sexual ethics. Special attention is given to spousal love, that total mutual self-gift that is the basis for the permanence and exclusivity of marriage.

Thus, the second theme is the unique character of spousal love, which is the only form of love with a sexual nature.

Since spousal love does have a sexual nature it is necessary to examine how our sexual powers can be used in a manner that is proper to our status as persons rather than objects for use. The third theme, therefore, is the Pope's "personalistic approach" to sexual ethics (PC 283). A person uses his or her sexual powers responsibly when he or she respects both the generative purpose of the sexual drive and the dignity of the person, who must always be affirmed for his or her own sake. A couple should be well disposed toward sexual morality anchored in the value of the person before they become husband and wife.

The fourth theme is the Pope's view of marriage as a covenantal communion rather than a contractual relationship. The Pope's account of the marriage covenant, based on mutual self-gift of spousal love, is profoundly enhanced by his theology of the body. From the logic of spousal love and the Gospel, it follows that marriage is defined by three fundamental properties: real unity, absolute fidelity, and fruitfulness. The Pope also gives us a deeper insight into sacramental theology. He explains why marriage is not only the "primordial sacrament," but also the "prototype" of all the sacraments of the new covenant (TB 511).[5]

This fruitful marital union achieves even greater fulfillment as a family. And so the fifth theme is the family as a community of persons where children must be valued for their own sake and shaped into mature persons who can become a gift for others. In order to fulfill this demanding educational mission, the family requires "sovereign power" (LF 17). The Pope's earnest reflections on family sovereignty and family rights add new depth and richness to the Church's social magisterium. The Pope also spotlights the family as a domestic church that participates directly in Christ's saving mission.

The sixth theme is the Pope's original defense of *Humanae Vitae*, which is grounded in the doctrine of personalism. The Pope believed that married couples who dismissed the teaching of this encyclical and turned to contraception were doing great harm not only to their marriages but to their own personal dignity. The problem is that contraceptive, sterilized

5   Marc Cardinal Ouellet, *Mystery and Sacrament of Love*, trans. Michelle Borras (Cambridge, UK: Eerdmans, 2015), 45–57.

sex is depersonalizing because a man and woman are transformed into sexual partners rather than husband and wife. Depersonalized sex, whose aim is pleasure, lacks any unifying power: it is not capable of creating or enhancing marital unity. Spouses must respect the unitive and procreative meaning of the sexual act and "live together in the inner truth of the 'language of the body'" (TB 658).

Finally, the Pope wisely exposes the interdependence between a strong marriage culture and a culture of life. The same cultural forces that undermine a commitment to the sanctity of life undermine the integrity of marriage. Positive convictions about the sterility of sex and artificial contraception provide the setting that promotes abortion and artificial procreation. A culture that respects life and the fruitfulness of marriage cannot be fostered without a responsible attitude toward human sexuality that recognizes the unbreakable connection between spousal love, sexuality, and procreation.

The unifying thread throughout these various discussions is spousal love. Some critics question the validity of total self-giving, claiming that it's either impossible or inconsistent with individual liberty. But in the thought of John Paul II, spousal love is tightly linked to marriage, parenthood, sex, and procreation. Without spousal love understood as mutual self-gift, the whole edifice collapses. Strip away total self-giving and dedication from marriage and the case against indissolubility becomes more plausible. Absent spousal love, the marriage vows begin to lose their sacramental quality. Spousal love preserves the generative meaning of the one flesh union that leads to the creation of new life. And the self-sacrifice required by spousal love prepares a couple for parenthood.[6]

Our main objective in the chapters ahead is to explore the qualities of spousal love along with these other basic themes so that we can better understand the natural realities of marriage and family. We will also review some interrelated issues such as John Paul II's reflections on the personalistic norm and the virtue of chastity. We begin by exploring some of the current threats posed to marriage in light of the Pope's neglected work, *Sign of Contradiction*. As this book explains, Jesus's teachings on the meaning and purpose of marriage are countercultural, a sign of contradiction in

---

6 Scott Yenor, *Family Politics* (Waco, TX: Baylor University Press, 2011), 250.

a secular age with its sexually permissive and anti-life tendencies. However, "Jesus proclaims the truth about marriage," and the Pope's aim is to reassert and defend that truth (LF 18).

Conclusions

Saint John Paul II truly is the Pope of the Family. This Pope always personified hope and moral clarity even in times of despair and desolation. During his long papacy, John Paul II was one of the foremost cultural voices resisting the tyranny of sexual progressivism and defending the Christian vision of marriage and human sexuality. He adamantly resisted the popular notion that marriage is a socially constructed institution that can be divorced from procreation and the education of children. Also, no Pope has ever spoken so passionately about "fairest love, which *always begins with the self-revelation of the person*" (LF 20). And no Pope has so resolutely defended the sacramentality of indissoluble marriage and the sovereignty of the family from the siege of secular triumphalism.

TWO

Marriage and its Enemies

O N A CHILLY WINTER MORNING UNDER A DOVE-gray sky, Cardinal Karol Wojtyła ambled along through a deserted Vatican square on his way to Saint Mathilda's Chapel in the Apostolic Palace. It was early March, 1976, and the Cardinal had been invited to preach the Lenten Retreat to Pope Paul VI and the senior members of the Roman Curia. The seventy-eight-year-old Pontiff wore his customary Lenten hair shirt under his white cassock. The Pope, somewhat frail and tired-looking, was in the twilight of his papacy. Cardinal Giovanni Battista Montini was elected Pope Paul VI in 1962 during the Second Vatican Council. Regrettably, his papacy was thrust into some turmoil over the torrent of hostility provoked by his 1968 encyclical *Humanae Vitae*. The Pope did little to quell the dissent or address the rising tide of secularism, as he watched scores of men and women abandon the priesthood and religious life.

As a result, the last eight years of his pontificate had been a time of growing discord and anxiety in the Church. Some Catholic theologians had brazenly proclaimed that the *Humanae Vitae* encyclical was a great mistake and an "albatross around the Church's neck." In the "spirit of Vatican II" they questioned the Pope's teaching authority and proposed that the Magisterium's teaching must be balanced against other points of view. One theologian flippantly remarked that the encyclical was just the private theological opinion of the Bishop of Rome. The clear implication of these statements was that rival teachings could be given the same weight as the doctrinal assertions of the Pope. However, these dissident theologians seemed to conveniently overlook the actual language of Vatican II documents like *Lumen Gentium*: "The Roman Pontiff, by reason of his

11

office as the Vicar of Christ, has full, supreme, and universal power over the whole Church" (LG 22).[1]

Despite the lingering controversy, Pope Paul VI, now peaceful and stoic, carried on as head of the Church. Although he appeared diffident in the face of dissent, the Pope was still determined to convey the moral strength and authority of the papal office. During the days and weeks prior to the retreat, Pope Paul had been making tentative plans for a trip to the United States. He hoped to attend the Eucharistic Congress that was to be held during the summer in Philadelphia. But the Pontiff was informed by his close aides and doctors that his health couldn't tolerate such an arduous undertaking and eventually these plans were cancelled. On March 5, just days before the retreat, a close confidant and Secretary to the Italian Episcopal Conference, Monsignor Enrico Bartoletti, unexpectedly passed away, adding to the Pope's travails. The Lenten retreat would be a welcome relief from all these setbacks and disappointments.[2]

The Cardinal meanwhile had the opportunity to prepare for this papal retreat in the beautiful resort city of Zakopane-Jaszczurowka, located at the foot of the imposing and snow-covered Tatra mountains. He stayed at the Ursuline Sisters' convent, enjoying the chance to pray and think about his upcoming sermons and meditations. In spite of the frigid weather, he frequently walked around the convent grounds to help collect his thoughts. Some days, during the wispy mid-day snow, the vigorous Cardinal Wojtyła would venture up in to the mountains for a brief ski break. On March 1, after a noon session with his bishops in Krakow, he departed for Rome by way of Warsaw. He spent a few days at the Polish College in Rome, revising his work before the retreat got underway. The retreat began on March 8 and concluded with a 9:00 a.m. conference on March 13. On his final day in Rome the future Pope had a brief audience with Paul VI before returning to Poland.[3]

---

1 See Ralph McInerny, *What Went Wrong with Vatican II* (Manchester, NH: Sophia Institute Press, 1998), 33–35.

2 Peter Hebblethwaite, *Paul VI: The First Modern Pope* (New York: Paulist Press, 1993), 658–63.

3 Adam Boniecki, *Making of the Pope of the Millennium: Kalendarium of the Life of Karol Wojtyła* (Stockbridge, MA: Marian Press, 2000), 697. See also George Weigel, *Witness to Hope* (New York: Harper Collins, 1999), 223–25.

Cardinal Wojtyła's prophetic and mystical mind was on full display in the sermons and colloquies he delivered to Pope Paul VI and his Curia. To some extent, the retreat represented an impassioned resistance to the cultural and social forces gathering momentum in the 1970s. The Cardinal's realism collided with the more optimistic tone of Vatican II's *Gaudium et Spes*. But Wojtyła seemed to sense that the repudiation of *Humanae Vitae* was a portent of things to come in the escalating battle between the Church's teachings and the principles of sexual liberation. Wojtyła peered into the abyss and saw the imminence of a more secularized and disruptive culture with the Church in "the front line [of] a lively battle for the dignity of man" (SC 24).

In the peaceful and secluded chapel, adorned in Lenten purple, Cardinal Wojtyła's first invocation paid tribute to Pope Paul VI for his humble service to the Church. His supportive words must have comforted this beleaguered Pope. After reflecting on Psalm 139, Wojtyła turned to the hymn of Simeon in Luke's Gospel. His special focus was on the reference to the infant Jesus when He is presented at the Temple by Mary and Joseph: "Behold, He is set for the fall and the rising of many in Israel, and as a sign of contradiction" (Lk 2:34). In these troubled times, the words of Simeon acquire renewed relevance. This prophecy will be the "connecting thread" of all the meditations to follow (SC 7).

It's not hard to see that by evoking this image Cardinal Wojtyła was referring to the Pope's contested teaching on contraceptive intercourse. Simeon's prophetic remark is the "key to understanding the various symptoms displayed by modern life,... which are of continual concern to the Holy See" (SC 7). Cultural currents distant from the Catholic faith have "contradicted" the unambiguous teaching of Jesus Christ on sexual morality in favor of human autonomy and the quest for sexual satisfaction. Inspired by this dramatic shift in the culture, many Catholics rashly concluded that the traditional teaching on contraception was no longer valid. Simeon's prophesy, therefore, points to the recalcitrance against *Humanae Vitae*, which resisted this popular sentiment. The encyclical refused to relax Church doctrine on the procreative purpose of sexuality and the immorality of positive contraception. It steadfastly opposed cultural "progress" in the name of the Gospel. Yet this teaching continues to be criticized for two reasons. First, it does not take into account the personal experience of many married couples. Second, it is at odds with the desire of Catholics to assume more responsibility for making their own moral decisions. "Inevitably," explains Cardinal Wojtyła, "the Church's activities and those of the Supreme Pontiff in particular, often become a 'sign of contradiction'" (SC 124). The problem is a failure to understand that the moral law involving contraception is not an encumbrance. Rather, it liberates man and woman so that they can become a total gift for each other.

His audience, including Pope Paul VI himself, seemed totally absorbed in Wojtyła's moving presentation, which reflected a self-confidence rarely found in the Church these days. Cardinal Wojtyła published these striking meditations in a short book known as *Sign of Contradiction*. That book clearly anticipates an escalating and determined resistance to Church teaching on marriage, family, and related doctrines. Wojtyła's penetrating inquiry can help to frame a concise review of the social trends aligned against marriage, these new and dangerous "symptoms" of modern life. When Cardinal Wojtyła became Pope John Paul II, he continued to elaborate many of these same themes throughout his papal encyclicals and exhortations.

The Message of Sign of Contradiction

In these richly allusive meditations Wojtyła sets out to interpret "the signs of our times" (SC 35). What he finds is a powerful clash between the whole truth of Christ and the secular spirit of this age, which is no longer open to the transcendent truth of revelation. Since the Church's authoritative teachings reflect that truth, they will be aggressively resisted, particularly by Christianity's erudite despisers. The implication for the Church's unwavering defense of an orthodox view of marriage is clear: the clergy and laity must expect unremitting opposition and even persecution for their efforts.

We can appreciate the dynamics of this conflict by consulting the Book of Genesis. One cannot grasp the human condition and the plight of modern humanity "without having first read and pondered very deeply the first three chapters of Genesis." The Cardinal goes on to say that "these [three chapters] are the key to understanding the world of today, both its roots and its extremely radical...affirmations and denials" (SC 24). Life is an ongoing conflict between the truth revealed by God and the web of Satan's deceptions, which seduce humanity into renouncing its dependence on the Creator.

A major theme of Genesis given prominence in *Sign of Contradiction* is the pre-established order of creation. Every being conceived by the Creator, including the human person, has a fixed nature and purpose in accordance with the divine plan. Moreover, this created world is not absolute. We are *creatures*, completely dependent on the Creator for our continued existence. At the same time, the innate goodness of all creation reveals that the motive of the Creator is love. The Creator does not create from necessity, but out of an overflowing goodness that is shared with all of existence. This loving God enjoys His own infinite goodness and wants to share it with other creatures made in his image.

The Creator's covenant with man is based on that love, but also on the moral truth inscribed in the natural order. The tree of knowledge symbolizes "being and value"; it represents an objective morality and our preordained destiny established by the provident Creator. This tree also represents the limits imposed on the creature by the Creator, limits that are designed for the creature's own good and fulfillment. The values revealed to man by his own human nature securely guide him to fulfillment and the fullness of perfection as a being made in God's image.

Yet, from the very beginning, humanity proceeds down a dark path of defiance and contempt. The human soul rebels against the order of the cosmos. It turns away from God and the "truth of creation" in order to follow its own pragmatic truth (SC 20). In the Garden, Adam and Eve ate the forbidden fruit believing it would transform them into God-like beings who could shape objective reality along with their own moral destiny. But the rebellion did not end there. Spellbound by Satan's deceits, man has continued to reject the givenness of his own human nature and to overthrow the limits of creation. Full of hubris, people become convinced that the moral meaning of the universe depends solely on their own subjective opinions and creative powers. By dispensing with the natural order, man gives birth to the dream of absolute freedom, which transplants the Promethean myth "into the soil of Genesis," and "prizes man as if he were God" (SC 32).[4]

There are many modern versions of this capitulation to the serpent's

4 Eric Voegelin, *Science, Politics and Gnosticism* (Wilmington, DE: ISI Books, 2004), 28.

temptations. The motives are always the same: self-sufficiency and independence from the moral law's restrictions. There is a desire to ignore
the cosmic order and invent one's own morality. Saint Paul describes
those who "exchanged the truth about God for a lie, and worshipped and
served the creature rather than the Creator" (Rom 1:25). This lie, which
promises unfettered freedom and power, is quite attractive. It takes hold
within communities and even whole cultures. As a result, in the course
of human history, the human person becomes subject to rule by "the
Word and the anti-Word, the Gospel and the anti-Gospel" (SC 29). In the
inverted world of the anti-Word, the requirements of the covenant and
its moral law are disavowed as man throws off his creaturely status and
recklessly tries to assume complete control of his future.

In this way Satan has infected humanity with a rebellious attitude that
positions him "outside the truth" (SC 30). The bold lie of Satan accepted
by Adam and Eve establishes the pattern for all later temptations and
transgressions against the divine order. The duplicitous "father of lies"
sets in motion a chain of events that gives rise to the world "as a terrain
of struggle between man and God," a terrain marked by the "created
being's defiance of his Creator" (SC 32). Tracing the route of the anti-Word
through history begins with this distortion of the truth about God and
His covenant and leads to man's ultimate denial of religious transcendence
and the necessity of eternal truth.

While this struggle is a familiar one throughout human history, Wojtyła
worries that Satan's message has now found a particularly hospitable climate
where it can take root and flourish. The tendency to dethrone the Creator
in favor of humanity's absolute freedom and self-sufficiency has already
made great strides in the twentieth century. "Perhaps," speculates Wojtyła,
"we are experiencing the highest level of tension between the Word and the
anti-Word in the whole of human history" (SC 34). Especially worrisome
at the time was the rise of atheistic humanism, which esteems godless man
who is closed to the notion of a universal morality based on our God-given
human nature. This exclusive humanism, given voice in the thought of
popular thinkers like Friedrich Nietzsche, Karl Marx, Sigmund Freud, and
Jean-Paul Sartre, strips man of his transcendent character and confines
his horizons to this world. Nietzsche's great wish is fulfilled, since man is
finally faithful only to the earth. Man without God, he writes, is a "bridge

to the highest hope, the rainbow after a long storm."[5] Now man is alone, "independent of good and evil, independent of God" (SC 35).

The human person is no longer seen as the perfection of creation but as a purely material and ordinary being. She is reduced to her biological needs and simple aspirations, which can be met by the heroic state (Marx). Or the person is regarded as a conscious being who is completely free to assert himself, to pursue his own ends rather than those inscribed in his nature by the Creator (Sartre). These Western intellectuals and their facile ideas deeply disturbed Cardinal Wojtyła. He confided to a close friend that he was chiefly troubled by the wildly popular thought of Sartre because he misrepresented the meaning of freedom and argued for a self-made morality. Perhaps few people today speak about Marx or Sartre, but traces of their ideas can be found in the "new atheism" and society's pursuit of a libertarian utopia.[6]

Marx and Sartre, of course, were not the only ones who sought to reconfigure our natural human condition. Radical feminism was on the rise during the 1970s, and the gay rights movement was stirring underneath the surface. For feminists like Simone de Beauvoir, marriage as envisioned by the Creator was not a response to every person's need for love. Marriage was a human "tragedy" that repressed women and needed to be reconstructed.[7] More recently, gay rights activists have redefined the meaning of sexuality and rejected the traditional family as a natural reality established by the Creator.

At their core, these ideologies embrace an anthropocentric liberty that idolizes the human being and her desires. They reject the natural order and refuse to affirm the created universe as a gift to human persons from the personal Creator. They also quietly set aside the ideals and norms of the Gospel, especially those pertaining to sexual morality. Also, in disclaiming the gift of the natural order, they ignore the truth of human sexuality, which is imprinted on our male and female bodies. In place of immutable moral rules symbolized by the tree in the Garden is the

---

5 Friedrich Nietzsche, *Also Sprach Zarathustra* (Stuttgart, Germany: Philip Reclam, 1951), 47.

6 Stanisław Grygiel, *Discovering the Human Person: In Conversation with John Paul II*, trans. Michelle Borras (Grand Rapids, MI: Eerdmans, 2014), 80.

7 Simone de Beauvoir, *The Second Sex* (New York: Vintage, 1989), 477–78.

presumption that every individual can choose for herself what her real "nature" is to be. People can make their own moral choices about how to keep pace with the explosion of sexual expression in the twenty-first century. They forget that "man's dignity can be preserved only if human freedom is exercised justly and responsibly" (SC 124).

According to this progressive worldview, marriage does not mean the one-flesh heterosexual union described in Genesis. Marriage is not a means for the person to realize his or her vocation to "exist 'in relationship,' in 'self-giving'" (SC 132). On the contrary, the structure of marriage and family is purely arbitrary and open to negotiation. Divine revelation is superseded by the superficiality of sexual politics and social convention.

In the United States, the principle of moral independence has been enshrined in the legal system. People now have a legal *right* to invent their own version of morality even if it stands in direct opposition to natural reality and God's divine law. In the U.S. Supreme Court case of *Planned Parenthood v. Casey* upholding abortion rights, the court grounded its dubious decision in broad liberties supposedly protected by the Constitution. It went on to proclaim that "at the heart of liberty is the right to define one's own concept of existence, of meaning, of the universe, and of the mystery of human life."[8] Echoing *Casey*, the court also claimed in a later case that "our obligation is to define liberty for all, not to mandate our own moral code."[9] When freedom is empty, and man has no limits on his conduct except what he voluntarily imposes on himself, the Promethean myth has become ever more deeply implanted in the soil of modernity.

Despite this rebellion, we must remember that God never abandoned his original plan for our salvation. "From the moment of the first denial, Truth — the divine Truth — will always seek in ways known only to itself, to penetrate world history, to enter the minds and hearts of men" (SC 48). To redeem fallen humanity, God penetrated history in a penultimate way by sending His Son. In the life of Jesus, we find a new and complete revelation of the "great heart," God the Father.

But the Messiah's message of disciplined love and self-sacrifice was also cast aside in favor of the continuing seductions and false promises of

8 *Planned Parenthood of Southeastern Pa. v. Casey* 505 U.S. 833 (1992).
9 *Lawrence v. Texas* 539 U.S. 558 (2003).

Satan. Nonetheless, Christ's self-revelation through the Paschal mystery serves as an inspiration and a *provocation* to a sinful world. Christ has confronted men and women, who prefer to follow the lead of their own pride and concupiscence rather than His radical self-giving love, which leads to the Cross. This is the fundamental contradiction "aroused by the teaching and behavior of the teacher from Nazareth" (SC 86).

The Redeemer's provocative teaching always reminds us that God made human persons with a privileged status and invites them to share in His divine life as His sons and daughters. All men and women are challenged by the Word, who proclaims the truth about "the great dignity of human nature" (SC 102). That nature is fulfilled not through sexual indulgence or the exercise of blind power, but through freedom that respects the natural created order. It is no surprise, therefore, that Jesus's instruction on marriage (such as Matthew 19) reinforces the teaching of Genesis, which reveals the "divine plan of truth and life" (SC 54). Ultimately, we can take refuge in God's fidelity. The Father's "great heart" that was open to man in the beginning never withdraws or closes when faced with the lie, "but sheds over the whole of human history…the light of boundless hope" (SC 48).

Marriage and the Anti-Gospel

The anti-Word refers to doctrines, beliefs, and even whole ideologies that are militantly at odds with the divine plan of creation, effective from the beginning and reaffirmed in the Gospel. The refusal to live by the moral law symbolized in the tree of good and evil was the "original sin." Through the Decalogue and other means, God continued to reveal that law through the chosen People. The self-revelation of God through His Son also includes the same clear moral principles, such as the absolute prohibition against adultery. Our "moral grandeur" has its foundation in conscience that obeys those objective moral principles based on the "divine law of love" (SC 140–41). Whatever contradicts and subverts that divine law is part of the anti-Word.

Those masters of suspicion, Freud and Marx, have laid much of the groundwork for overthrowing God's plan for marriage. The Freudian vision of sexual indulgence strikes at the heart of the Gospel's doctrine on the suitable use of man's sexual powers. Marxism seeks the abolition of culture and its traditional understanding of marriage and family because they are obstacles to its new classless society. Cultural Marxists, who still inspire many progressives, are not reticent about the need to "smash monogamy," and challenge outdated conventions about marital permanence. In their incredible book called *Commonwealth*, contemporary Marxists Michael Hardt and Antonio Negri argue that the family is a "pathetic" institution, a machine that grinds people down and undermines the common good. The world's spirit and vitality will be revived only when people are finally emancipated from the family.[10]

Many similar ideas have now been woven into a subversive anti-Gospel that contradicts the essential truth about marriage presented in the second chapter of Genesis. Not only was the created world a gift to Adam and Eve, but they were also gifts to each other through their masculine and feminine bodies. Their "reciprocity was to be the mark of their lives as human beings of different sexes" (sc 55). Men and women need each other for procreation, but also find themselves in the other. Jesus has also re-promulgated the Genesis teaching that a married man and woman are no longer two but one flesh, a whole new sacred reality (Mk 10:2–12; Mt 19:3–9). Opposition to this biblical idea of marriage represents the anti-Gospel because it transparently contradicts the Word of God. Let us consider some of the specific contemporary prejudices against this traditional view of marriage and how they have corrupted a proper understanding of marital union consistent with the natural law and the Gospel.

First, the imperial sexual revolution has convinced many people that sexuality has neither a procreative purpose nor a naturally given structure. The body and its sexual powers are instruments of the person's freedom and will. A person can use them for pleasure or for whatever purpose he or she deems appropriate. These deceptions open the door for immense confusion about marriage. The integrity of the conjugal act is destabilized when it is no longer seen as an expression of spousal love, a unitive and generative act proper only within marriage. If procreation is deliberately frustrated, marital relations can degenerate into a destructive hedonism.

---

10 Paul Kengor, *Takedown: How the Left Has Sabotaged Family and Marriage* (Washington, DC: WND Books, 2015), 98–104, 174.

Under the influence of Freud and his determined disciples, society endorses "free love" and recreational sex. Sexual relations outside of marriage have become normative. The result of this promiscuity is children born out of wedlock, children who do not have the benefit of being raised and formed by both a mother and a father. The proclamation of sexual liberation in the 1960s began to sound the death knell for traditional heterosexual marriage that same-sex marriage advocates would soon hear.

Second, many people no longer think that children fulfill a marriage or that the meaning of marriage is the family. Thanks to certain elements in the radical feminist movement and the work of organizations like Planned Parenthood, children are often perceived as a burden rather than a blessing and the fruit of conjugal love. Feminist orthodoxy insists that women should have the same rights as men. Therefore, they should be free to enjoy sex as men do, and this means that they should not be penalized with unwanted offspring. This specious argument based on a false egalitarianism provides the rationale for artificial contraception and abortion. In recent years, women have claimed the right to free contraception, and those who oppose this right are accused of orchestrating a "war on women."[11]

The eugenicist and Malthusian movements have also propagated the idea that children are a social and economic burden for the whole society. Margaret Sanger, the founder of Planned Parenthood, was a well-known eugenicist who believed that birth control was the key to preventing the planet from being overrun with what she called the "feeble-minded." The neo-Malthusians, inspired by the economist Thomas Malthus, worried that overpopulation would contribute to social chaos and economic misfortune. A surplus of people can be avoided through preventative measures such as abortion, birth control, and childless marriages. While Malthusian projections about a "population bomb" have been sensibly discounted, there remains a belief that overpopulation is at the center of humanity's most intractable problems, from genocide to environmental degradation and global warming. These apocalyptic environmental fears have inspired a strident anti-family rhetoric that also tears at the fabric of marriage.

11 Ryan Topping, *Rebuilding Catholic Culture* (Manchester, NH: Sophia Institute Press, 2012), 182–91.

Third, opposition to the traditional and biblical vision of marriage also comes from those who assert that sexual reciprocity is not essential to marriage. Marriage is no longer universally regarded as the gift of man and woman to each other, "the gift of one's humanity, the man's masculinity, the woman's femininity, the procreative ability of both" (SC 56). Advocates of same-sex marriage have taken the extraordinary step of redefining marriage, which is no longer an exclusive and unique heterosexual bond. Instead, marriage has become merely an association between two individuals who form an intimate, emotional connection. This thin and indefensible definition negates the divine plan that puts procreation and the rearing of children at the heart of marriage. Marriage is about fruitful spousal love in which a man and woman unite spiritually, emotionally, and physically in a personal union that is fulfilled by children.[12]

The redefinition of marriage crystallizes the bold disobedience of this new age, which rejects the preordained duality of man and woman who unite to become a total bodily gift for each other as spouses. This vision of marriage, so clearly expressed in Genesis, is reinforced by Jesus Himself (Mt 19:3–9), who is "the teacher of truth" (SC 85). By repudiating marriage as a one-flesh union (Gn 2:24) for the sake of fruitfulness (Gn 1:28), humanity "places itself outside the truth...outside the law of dependence on the Creator" (SC 30).[13]

Added to these biases is another that is quickly gaining traction. The drive for "gender expression" also calls into question the natural division of the human species into male and female genders determined at the moment of conception. Transgender ideology rejects the full truth of sexual differentiation. It repudiates the idea that a person has a given nature determined by his or her physical reality and falsely claims that a human person can change his or her sex. The transsexual person discards the physical reality of masculinity or femininity given in nature and instead assumes to be someone different. A transsexual woman, for example, believes that because "inside" she feels like a man, she should have a male body. Others are convinced that, contrary to nature, they do not fit into either gender and cannot be referred to as "he" or "she."

---

12 Patrick Lee and Robert George, *Conjugal Union: What Marriage Is and Why It Matters* (New York: Cambridge University Press, 2014), 47.
13 Kengor, *Takedown*, 198.

Such gender fluidity with no fixed borders for sexual identity or expression seems to inspire some people who falsely believe that this is a step toward greater freedom. The spiritual self, unconstrained by physical reality, fashions its own identity through a creative assertion of the will. However, transgenderism and its permutations are yet another manifestation of the anti-Word that seeks to undermine the sexual nature of the human person in its duality of man and woman. There is an obvious refusal to recognize the "impassible limits" on man's freedom, which cannot contradict the order of creation. [14]

Traditional marriage, therefore, must now contend with these strong cultural currents aligned against the gift of monogamous and heterosexual marriage as it was given to humanity at the dawn of creation. According to these expressions of the anti-Gospel, sensuality is a good in itself and need not be integrated into spousal love, children are often a burden rather than a blessing, and the use of our sexual capacities does not have a natural, generative purpose. Not only is marriage redefined, but so are family relationships, which are often simply reduced to functional roles. The result, however, is often endless confusion, especially about the identity of a child's mother and father. Is the father the man who donates his seed, or the one who cares for the child? Is the real mother the surrogate who bears the baby in her womb, the woman who donates her eggs for artificial reproduction, or the woman who brings up this child? Regrettably, the Creator's plan for marriage as a one-flesh heterosexual union open to new life has been artfully deconstructed and proudly re-fashioned by judges and activists. Those who dispute that plan have been duped yet again by the temptation "to prize man as if he were God" (SC 32). This is an ominous moment that opens a new chapter in the drama of history that is all too often shaped by rebellion against the Creator.

As a result of these contradictions to the Word, many no longer believe that the institution of marriage has its own fixed nature. They do not accept marriage's natural reality as revealed in Genesis. They easily fall

---

14 Claire Chretien, "Satan's 'Last Barrier' to Destroying Mankind is Male/Female Duality," *LifeSite News*, September 18, 2017, accessed September 20, 2017, https://www. lifesitenews.com/news/deceased-dubia-cardinal-destruction-of-natural-human-sexuality -is-the-last-barrier-to-destroying-mankind. See also Katherine Kersten, "Transgender Conformity," *First Things*, December, 2016, 25–31.

for the manipulation of the truth by the mass media that "panders to the cult of sensationalism" (sc 121). But Christ emphatically proclaimed the truth about marriage, which like all divine truth must be "accepted as the greatest treasure of the human spirit" (sc 120).

Christ's Church has been determined to resist this dramatic change in the perception of marriage. Given these irreversible cultural trends, this resistance assures that it will become a persecuted countercultural Church as Wojtyła predicted. Anyone committed to defending the sanctity of life and the moral propriety of traditional marriage will become a human sign of contradiction. Triumphant secularism has even become a threat to intellectual freedom, as it strives for the abolition of truth. Those who sincerely attempt to conserve the truth about marriage and family risk condemnation and marginalization. But all Christians are called to defend "the truth of the faith and the moral life" with courage and clarity (sc 124).

However, there is an unfortunate tendency for some Catholics, including the clergy, to go along with secular morality, to breezily exchange "relevance for truth" (FR 77). They seek compromise with secular culture's moral innovations. As a result, they fail to defend the moral truth about sexuality and marriage revealed in Tradition and Sacred Scripture. Egoism and concupiscence lead some astray. Others are convinced that marital permanence and fruitfulness are "ideals" that are just too difficult for many couples in the modern world. Still another segment of the faithful adopts a posture of indifference or complacency. They fail to grasp the depth of this struggle and the urgent need to commit themselves fully to Jesus Christ, "the great Prophet" (sc 120). They do not understand that in a fallen world Satan's anti-Word still poisons the air. Human pride and self-sufficiency always raises its voice in contradiction to the crucified Christ's call for humility, self-giving love, and submission to the truth of creation. Christ paid a high price for our redemption and we too must sometimes pay a price for fidelity to the true Word.

Conclusions

Cardinal Wojtyła's pastoral meditations during the Lenten retreat must have left a deep impression on his captive audience in Saint Mathilda's chapel. The mature Cardinal's sermons, sometimes full of emotion, brought these listeners "face to face" with the truth contained in the utterance of Simeon about man's rebellious spirit (sc 8). They also provided insight into the relevance of the Genesis narrative, the opening book of the Bible that never ceased to captivate Wojtyła even when he became Pope. A careful study of creation, the first covenant, and the Fall is of paramount importance for rediscovering our identity as human persons endowed with great gifts but subordinate to the Creator. Genesis is also the key for interpreting the antagonistic relationship between the Church and modern culture. From the moment of the first disobedience, the world became "a terrain for struggle between man and God," where "human pride seeks not the glory of God but its own greater satisfaction" (sc 32). We see this epic struggle now playing out in the acrimonious debate about marriage. The clear norms of heterosexual union, marital permanence, and monogamy are part of a moral hierarchy that has lost its relevance in a hyper-sexualized culture. Thus, the words of Genesis and Jesus ring hollow as the secular anti-Gospel gains greater prominence. The ultimate message of *Sign of Contradiction* is that the Catholic Church faithful to the Word must always be a countercultural Church that fears God more than man.

THREE

Personhood, Freedom, and Sexual Identity

C ARDINAL WOJTYŁA BECAME POPE JOHN PAUL II in the fall of 1978. His first few years in the papacy were filled with the trials and tribulations common to being a world leader. The rebellious Solidarity labor movement in Poland had made great strides, thanks in large part to the Pope's visit there in 1979. The Soviet Union was growing increasingly impatient, and in December 1980, a planned Warsaw pact invasion of Poland was barely averted. The Pope sought to defuse tensions in East Europe with a letter to Leonid Brezhnev urging him to stay out of Poland's internal affairs. Political turmoil persisted in Central America with the Church often in the crosshairs. In 1980, four American churchwomen were ruthlessly murdered in El Salvador. The Pope was also distraught over the state of the Church in Hungary. Since the departure of the anti-Communist Cardinal Mindzenty, Catholic leadership refused to assert itself against the Communist regime. The Pope sent the Hungarian bishops a strongly worded letter urging them to fight against state regulations of religious education. But John Paul II's greatest trial still lay ahead.[1]

On May 13, 1981, the Feast of our Lady of Fatima, Mehmet Ali Agca, a young Turk, carried out his plan to assassinate the Pope. Like any pilgrim, he had easy access to St. Peter's Square, where the Pope was set to appear for his usual Wednesday audience. The spring sun was rich and mellow that afternoon as the platform was set up for the Pope's brief address. The Pope was in cheerful spirits. For lunch, he dined with his good friends,

---

1 Weigel, *Witness to Hope*, 371–72.

Professor Jerome Lejeune and his wife. At 5:00 p.m., the compact pope-mobile drove through the Archway of the Bells into the square, where a joyful throng greeted the Holy Father. Agca stood behind the first row of pilgrims and fired two shots at point blank range. The Pope was struck in the abdomen and was thrust back into the arms of his startled secretary, Monsignor Dziwisz. He was immediately rushed to Gemelli Hospital. In the ambulance he continually pronounced the same words in Polish: "Jesus...My Mother..."

The press was quickly informed that the Pope had been taken directly into surgery. Several anxious hours followed. Distraught Catholics poured into Vatican Square to await some official word of the Pope's condition. Shortly after midnight there was good news. The surgery had been a success and the Pope's full recovery seemed likely. He had suffered a devastating wound, but the bullet missed the main abdominal artery by a fraction of an inch. Had the artery been struck he would have bled to death before reaching Gemelli. The Pope was convinced that his life was spared by Our Lady of Fatima. "One hand fired and another guided the bullet," he would later confide to his friends (MI 159).

This fateful day in May was supposed to have been memorable for a different reason. The Pope had planned to announce the formation of The Pontifical Institute for Studies on Marriage and Family. But given the dramatic events, the announcement was postponed until October 7, 1982 when the Institute's Apostolic Constitution, *Magnum Matrimonii Sacramentum*, was finally published. In that constitution, the Pope explained that the institute was established "so that the truth of marriage and family may be given closer attention and study."[2] It was located at the Pontifical Lateran University in Rome. In addition to Rome, the institute now holds sessions in many countries, including the United States, Spain, Mexico, and Brazil.

John Paul II's close friend, Stanisław Grygiel, recounts that the Pope had long dreamed of such a university, dedicated exclusively to intensive study of marriage and family. He also dreamed of a special university where the truth of man would shine forth. The Pope recognized that we cannot

---

2 John Paul II, "Magnum Matrimonii Sacramentum," *Acta Apostolicae Sedis* 74 (1982): 918–30.

understand marriage and family without knowing the most important truths about the human person. Those truths will reveal how marriage is firmly grounded in human nature. Philosophical anthropology, which considers the question "what is a human being?" had always been the chief focus of his academic studies and scholarly writing. Also, the Pope once remarked that as he discovered his vocation to the priesthood, "man became the central theme of my pastoral work" (CTH 199).[3]

The truth about the human person had been suppressed under the totalitarian regimes that menaced Poland and other Communist countries during the last several decades. Life was all about serving the collective rather than fulfilling the needs of the individual or the family. The utopian state was conceived as the answer to each person's deepest aspirations. This negation of individuality undoubtedly accounted for the Pope's passion about this issue. But in the West that truth had been subverted by the opposite sentiment: an inflation of individual sovereignty, which promotes self-sufficiency and independence. This mentality has now become entrenched in Western culture. It has also formed the values and governed the lives of several generations. Individualism easily devolves into narcissism or an exclusive obsession with vanity and self-entitlement. In America, this brand of individualism began to emerge in the 1950s. The "big idea" books of this era, such as David Riesman's *The Lonely Crowd*, claimed unabashedly that the highest moral good was personal enrichment and self-advancement. Other writers began to draw attention to the simple formula of self-achievement as the bridge to authentic fulfillment.[4]

There is little doubt that these views have had a destructive impact upon social institutions like marriage and the family. Individualism tends to loosen personal bonds rather than to strengthen them. The self-absorbed individual might be true to himself, but he cannot possibly be true to the ideals of marriage. For such an individual, the purpose of marriage and conjugal love becomes self-satisfaction rather than mutual self-donation. Marriage must satisfy one's own emotional, psychological, and spiritual needs. Each partner in such a relationship seeks to "get" rather

---

3 Grygiel, *Discovering the Human Person*, 120–21.

4 Barton Swaim, "The Roots of the Culture War," *The Wall Street Journal*, April 7, 2014, A17. See also Charles Taylor, *Ethics of Authenticity* (Cambridge: Harvard University Press, 1991), 2–4.

than to "give." Of course, those who have brushed aside the centrality of self-sacrifice and self-donation have greatly misunderstood the essential meaning of marriage.

Individualism is usually linked with a deformed view of the human person. We might label this "secular anthropology," which is the antithesis of the "anthropology of the Gospel" (TB 545). The person is falsely conceived either as a purely material being or as conscious freedom, with a body exterior to his or her real inner self. The self is a mind or spirit that is free to manipulate and subdue the non-personal body and even choose its own gender. Moreover, the person is seen as an isolated individual who is only accidentally related to others. Relationships are not a natural human good that perfects us. Rather, they are formed for the sake of utility and mutual pleasure. Thus secular anthropology is dualistic, individualistic, and hedonistic. It is totally divorced from the reality that fulfillment is achieved in the gift of self, which creates communion with others.[5]

This narrow anthropological vision, now a part of secular society's desolate landscape, conceals the truth about the human condition. It creates intellectual confusion that "profoundly disturbs the human soul," and causes the soul to "wander in myths" (VS 30). And since the person is now a being "unknown to himself," marriage and family remain an "unknown reality" (LF 19). We must disentangle these myths and retrieve the proper anthropological foundation of marriage that has been eroded by this complete subversion of the Genesis narrative. Antecedent to an adequate understanding of marriage and family is a careful discernment of what it means to be a person, "somebody" rather than "something." As a rejoinder to secularism and individualism, the Pope presents a personalist anthropology that defends the person's elevated status and social nature.

Who is the Human Person?

Karol Wojtyła's major philosophical work, *The Acting Person*, is one of two books that explore his philosophy of personalism with its emphasis on the dignity and "interiority" of the human person. This philosophy seeks to

5   Antonio Lopez, "Marriage's Indissolubility: An Untenable Promise?" *Communio* 41 (2014): 274–76. See also Robert George, "Gnostic Liberalism," *First Things*, December, 2016, 33–38.

approach the person as she experiences herself from within, in her own existential uniqueness but always in relation to others.[6] Wojtyła's difficult book is focused primarily on the theme of human action and is beyond the scope of our discussion. Equally brilliant, *Love and Responsibility* is a far more accessible work, a polished account of responsible sexual conduct. *Love and Responsibility* was published in Poland in 1960, expanded in 1962, and first translated into English in 1981.[7] This meditation on love, unflinching in its criticism of sexual license, begins with a discourse on the nature of the human person.

Every person, explains Bishop Wojtyła, belongs to the human species, and this accounts for our common identity that Adam first observed when he encountered Eve. If we were not all essentially alike, we couldn't point to the reality of our common "humanity," and thereby vanquish spurious claims of racial superiority or ethnic inferiority. But a human being is more than just a member of the human species. Wojtyła explains that "the human being holds a position superior to the whole of nature" (PC 178). The reason for this superiority is that a human being is also a person. The term "person" signifies that there is something more to man than belonging to a species, a "particular fullness and perfection of being" (LR 4).

Every being has a certain nature, essential qualities that make it this kind of being and not some other kind. Cats and trees are very different because they do not share the same essential features. What sets the person apart from all other creatures and accounts for its excellence is its rational nature made possible by the soul. In this life, the soul, which is created directly by God at the moment of conception, is inseparable from the body. The soul is the natural form of the body and shares its spiritual existence with that body so that it becomes a spiritualized human body, quite different from an animal body. When the soul dies it retains its own act of spiritual existence, which it no longer shares with the body. Human acts, such as knowledge and creative imagination, are performed by the

---

6 W. Norris Clarke, "The Integration of Person and Being in Twentieth-Century Thomism," *Communio* 31 (2004): 434–44.

7 The edition and translation used throughout this book will be the following: Karol Wojtyła, *Love and Responsibility*, trans. Grzegorz Ignatik (Boston: Pauline Books and Media, 2013). This is a more precise rendition of the original Polish than the first English translation published in 1981.

whole "I" through a close collaboration of soul and body. The person, therefore, is a natural unity of body and soul, a finite *embodied spirit*.[8]

The soul has primacy, however, because of its higher powers of intellect and will that begin with the body but well exceed its capabilities. Thanks to the soul, the "human being is a person, a subject who decides for himself" (MD 18). A person, for example, might make a series of free choices such as going to a doctor and taking unpleasant medicine for the sake of improving her health. Only a person can consciously envision something as a good (such as restoring her health) and carry out intentional actions designed to achieve that goal. The person lives out his or her life from within and is "more interiority than a body" (LR 245). Thus, we cannot judge a person only by her external actions but by her intentions as well. A humorous but poorly phrased congratulatory note might be a means of ridicule or a clumsy attempt at praise. It all depends on what this person *intends* to communicate through her words.[9]

The person is also incommunicable. "No one else can will in my stead. No one can substitute his active will for mine" (LR 6). I can't transfer my inner life to another person—I do my own willing and thinking. These activities, rooted in powers of the soul, cannot be delegated to someone else. Incommunicability is closely linked with free will and self-reliance. James may want Jane to love him and care for him, but no matter how persuasive he may be, he cannot make this choice for Jane. She must make the choice to love him through her own free will. Part of the mystery of personhood is this "impassable boundary" between people like James and Jane "that is determined precisely by free will" (LR 6).

Despite the soul's preeminence we must not neglect the contribution of the body, which belongs essentially to the human person. Our bodies can sometimes seem like machines, and they can make us vulnerable to objectification. However, the body is "authentically human and…determines man as a person" (TB 164). The soul bestows a spiritual meaning upon the body. As John Paul II expressed in *Letter to Families*, "the body can never be reduced to mere matter: it is a *spiritualized body*, just as

8 W. Norris Clarke, *The Creative Retrieval of St. Thomas Aquinas* (New York: Fordham University Press, 2009), 177.

9 John Finnis, *Intention and Identity* (Oxford: Oxford University Press, 2011), 134. See also Clarke, *Creative Retrieval*, 177–79.

man's spirit is so closely united to the body that he can be described as an *embodied spirit*" (LF 19). The spiritual soul endows the body with its form or structure. It is through the body animated by this soul that the person gives himself. The person discovers in the body "the anticipatory signs, the expression and promise of the gift of self" (VS 48). What the Pope means is that the body is ordered to the communion of persons, including the most intimate communion of marriage.

Thus, the body shares in the person's moral subjectivity, especially because of its capacity for self-gift that has been inscribed by the Creator. This is why the person is "also in all [her] bodiliness similar to God" (TB 164). As we will see, the body expresses the truth of a sacramental marriage. The conjugal act that consummates marriage is not produced by either the body or the soul alone, but by both together in a single integrated act. And since the body is part of our personal reality, we cannot treat human bodily life at any stage of its existence as sub-personal.

The soul makes possible self-possession, which is the most fundamental characteristic of personhood. This self-possession, which becomes evident in the examination of human experience, is expressed in two ways. First, the person has self-awareness or self-knowledge. Only a person can identify herself. Unlike animals, she can utter the word "I" and know that it refers to her. Second, a person "possesses himself and determines himself" because he has mastery or control over his actions (LR 280). This power of self-determination, which is actualized by the will, enables the person to be responsible for his or her choices and actions. Each person is her own master and therefore shapes her own destiny.[10]

Freedom, therefore, is a distinctive mark of personhood. But freedom is widely misunderstood and often exaggerated as sheer spontaneity and open-ended possibility in opposition to all naturally given limits. The modern person imagines herself free enough to determine the sexual meaning of her own body. In *Veritatis Splendor* the Pope warns about opposing freedom to our bodies or physical nature. He criticizes those who treat "the human body as a raw datum devoid of any meaning and moral values until freedom has shaped it in accordance with its design"

---

10 See Thomas Aquinas, *Summa Theologiae*, 5 vols. (New York: Benziger Bros., 1948), I, q. 30, art. 4.

(vs 48). On the contrary, the freely acting human subject is always a body-soul unity in which body and soul cooperate with each other. For example, a person is not "free" if she exercises control over her fertility through contraception or sterilization. There is a failure to see that the body and its fertility is part of her identity as a moral subject and part of the gift of self that can be fruitfully given to another.[11]

Freedom aims at those goods that fulfill us, and love is the highest good. As Wojtyła explains, "freedom is for love, for through love man most fully participates in the good" (LR 117). Every person needs the love of others because fulfillment is achieved through personal communion, which is created by mutual self-giving. But love requires self-mastery, "the mature possession of one's own 'I' in its bodily and emotional subjectivity" (TB 652). No person is truly free unless she is able to rise above unruly passions or biases that interfere with sincere self-donation. Freedom always possesses this "*relational dimension*" because it seeks true goods such as marriage and friendship that build up communion and community (EV 19).

Universal Human Identity and Sexual Difference

No anthropology is complete without a thoughtful consideration of the human person's sexual identity. According to the provident Creator's divine plan, "the human being should always and only exist as a man or a woman" (MD 1). Masculinity and femininity represent two distinct "incarnations" or two different ways "in which the same human being, created in the image of God is a body" (TB 157). Our sexuality, therefore, is not something incidental or superficial, but part of our substantial nature as a human person. There is no human personhood apart from sexuality. Someone can still be a person without any hair on his head, but that someone must always be a man or a woman. We can never discount our sexual embodiment in developing a full understanding of what it means to be a person. In addition, sexuality is personal, not sub-personal: it cannot be reduced to what is "merely biological" and outside of our personal being. Maleness or femaleness affects the whole person.[12]

11 Michael Hanby, "A More Perfect Absolutism," *First Things*, October, 2016, 25–31.
12 Earl Muller, "The Nuptial Meaning of the Body," in *John Paul II on the Body*, ed. John McDermott (Philadelphia: St. Joseph's University Press, 2007), 87–120.

The Pope often describes man and woman as a dual unity or "unity of the two" (MD 7). They are identical because they share the same essential human qualities of reason and free will. But they are also different, and that difference is discovered primarily through the body. They are both persons, but they are sexually diverse persons. When Adam encounters Eve he immediately recognizes their identity ("this at last is bone of my bones, flesh of my flesh," Gn 2:23). He readily perceives that this woman is "another I" who is just like him. But he also observes that she is quite different, for there is another way of being human, another way of being a person that is simply not available to him. This "lack" or incompleteness is part of our human finitude. If a person looks deeply enough into himself he will appreciate this limitation and insufficiency. But this lack is not the end of the story. When a man and woman join together in marriage, they complement each other. According to the Pope, "*'masculinity' and 'femininity' are distinct*, yet at the same time they *complete and explain each other*" (MD 25).[13]

It is important, however, not to assume that sexual difference amounts only to having a different male or female body. As the Pope pointed out in a 1995 Wednesday audience address, "sexuality...reaches the deep structures of the human being" (JPSW 274). Similarly, the philosopher Edith Stein (St. Theresa Benedicta of the Cross) has demonstrated how sexual differences are not determined just by the physical body, but also by the way the soul operates and expresses itself through a male or female body. Body and soul, which form a natural unity, contribute to the meaning and structure of each other. Sexual differences, therefore, must go much deeper than the body and its sexual attributes, because they affect one's whole personality and self-expression.[14]

How are men and women different? In Edith Stein's view, women are more subjective than men, far less interested in abstract ideas or concepts. Women are more motivated by being with other persons and serving them. While men tend to be intellectual and emotionally aloof, women are more reliant on their emotions as a guide to their behavior. Women are also far more sensitive and attuned to the emotional needs of others,

13 Angelo Scola, *The Nuptial Mystery* (Grand Rapids, MI: Eerdmans, 2005), 33–35.
14 Edith Stein, *Self-Portrait in Letters 1916–1942* (Washington, DC: ICS Publications, 1994), 98–100. See also David Schindler, *Ordering Love* (Grand Rapids, MI: Eerdmans, 2011), 244-46.

including their children. According to Stein, "The strength of woman lies in the emotional life...."[15]

This sexual difference makes possible a total union of persons, which overcomes our solitude. Man and woman are whole unified beings, not androgynous parts of a whole. But this complementary sexual differentiation is the pathway to a more complete and higher unity based on an intimate mutual gift mediated through the body. Only a man and woman can form such a unique and intimate union. As the Pope explains, "This conjugal communion sinks its roots in the natural complementarity that exists between man and woman" (FC 19).[16]

Every person's innate need for the other implies that he or she becomes a more complete self only with another's help. Unlike the low anthropology favored in secular society, Christian personalism insists on man's relational nature. "Man cannot exist alone"; he can exist *only in relation to another human person* (MD 7). Thus, there is no authentic "I" without a "We," since the person knows herself only in dialogue and communion with others. And the paradigmatic human relationship is the communion of love between a man and a woman.

Secular anthropology, which amounts to self-centered individualism, easily loses sight of the reality that fulfillment is not found in isolation but only in communion with other human persons. It is also bedeviled by a crude dualism that separates the material body from the conscious mind that controls it. Its failure to integrate biological forces and sexual difference into the unity of the person obscures the role of the body and sexual difference in the language of human love and the gift of self. But the Christian idea of the human person, defended by the Pope, always sees that person as an integrated whole of body and soul. Therefore, masculinity and femininity are part of the richness of the total gift of self that creates this conjugal communion of love.[17] Given the human condition, including our incompleteness and relational nature, we can understand

15 Edith Stein, "Spirituality of the Christian Woman," in *Essays on Woman*, trans. Freda Oben (Washington, DC: ICS Publications, 1996), 96. See also Regina van den Berg, *Communion with Christ* (San Francisco: Ignatius Press, 2015), 62–64.

16 Scola, *Nuptial Mystery*, 13, 94.

17 Michael Hanby, "The Civic Project of American Christianity," *First Things*, February 2015, 33–39.

why the gift of marriage, first given to Adam and Eve, is so important for our fulfillment and personal maturity.

Personhood and Being

Pope John Paul II realized that we could never achieve a full appreciation of the human person without a metaphysical perspective. This intellectual commitment stands in direct contrast to the anti-metaphysical bias of the current age. While the Pope was open to new philosophical approaches, he never turned his back on the core metaphysical teachings of St. Thomas Aquinas. Metaphysics simply refers to the study of being, and considers this fundamental question: What do all beings or all things that exist have in common? To complete the picture of what it means to be a person we need the help of metaphysics.

According to the Thomistic tradition, every being, whether it is a rock, a tree, a cat, or a person, is an *act of existence*. As such, it is actively present to other beings, and stands out from sheer nothingness. Everything that exists manifests itself and makes a difference in some way. It is the nature of being, therefore, to naturally express itself in self-communicating action. According to Aquinas, "from the very fact that something exists, it is active."[18] Every being spontaneously overflows into action for two reasons: That being is poor and seeks to enrich itself as much as possible by those around it; and that being is also endowed with the richness of existence, which it tends naturally to share with others. This doctrine can be explained as the self-diffusiveness of the good: every being by virtue of its existence is good and seeks to share its riches and perfections. According to Wojtyła, "the natural perfection of being is expressed…according to the well-known Latin saying *bonum est diffusivum sui* [the good is diffusive of itself], which was readily invoked by St. Thomas" (LR 245).[19]

In the life of the person, the act of existence becomes enlightened self-presence, a presence not just to others but also to oneself. Only a

---

18   Thomas Aquinas, *Summa contra Gentiles*, trans. James Anderson (Notre Dame: University of Notre Dame Press, 1975), I, 43.

19   W. Norris Clarke, "Introduction" to *The Metaphysics of St. Thomas Aquinas*, ed. J. Anderson (Washington, DC: Regnery, 1997), xvi–xix. See also W. Norris Clarke, *Person and Being* (Milwaukee: Marquette University Press, 1993), 10–11.

person with a spiritual soul is capable of this self-possession, which takes the form of self-awareness and self-determination. The person transcends the realm of nature and exists more intensely than other beings because she has fewer limitations than beings that are totally submerged in matter. Without the constraint of matter that keeps other creatures in darkness, active presence in the world becomes a free and self-conscious communication of a person's being. And since everything created by God is good, the person is really sharing the goodness that he or she possesses. For self-communication to be truly personal, this sharing must come forth from the deepest roots of one's being. Thus, the person gives to others from the wealth of her inner spiritual resources: her wisdom and compassion along with her very presence that creates the joy of togetherness. Personal self-communication, therefore, amounts to love — going out towards others to share one's gifts and to help others to acquire the goods they need for their own fulfillment. All beings are ordered to self-communication. A cat, for example, communicates its affection along with its needs, and communes with its fellow cats and other creatures. But only a person can communicate or express love that freely proceeds from her "interiority" or the inner recesses of her being. It follows that only this self-possessed and free person is able to truly "give itself, that is, to make itself a gift" for others (LR 282).[20]

Personal being, therefore, is nothing more than being itself, emancipated from the restrictions of matter that confine other creatures to a lack of self-awareness and diminished active presence. But a person can transcend herself and can be more actively present to others by loving them and caring about their good or well-being. According to Wojtyła, "inscribed in the nature of personal being [is] the potency and power of giving oneself" (LR 44). Given our nature as beings made to share our goodness, our perfection as human persons is achieved only by self-giving love. As we will discover, the fullest expression of self-giving love is the total mutual self-gift of spousal love. That love between a man and woman creates a lasting and exclusive personal communion that leads to fulfillment. Wojtyła refers to this basic principle as the "law of the gift"

20 Clarke, *Person and Being*, 75–82. See also W. Norris Clarke, *The Universe as Journey* (New York: Fordham University Press, 1988), 78–82.

(LR 281). Since this unselfish self-giving leads to the formation of many different forms of human bonds, including intimate personal communion, we might add that it is also the "law of communion." On the other hand, to be egocentric and locked up within the self is to be impersonal and to unnaturally oppose the "expansive generosity" of being itself.[21]

This metaphysical premise about the generosity of being is confirmed in Sacred Scripture, where we see that man's whole being is structured by the fact that he is a gift from God and is destined to be a gift for the other. According to John Paul II, *"existence is already a gift, the first gift of the Creator to the creature"* (LF 11). The creation of the woman allows man to exist as a gift for her (and she for him) in a way that is symbolic of the creative giving of the Father. The person can be a gift for others only because of the presence in him of God's generosity.[22]

Thus, Wojtyła's committed belief in our vocation to spousal love and the sharing of our personal gifts is rooted in the metaphysical insights of Aquinas. We now see the spiritual devastation of secular humanism where self-sufficiency and independence overshadow interpersonal self-donation. Individualism and self-absorption are contrary to the dynamic of personal being. A life well lived is a life lived in communion and community where people are bound together by love and self-sacrifice.

The Human Person "In the Beginning"

So far we have concentrated primarily on the Pope's philosophical writings about the nature of the human person. But the Word of God also brightly illuminates the meaning of personhood. Man the creature cannot fully understand himself apart from the Creator to whom he owes everything: "When God is forgotten, the creature itself grows unintelligible" (EV 22). The early chapters of Genesis are especially critical for comprehending man's origin and destiny. These insights, of course, are confirmed in the whole Bible, which "expresses the truth about man as creature, man as a being who is relative and contingent" (SC 14).

---

21 Jacques Maritain, *Creative Intuition in Art and Poetry* (New York: Meridian, 1955), 105. See also Clarke, *Person and Being*, 80–82.

22 Walter Schu, *The Splendor of Love: John Paul II's Vision for Marriage and Family* (Cheshire, CT: New Hope Publications, 2003), 82. See also Schindler, *Ordering Love*, 262.

In *Man and Woman He Created Them*, the Pope divides human history into three distinct periods: original innocence before the fall, the era of the person's threefold concupiscence, and the time of resurrection. Our present human experience is different from our experience in the beginning, and in the future when Christ will come again. The important thing for the Pope is not so much that these experiences belong to our history but that "they are always at the root of every human experience" (TB 169). We can better understand the human condition by looking at our origins, which remain with us in some way, for "every man carries within himself the mystery of the beginning" (TB 217).[23]

John Paul II carefully describes the first phase of human history, the experiences of man and woman in the beginning. His point of departure is the most fundamental principle of human dignity: man and woman have been created in God's image (Gn 1:27). According to the Pope, "the revealed truth concerning man as 'the image and likeness' of God constitutes the immutable basis of all Christian anthropology" (MD 6). The first man and woman, Adam and Eve, come to realize this truth about themselves through several primitive experiences involving their own solitude and unity. The Yahwist account of our origins in Genesis delineates several stages in the development of human subjectivity, which is made known to man through the body. The Pope first reflects on the meaning of original solitude.

It is in solitude that Adam first begins to discover himself. Man was the *object* of Yahweh's creative act, but his subjectivity, based on his ability to act through himself consciously and freely, is apparent in the making of the first covenant. Although tethered to the physical world, man finds himself in a unique and exclusive relationship with a spiritual God as a *"partner of the Absolute"* (TB 151). He is not just a passive or inert being like the other visible creatures around him, but an active *"subject of the covenant"* who is free to accept or reject God's commands (TB 151).

That subjectivity finds further expression in the naming of the animals as man "gains the consciousness of his own superiority" and begins to discover

---

23 Jarosław Kupczak, *Gift and Communion: John Paul II's Theology of the Body* (Washington, DC: Catholic University of America Press, 2014), 77–82. I am indebted to Kupczak's penetrating analysis of the Pope's theology of the body, here and in other sections of this book.

himself even more profoundly (TB 148). Adam achieves self-knowledge in this act of naming, since he knows that he cannot identify himself with the rest of the visible world. Also, through his conscious awareness, the first man realizes that he has the power of knowing, and with this knowledge man "*reveals himself to himself in all the distinctiveness of his being*" (TB 150). Man is alone and set apart because he is so strikingly different from the rest of the created, visible world. This experience "in the beginning" is preserved through time, since the person always perceives herself as superior to the rest of earthly creatures.

Man's subjectivity is also unveiled in the call to work and to have dominion over nature. Unlike other creatures, man alone is called upon to "cultivate the earth" (Gn 2:5) and to "subdue it" (Gn 1:28). According to the Pope, "one can say that from the very beginning the awareness of 'superiority' inscribed in the definition of humanity has originated in a typically human praxis or behavior" (TB 154). Man senses his subjectivity in his ability to work purposefully and to impose a sense of order on the material world.

God's instruction about the tree of knowledge of good and evil leads to the realization that man has the power of choice and self-determination. This represents another milestone in the unfolding of human subjectivity. Man is free to determine himself, and the stakes are quite high. Adam is told that if he eats of the forbidden fruit he will "certainly die" (Gn 2:17). Man's ultimate destiny depends to some extent on his own free choice. He can experience death through disobedience or follow God's commands and achieve immortality.

Thus, in original solitude personal subjectivity comes into sharp focus through this conscious awareness of a covenant with the Creator, his dominion over creation, and his power of self-determination. Man can begin to appreciate that he bears a certain likeness to God through his self-experience as a moral subject. He lives life from within through his thoughts, deliberations, and intentional choices. It is important to highlight that in all of these experiences man discovers his subjectivity or inwardness through the body. As the Pope explains, "Man is a subject not only by his self-consciousness and self-determination, but also based on his own body" (TB 154). In the naming process, for example, he would first come to know differences among the animals through his senses. The body, therefore, is an integral part of the human "I" that acts and thinks. The body expresses the person, and "*the structure of this body is such that it permits [the person] to be the author of genuinely human activity*" (TB 154).

The second set of experiences in the beginning is part of the original unity. When God says "It is not good that man should be alone" (Gn 2:18), man's solitude is confirmed. Yet in his solitude Adam is dimly aware that he is oriented by nature to the other.[24] He is open to another like himself, and so God creates Eve, "a helper fit for him" (Gn 2:18). She is created "with the rib" taken from Adam. This metaphorical expression implies the homogeneity of human personhood. When Adam sees Eve, he recognizes immediately that she has been created for him: "This at last is bone of my bones and flesh of my flesh" (Gn 2:23). The "definitive" creation of man consists in this creation of the "unity of two beings" (TB 161). Their unity reveals the identity of human nature, while their duality shows what "*constitutes the masculinity and femininity of created man*" (TB 161). Solitude, where man first finds himself and appreciates his distinctiveness, is overcome when man and woman become a sexually differentiated communion of persons. This is the Creator's original and only plan for marriage.

Fulfillment through this communion confirms our social nature. The person is not meant to be alone. She is not fulfilled through a solitary existence where it is impossible to develop and share her great gifts. As we have seen, the person is by nature a relational being who seeks out others and thrives in communion with them. Thus, we image the Trinitarian God not just through our freedom and rationality, but by living in a communion of intimate love. The Pope explains that "*man becomes the image of God not only through his own humanity, but also through the communion of persons* which man and woman form from the beginning" (TB 163). Revelation confirms that man is by nature open to communion with others. A person cannot fully image God, who is a communion of love and sharing, without a relationship with others. The person, therefore, becomes God-like not so much in the moment of solitude as in the moment of communion.[25]

---

24 The Hebrew word *adam* means man in the generic sense, not male.

25 Scola, *Nuptial Mystery*, 21–31.

The third set of experiences revolves around the person's original naked-ness: "The man and his wife were both naked, and were not ashamed" (Gn 2:25). Adam and Eve saw each other as persons and so there was no shame, no fear of sexual manipulation. In this state there is a "particular fullness of interpersonal communion," through which the body expresses the "personal I" that is perceived by the other (TB 176). The ability for man and woman to recognize each other as bodily persons, who deserve mutual respect and affirmation, makes an intimate communion of persons possible. Communion is a personal I-Thou relationship where two persons are dedicated to each other and live together "in truth and love" (LF 9).

The body transparently reveals the "living soul" of the person in this stage of original nakedness, but it also expresses "femininity for masculinity and vice versa" (TB 183). The Pope explains that the body has a spousal meaning: the body "contains 'from the beginning' the 'spousal' attribute, that is, the power to express love: precisely that love in which the human person becomes a gift and — through this gift — fulfills the very meaning of his being and existence" (TB 185–86). All creation is a gift that reveals God's overflowing love. The body's innate spousal meaning reflects this "gift-character" of creation that allows man and woman to become a reciprocal gift for each other. In the marriage covenant they share in God's creative and life-giving powers.[26]

After the fall, however, man is burdened with the triple concupiscence described by St. John: "the lust of the flesh and the lust of the eyes and the pride of life" (1 Jn 2:16). The body no longer fully carries within itself "an unquestionable sign of the image of God" (TB 241). Through the experience of concupiscence, lust, and shame, man realizes that his body is not as submissive to the spirit as it once was in the state of original innocence. The body resists the spirit and the person sometimes yields to temptation. Sexuality becomes an obstacle in man's personal relationship with a woman. Thanks to the body's sexual attributes, the person can be easily objectified and so it becomes difficult to welcome in one's heart the reciprocal gift of persons. As a result, *"the relationship of the gift changes into a relationship of appropriation"* (TB 260). The Pope points out, however, that the body's spousal meaning has not been totally suppressed by concupiscence but

26 Schu, *The Splendor of Love*, 81–85.

only threatened. The ability to make a gift of one's whole bodily-spiritual personhood to another is weakened but not abolished.

What are the chief lessons of the Pope's theology of the body for our purposes? First, by examining the human experience of man recounted in the biblical passages of Genesis, the Pope reaffirms those conclusions about the person that were derived from philosophy. The key revelation is the truth of our embodied subjectivity: the body is always part of the human "I" that acts and thinks. Second, we must remember that our understanding of personhood is greatly enhanced by looking at the three ages of historical man. The beginning was the time before the fall and in the future there will be a new spiritualization of man. These moments are not just part of humanity's history, because they are always "at the root of every human experience" (TB 169). The experience of the beginning is always present within man, and the resurrection is an object of longing, hope, and consolation for all people. Original innocence, therefore, is something every person "carries within himself" (TB 217). Hence the person retains his sense of superiority to the rest of earthly creation, and the spousal nature of the body does not lose its perennial meaning.[27]

Third, revelation confirms the insights of Christian philosophy, which postulates man's relational nature. We are not destined to be solitary creatures; rather, with the aid of a "helper" (Gn 2:18), the person becomes complete in relation to the other and thereby images his Trinitarian Source. "To be human," explains the Pope, "means to be called to interpersonal communion" (MD 7). And the exemplary interpersonal communion is the "intimate partnership of married life and love" (GS 48).

Finally, in the present age there is a propensity to perceive a person of the opposite sex as merely an attractive body, thereby "reducing the wealth of the perennial call to the communion of persons to the mere satisfaction of the body's sexual urge" (TB 298). Concupiscence and lust interfere with the freedom necessary to live up to the vocation of interpersonal self-sharing, and receiving that is the pathway to our fulfillment. The age of innocence is over and every person must squarely face this struggle. Love demands help from the virtue of chastity, which enables a fallen humanity to overcome the powerful temptation to use another person simply for pleasure.

27 Kupczak, *Gift and Communion*, 77–82.

The Pope's theology of the body confirms that the human person has been created for marriage. Like Adam and Eve, contemporary man and woman, who complement each other in body and spirit, need the other as a "helper." Each person is made for the total bodily gift of self that fulfills our human nature by creating an intimate communion, thereby overcoming our unnatural solitary state. Marriage and family are not extraneous to our fallen human nature, because the person flourishes only through the deepest immersion into communion and community.

Conclusions

The modern person tends to define herself by her freedom and independence. She is self-centered and focused on what is good *for her*. Self-fulfillment is realized through the succession of personal choices that ratify this freedom. Relationships with others are motivated primarily by utility and mutual advantage rather than selfless love. She prizes self-sufficiency and seeks maximum control over her destiny. The moral direction of her life is not shaped by her God-given human nature and its laws, but by her own private judgments that typically conform to the conventions of society. Obviously, this common conception of what it means to be a person in the twenty-first century contributes to distorted views about marriage. The ephemeral marriage bond depends entirely on free will and the persistence of a mutual benefit for both spouses.

This secular anthropology with its anti-metaphysical bias is rife with dualism, individualism, and an inflated sense of freedom that is detached from truth. Arguments spun on its behalf echo the ancient philosophy of Gnosticism, which divides the material body from the spiritual self. This libertine anthropology also endorses the emancipation of sensual desire as the fundamental principle of our permissive culture. It downplays sexual complementarity and regards romantic love as a spiritual reality that is not tied to the language of the body. Secular anthropology, which is broadly assumed by many ethicists and intellectuals, strongly resists the logic of marriage based on our human nature that is ordered to a sexually differentiated communion of persons.

On the other hand, authentic Christian anthropology, brought to light by John Paul II, is centered on the "categories of *communio*, person, and gift" (PC 325). It accentuates the unqualified dignity of the human person as a body-soul composite, the creation of personal communion through mutual self-gift, and the relational dimension of freedom. This anthropology acknowledges both the power and limits of human freedom, whose supreme moment comes in the gift of self. In marriage, spouses give themselves to each other in their totality as bodily-spiritual beings. Christian anthropology has no room for sexual liberation that breaks down marriage and family.[28]

The ultimate foundation of the Pope's anthropology is the generosity of being itself, which takes on a new dimension at the level of the person. Each person is called to be a gift, "living in a reciprocal 'for,' in a relationship of reciprocal gift" (TB 182). And marriage is the most fundamental dimension of this call. Marriage given to us by the Creator perfectly fits our human nature and represents the answer to our natural desire to live in communion. But how can the human person live up to this high calling of marriage? How can the person comport herself to the other in a way that makes her worthy of being a gift? These questions bring us into the heart of marital and sexual ethics. Before we turn to those issues, we must consider the more general moral standard proposed in Wojtyła's philosophy that provides secure guidance for *any* moral decision affecting other persons.

---

28 Martin Rhonheimer, *Ethics of Procreation and the Defense of Human Life* (Washington, DC: Catholic University of America Press, 2010), 72–73.

FOUR

The Personalistic Norm and the Sexual Drive

O NE OF THE DEFINING MOMENTS OF THE SEX-
ual revolution in Britain was a famous 1960 court decision that
overthrew a nationwide ban on D. H. Lawrence's novel *Lady
Chatterley's Lover*, published by Penguin Books. The contentious trial,
which took place at London's Old Bailey, was a major public event in
Britain. A jury of three women and nine men reached a verdict of "not
guilty" after spending many days in the courtroom. They concluded that
the book did not violate Britain's Obscenity Publication Act because it
met the exception for literary merit.

The full, unexpurgated version of Lawrence's racy novel had been
blacklisted in libraries, bookshops, and schools since its initial publication
in 1928. It was judged to be obscene and inappropriate reading for both
adults and children. The novel depicted in graphic detail the adulterous
relationship of a rich woman, Lady Chatterley. Her handsome husband,
Charles Chatterley, had been paralyzed during the war, and he neglected
his wife both physically and emotionally. Their fraught relationship thrust
Lady Chatterley into the arms of her husband's gamekeeper, Oliver Mel-
lors. Lawrence's lurid tale of this affair seemed to encourage a reckless
bohemian spirit, indulging one's desires for sexual intimacy even outside
of marriage. After the ban was lifted, the popular novel promptly became
a successful bestseller.

Meanwhile, in the United States, novels like *Peyton Place* and *Valley of
the Dolls* began to appear in bookstores and libraries. They depicted small
American towns and suburbs seething with promiscuity and adultery that

lurked beneath a deceptively serene facade. It became commonplace to celebrate these books for their candor and their willingness to expose the natural goodness of sensuality and the wonders of sexual pleasure. Marital fidelity, on the other hand, was portrayed as a source of repression and dull conformity. Clearly, the idea that sexual activity was connected with procreation and should be reserved for marriage was becoming quaint and almost indefensible.

For more thoughtful individuals, what emerged in the public furor over the banning of books like *Lady Chatterley's Lover* were some fundamental moral questions: is sensuality a good in itself, and is it morally suitable to have sex with someone just for pleasure? Aside from the adultery, was there anything wrong with Lady Chatterley's passionate fling with her young and handsome paramour? The spread of recreational sex had been energized thanks to the introduction of effective contraceptive techniques that allowed couples to have sex without commitment or procreation. The false prophets of the sexual revolution, such as Helen Gurley Brown and Hugh Hefner, expounded regularly on the virtues of sexual liberty and promiscuity. Many of the intellectual and cultural elite were easily converted. Ms. Brown was the editor of the edgy *Cosmopolitan* magazine, and her Cosmo cover girls became icons of sexual freedom. A Cosmo girl, Brown once said, wouldn't hesitate to get involved with a married man if it suited her fancy.

Recreational sex was even implicitly endorsed in several US court cases such as *Eisenstadt v. Baird* (1972), which declared that laws prohibiting the sale of contraceptives to unmarried couples were unconstitutional. Marriage was loosely defined in this case as an "association between two individuals." But whether or not a person was in such an "association" was irrelevant to the court. The Justices insisted that "it is the right of the individual, married or single, to be free from unwarranted government intrusion into matters so fundamentally affecting a person as the decision whether to bear or beget a child."[1] In the name of privacy rights, *Eisenstadt* and subsequent cases inferred that there was a constitutional right to engage in promiscuous behavior without the burden of children.

Also popular at the time was the dubious moral theory of situation

---

1   *Eisenstadt v. Baird* 405 U.S. 438 (1972).

ethics, which suggests that each situation or context supplies its own "norm of action" (LR 101). Whether an action is right or wrong is always relative and dependent on the circumstances. When these ethicists were asked about the moral validity of recreational sex they answered with their customary ambivalence: it all depended upon many different factors such as the maturity or commitment of the individuals involved. Ethicists of this school of thought seemed unwilling to endorse an absolute prohibition on non-marital sex regardless of the circumstances.

For Wojtyła, the issue of casual or non-marital sex hinged on a more general question: how do we interact with others who are endowed with a spiritual soul and the freedom to choose their own destiny? In Wojtyła's mind, the moral challenge for all of us is how to consistently treat the other person as a "somebody" worthy of respect rather than "something." As we saw in the previous chapter, the person has an elevated status that implies certain duties or obligations. Those duties require careful control over fickle and selfish instincts.

In *Love and Responsibility*, Wojtyła argues that the only acceptable posture toward the other person is an attitude of loving kindness. He posits a sharp dichotomy between love and use. Either we love another person or we use that person merely as a tool, a means to advance our own ends. If Frank tells his girlfriend, Amy, how much he cares for her only in order to get her to sleep with him, he is shamelessly using her merely as a means to acquire sensual pleasure for himself. By his guile and charm he callously manipulates her powers of reason to get his own way. Even if Amy were not having sex with Frank under false pretenses there would still be something wrong. Sexual relations for mutual gratification is a distortion of the "moral meaning" of the body, which has been created for self-giving and not as an instrument for pleasure (VS 49).

The issue of sexual morality is closely related to the themes of marriage and family. Sexual impropriety can cause great harm to marriage. The spirit of "free love" and "safe sex" encourages adultery and makes persons "slaves to their weaknesses" (LF 13). Casual sex by unmarried couples can hinder their prospects for one day coming together in a "communion of love" (MD 7). Also, a married couple will find it difficult to enjoy the great benefits of marital communion if they misuse their sexual powers. As we will see in this chapter, Wojtyła's standard for sexual morality is based on his personalistic norm linked with an affirmation of sexuality's procreative purpose. Thus, before we explicitly treat the topic of marriage, it is useful to briefly consider this standard that should guide sexual behavior, including the behavior of married couples.

Loving vs. Using: The Personalistic Norm

The principle that persons should not be "used" has a distinguished pedigree in moral philosophy. The great philosopher Immanuel Kant insisted that persons are never to be treated as merely a means to achieve our own goals. When our actions are directed at another person, we must bear in mind that this person is not just an object of such action but a moral subject, a "someone," capable of reason and self-determination. As we saw in the previous chapter, we discover these two properties in the inner life or "interiority of the person" (LR 10). The person exists for his or her own sake, not for the sake of others. Hence, we must steadfastly avoid any forms of lying, intentional deception, promise-breaking, and coercion. These actions undermine a person's ability to exercise her freedom responsibly in the pursuit of happiness. Quite simply, we must not interfere with a mature person's reasonable self-chosen ends.

To illustrate how an improper action disturbs a person's capability for determining his or her own valid aims, consider the problem of lying. Lying is morally unacceptable not only because it erodes trust, but also because it is so manipulative. For example, let's assume that a doctor lies to his patient and tells her that there is only one very expensive way to treat her illness, when in fact there are other less expensive options. The doctor is blocking this patient from considering those other options that she might have chosen had the deception not occurred. The patient becomes only a means for this doctor to accumulate more money. If we approach other persons merely as pawns to be maneuvered for our advantage, they become depersonalized. We end up trying to control them in the same way we might control a scientific experiment.

Of course, a person cannot choose *any* good or end, but only those that lead to his or her fulfillment and perfection as a person. As Wojtyła points out, "it must be demanded from the person...that those ends be truly good" (LR 10). These ends or goods are referred to frequently by

Wojtyła as the *bona honesta* (true goods), and they include life and health, knowledge, marriage, friendship, and internal harmony (PC 58–60). The reasonable and conscientious pursuit of these goods should always direct our actions and choices. When a mature person prudently seeks out ends that are truly good, his or her choice deserves our sincere respect and approbation.

Wojtyła expresses this moral imperative as the personalistic norm. This norm states that the person "is incompatible with using [and] may not be treated as an object of use, as a means to an end" (LR 25). The norm can also be stated in more positive terms: "The person is a kind of good to which only love constitutes the proper and fully-mature relation" (LR 25). The essence of love is to affirm the value of the person, to esteem that person for his or her own sake. We affirm our friends by caring about their well-being and by helping them to achieve their worthy goals. On the other hand, if we treat a friend only as a means and use her just for our own purpose, we will destroy that friendship. Love builds up relationships, but selfish using will fragment them. Marriage too cannot sustain itself on the brittle ideal of being "true to oneself."

This personalistic norm is the measure of all human action and the governing principle of Wojtyła's whole moral philosophy. A person who is faithful to this norm will not deny someone else the space to be herself so that she can *freely* choose morally reasonable ends. We must repel the temptation to see that person as an object or empty vessel who exists solely or almost exclusively for the advancement of our own selfish aims and projects. By following this simple standard, we begin to fix our attention on the valid needs and goals of the other person. Our deference to the personalistic norm represents the first traces of the interpersonal sharing that could blossom into mature friendship or even the mutual self-giving of spousal love.

The Perils of Utilitarianism

For many years Karol Wojtyła lived under a Communist government in Poland. As a priest, bishop, and cardinal he dealt fearlessly with political leaders and bureaucrats who dedicated themselves to this political system with bleak fanaticism. From the time he assumed his duties as Auxiliary

Bishop in Krakow, Polish Communist authorities took great pains to spy on his activities. They made every effort to blunt his popularity with the Polish people. But Bishop Wojtyła was always a step ahead of the Polish Intelligence Service, and he was usually able to elude its prying eye when necessary. He frequently confronted Communist repression and distortions of truth in his homilies and speeches. "I'm often chided," he once said, "for talking about these things, but how could I fail to speak out?"[2]

One common distortion was Communism's appeal to pragmatic moral principles such as the "end justifies the means." Leaders were informed that they sometimes had to have "dirty hands" to bring about the greater good of political stability or egalitarianism. This preoccupation with ends over means mirrors the philosophy of utilitarianism, a moral theory uprooted from any spiritual or metaphysical foundation. The Pope witnessed the destructive effects of this unprincipled reasoning, and this accounts for why he had such a strong antipathy to the soft relativism of utilitarian ethics.

According to the utilitarian model, developed in the nineteenth century by philosophers such as Jeremy Bentham, the supreme norm of morality is the maximization of happiness (or pleasure). There are several versions of utilitarianism, but hedonistic utilitarianism is Wojtyła's main focus. It assumes that the right action is the one that brings about the greatest overall balance of pleasure over pain for all persons affected by that action. Since we all seek pleasure and avoid pain, utilitarianism concludes that pleasure should be the basis of morality. According to Wojtyła, the principle of utility affirms the "maximum of pleasure for the greatest number of people" (LR 20). Pleasure is the one true good and the "proper end of man's action" (LR 20).

Utilitarian philosophy dismisses the idea that there are more fundamental goods than pleasure. Similarly, the notion of natural rights as a limit to our actions no matter how much they maximize pleasure was rejected by Bentham as "nonsense on stilts." According to this logic, nothing is sacred. One can lie, cheat, commit adultery, and even take a human life as long as the sum total of satisfactions outweigh the costs. The simple motto of utilitarianism is "Maximize pleasure!" But the motto of the personalistic norm is "respect the dignity of each individual person without exception!"

---

2 Stanisław Dziwisz, *A Life with Karol* (New York: Doubleday, 2007), 42.

In his sustained critique of this theory, Wojtyła makes a convincing case that pleasure cannot be the supreme good because it is linked to concrete acts. There is no way to determine in advance whether an act will produce pleasure much less calculate those pleasures, which are always "rather elusive" (LR 21). In addition, utilitarianism is just a form of egoism in disguise, "without any possibility of turning into authentic altruism" (LR 22). The principle of utility easily slides into egoism because in order to maximize pleasure I am bound to help someone else experience pleasure only on the condition that I also experience pleasure. Sexual interaction, therefore, is always based on a *quid pro quo*: I will strive to give you pleasure only if I receive pleasure in return. As a result, this semblance of romantic love is a "harmonization of egoisms" instead of an authentic communion of persons (LR 23). Utilitarianism, therefore, has close affinity to individualism. Your pleasure might be part of the moral equation, but what is always a factor is *my* pleasure and self-fulfillment.

The philosopher-pope does not retreat from his assault on utilitarianism in several of his most important papal discourses. In *Veritatis Splendor* he explains the severe defects of this ethical perspective, such as the problem of evaluating moral actions based on the consequences they bring about. He sharply criticizes these theories "that draw their norms to evaluate the rightness of an action from the weighing of the goods to be gained" (VS 74). It is practically impossible to objectively weigh and assess the diffuse consequences of our moral actions, since they extend outward in many directions. Utilitarianism, therefore, offers us only "false solutions" to moral problems (VS 77). A married woman conflicted over whether to abort her baby with a potentially serious birth defect might be tempted to make her decision based on thinking through the consequences of two alternatives: abort the baby or carry it to full term and accept it as a member of the family. But how could she possibly measure those consequences? If she opts for an abortion, can she predict the psychological damage that might ensue for herself along with her husband and children? How can she measure what this child could contribute to the family community before it is even born?

In *Letter to Families* the Pope explains that the utilitarian norm stands in direct opposition to Christian morality based on love of neighbor as oneself and sometimes called the Golden Rule. "Do to others as you would wish them to do to you" is the way Aquinas formulates this principle.[3] Utilitarian reasoning creates a culture that poses a grave threat to marriage and the family. No one can find security in a culture that promotes the sacrifice of a family member's well-being to ensure that pleasure or satisfaction is duly maximized. In that milieu, family members can be easily objectified: "Woman can become an object for man, children a hindrance to parents, the family an institution obstructing the freedom of its members" (LF 13).

Following the same line of reasoning, John Paul II also argued that utilitarianism in all its variations supports positions that harm the weak and the vulnerable. In a moral environment fashioned by utilitarian logic, people tend to be measured by their "usefulness" or contribution to the good of society. Where that contribution is lacking a person is seen to have little worth, and his or her interests become easily subordinated to the greater good. In our interactions with others, "the criterion of personal dignity...is replaced by the criterion of efficiency, functionality, and usefulness" (EV 23). The encounter with another person lacks any sense of the sacred. If a utilitarian perspective shapes our relations to other persons, they will be depersonalized and always regarded to some degree as a "means" to achieve our own ends. They become more like things to be used rather than persons to be loved and affirmed for their own sake.

What is the genesis of this pernicious theory? Utilitarianism and similar ideas fill the void left by what Nietzsche calls the "death of God": man's rejection of the Creator along with the laws of nature. This event has ushered in an era of metaphysical nihilism that has crippled Western thought. Without belief in God and the natural order, Christian moral principles lose their vitality and their power to help humanity find its moral bearings. Philosophers like Nietzsche boldly declared the emptiness of all traditional values. As a result, people search frantically for a replacement. One source of new values is found in the turn to "practical materialism," which breeds utilitarianism, individualism, and hedonism (EV 23). Hedonism and utilitarianism make a powerfully attractive combination that easily leads to contorted descriptions of romantic love. For example, Frank and Kathy get pleasure through mutual sexual satisfaction. They believe that this cooperation in providing pleasure for each other

---

3 Thomas Aquinas, *Summa Theologiae*, I-II, q. 99, a. 1, ad 3.

and finding pleasure through another is what love is all about.[4] This erotic entanglement, however, only disguises itself as love, which is always based on benevolence and the durable union of persons.

Pragmatic moral principles like utilitarianism, no matter how fashionable, only cater to our weakness of will and bad habits. For the most part, they simply rationalize the pursuit of selfish desires. Utilitarianism, especially when linked with the idolatry of pleasure, is an anti-social and erratic philosophy that represents an unfortunate detour in the history of ethics. Those who follow the utilitarian way quickly lose appreciation of the other person's dignity as well as their own. This philosophy cannot be the foundation for human solidarity or authentic community life.

The personalistic norm, on the other hand, is far superior to utilitarianism because it captures the "*unconditional respect due to the insistent demands of the personal dignity of every man*" (vs 38). This fundamental principle, anchored in the truth about the natural superiority of the person, requires that each person "must be nothing other than the end of every act" (LF 12). Following this norm assures that the dignity and freedom of the person will always be preserved. It also guarantees the most elementary form of justice, which is giving others what is rightfully due to them. Abiding by the personalistic norm begins to promote a "culture of love" in which marriage and family flourish. The pragmatic reasoning of utilitarianism, on the other hand, fosters a "civilization of production and use," in which people relate to others primarily by subtle manipulation (LF 13). In such fragmented cultures there is a tragic loss of truth about the person and the family and a risk that love too will ultimately be sacrificed on the altar of utility.

Personalism and Sexuality

This entire reflection on the opposition between love and use must be applied to sexual relationships where the temptations for use can sometimes be overpowering. According to Wojtyła, "use" has a second meaning that brings us into the heart of sexual morality. In the second form of use "the person becomes a proper source of variously colored pleasure or even

4 Josef Seifert, *True Love* (South Bend, IN: St. Augustine's Press, 2015), 7.

delight" (LR 16). Unlike animals, a man or woman who engages in sexual relations can isolate pleasure in the sexual act and treat it "as a distinct end of action" (LR 17). If Joe has sex with Kathy purely for the pleasure of an orgasm, Kathy's body is simply a means for his self-gratification. Thus, we cannot use people in a general way by manipulating them for our own purposes, nor can we use them for the sake of a pleasurable sexual experience. Using another person as an object to maximize pleasure is egoism and a gross misuse of one's sexual powers. Sexual union is a deeply interpersonal act, which is trivialized when someone treats his partner merely as a source of bodily pleasure. When this occurs, self-satisfaction displaces love: "Bodily use alone based on the intensive co-experience of *sexus* takes over the essential personal role of love and precisely in this way annihilates love" (LR 157). As we will see in chapter six, casual sex also undermines the good of marriage and makes it more difficult to experience the unifying power of sexual intercourse.

To some extent, the tendency to approve recreational sex is reinforced by modern rationalism, which demands empirical evidence and does not tolerate mystery. Since the unobservable soul is too enigmatic for the rationalist, he reduces the whole person to "mere matter," which is satisfied by physical pleasure (LF 19). On the other hand, the Gnostic or dualistic approach divides body and spirit, which are regarded as two separate substances. The body and its sexual powers are not perceived as part of our personal reality, but rather as a sub-personal domain. The body serves at the pleasure and whims of the conscious, spiritual self. According to this perspective, the body is neither fully human nor is it an essential part of the meaning and language of human love. Lost is our ability to "discover in human sexuality a treasure proper to the person" (LF 19).[5]

But this dualistic vision that so captivates the modern mind is a tragic error. Far more tenable is a holistic vision of the person where human activities like the acquisition of intellectual knowledge become intelligible only when regarded as a single power of a unified human nature.[6] The physical body is not just an instrument or material stuff separate from the soul. Rather, it is always a "spiritualized body" with a spousal meaning,

---

5 George, "Gnostic Liberalism," 33–34.
6 Clarke, *Creative Retrieval*, 201.

suited for the expression of self-giving love despite the incessant pull of concupiscence (LF 19). The body is an integral part of the human "I." Thus, when we use someone's body for sexual pleasure, we are using that person, who is a body-soul composite.

The Sexual Drive

The personalistic norm is an indispensable principle for guiding sexual behavior. But we must also understand the role of the body's sexual drive in order to construct a suitable sexual morality. This drive, which is the foundation of conjugal or spousal love, orients us to the sexual properties of a person of the opposite sex. Once this seed of attraction is planted, it can mature over time into full mutual self-giving or spousal love. But the sexual drive doesn't just give birth to spousal love — it is also the foundation for the transmission of life, which is its primary purpose. Although Wojtyła's exposition on the sexual drive is not explicitly based on natural law reasoning, he does not ignore human nature, which includes the sexual drive whose primary purpose is procreation. Just as we have senses to see, hear, and feel, we have been endowed with a certain sexual design in order to procreate. Contrary to thinkers like Freud, Wojtyła insists that the sexual drive "does not possess a purely libidinistic character, but it possesses an existential character" (LR 47). The drive does not exist for sexual delight but for the transmission of life. Any rational person can apprehend the sexual drive's indispensable role in the ongoing work of creation.

Thus, the ultimate meaning of the sexual drive is closely linked with human existence and with preserving the human species. The sexual drive is not just a biological function at our disposal. It surpasses the biological because "the proper end of the drive...is something supra-personal; it is the existence of the species *Homo sapiens*, the constant extension of its existence" (LR 35). The sexual drive ensures the continuing existence of human beings, and existence is "the first and fundamental good" for any creature (LR 35). Wojtyła suggests that we must regard existence not as a fact but as the metaphysical principle by which any being, such as a plant, an animal, or a person, is really present in the universe. As we have seen, this inner act of presence, the root source of all the perfections within every being, is ordered to self-communication, that is, to sharing its perfections with others. At the personal level that self-communication becomes self-conscious and free, assuming the form of love, a sharing of one's inner gifts of wisdom and charity with others. Wojtyła often refers to the "greatness" of this drive because it can bring into being this most intense personal form of existence.[7]

To interpret the drive solely as a means for self-gratification is to contradict nature by refusing to acknowledge the objective end of this drive. Sexual relations must be reserved for marriage, and the purpose of marriage is to form an intimate *communio* that can also serve existence. A married couple always lives out this vocation through the total self-giving of spousal love, which is permeated with an affirmation of the other person in accordance with the personalistic norm. Such love ensures that both persons in the relationship will not be used for pleasure or merely as a means for procreation. Those who insist that this drive exists only for pleasure and amusement overlook an important fact: only preservation of the procreative dimension of sexuality can make love truly marital. The conjugal act is differentiated from casual sex only if it is truly unitive, and it cannot be unitive unless it is also generative.

Sexual (or conjugal) morality, therefore, is based on a "synthesis of the finality of nature with the personalistic norm" (LR 51). The personalistic norm directs us to love all persons, but how that love is expressed depends on the form that it takes. Sexual union is valid only for spousal love, where it is a sign and a means to the full union of persons in marriage, where children are welcomed and cared for.[8]

When sexuality is detached from its procreative meaning, it can no longer be an expression of spousal love, which is a total and mutual self-giving, including paternity and maternity. To love the other fully is to love that individual in his masculine or her feminine personhood, as a potential father or mother, and as a source of human life. When that quality of love is absent, the logic of pleasure and self-gratification begins to dominate a couple's sexual behavior. Sensual appetite, however, does not seek the good of the other but always its own good, and so what looks like love is really

7 W. Norris Clarke, *Explorations in Metaphysics* (Notre Dame: University of Notre Dame Press, 1994), 3–12. See also Richard Spinello, *Understanding Love and Responsibility* (Boston: Pauline Books & Media), 38–40.

8 Kupczak, *Gift and Communion*, 100.

self-centeredness. A married couple avoids that logic only when they come together as two dedicated lovers who join together in sexual union for the larger purpose of serving human life. This makes their love spousal and marital and sets it apart from all other forms of sexual activity. However, when the objective "finality" of the sexual drive is suppressed, only pleasure is left, and this can hardly qualify as an expression of marital love.[9]

A thorough defense of Wojtyła's position on the sexual drive's existential meaning is beyond the scope of this book. But it is certainly logical to assume that the primary purpose of our sexual capacities is procreation, and not pleasure as some like Freud have supposed. Seeing certain sights or hearing certain sounds give us pleasure, but no one would argue that the purpose of the senses of sight or hearing is for our pleasure. Similarly, while our sexual capacities provide some degree of pleasure during the sexual act, pleasure is certainly not their purpose. While pleasure in conjugal love can be "a *fruit* of striving to affirm the other person, it should not be...the fundamental *end* of this striving" (LR 140).[10]

When pressed, most people will admit the obvious procreative meaning of sexual intercourse. Yet they still act as if this is not true because they prefer to follow their sexual desires. However, a person cannot operate by instinct in these matters and follow the promptings of the sexual drive wherever it leads. Such behavior contradicts who man is: a rational being with powers of reason and will. Every person must take up "full responsibility for the way he uses the sexual drive," and this responsibility is the "vital component of man's sexual morality" (LR 47). In the chapters ahead we will explore more specifically why misuse of the sexual drive causes so much turbulence in the inner life of the person. We also explore why this misuse strikes at the heart of marriage.

Conclusions

The personalistic norm offers us an unambiguous standard of morality, which states that the dignity of the human person is the unyielding criterion of right and wrong. It also signifies a caring concern for the other person,

---

9 Rhonheimer, *Ethics of Procreation*, 107–13.
10 J. Budziszewski, *On the Meaning of Sex* (Wilmington, DE: ISI Books, 2012), 24–26.

which can lead to higher forms of self-donation. The personalistic norm linked to a proper understanding of the sexual drive becomes the basis for sexual morality. All of us should readily acknowledge the moral problem that occurs when a person "'makes use' of another human being, 'using her' only to satisfy his own 'urge'" (TB 292). Only real love, which always triumphs over concupiscence, excludes the use of one person by another.

The sexual drive is the foundation for both spousal love and procreation, which are closely linked. When sexuality is detached from its procreative meaning, it loses its unifying powers and cannot serve the mutual self-giving love between a man and woman. There cannot be a gift of love to the other in the totality of a couple's bodily-spiritual personhood when the person is not loved as a spouse, as a potential mother or father, and as a source of new life.[11] Only the egoism of sensuality remains. On the other hand, real love that is true to the purpose of the sexual drive creates marital communion and family community, which fulfill both persons in the relationship.

Wojtyła could have reached some of these same conclusions by natural law reasoning. But instead he chose the philosophy of personalism, which is complemented by clear principles that preserve the ideas of nature and cosmic order. He undoubtedly preferred this approach because the personalistic norm could more effectively counter the spread of utilitarianism. Also, everyone can intuitively appreciate the simple idea that "the person is a being for whom the only suitable dimension is love" (CTH 201). No rational, mature person should ever want to be used exclusively as a means by someone else, even if he or she appears to gain something from that use in the bargain. The negative effects of being used, the damage to self-respect and integrity, far outweigh whatever gains there may be. On the other hand, no person can live without love. Life is unintelligible and empty unless one "encounters" love, "experiences" love, and "participates intimately in it" (RH 10). However, like "freedom" and "person," "love" is another concept widely misunderstood. In the next chapter, we examine Wojtyła's clarification of love with its special concentration on the nature of spousal love.

11 Rhonheimer, *Ethics of Procreation*, 115–16.

FIVE

True Love

I N THE MIDST OF A MID-DAY SNOWFALL, AN odd-looking couple stood outside a mid-town hotel in New York City answering a curious reporter's intrusive questions. The reporter was doing a feature story for a network news magazine on mail order brides. The lanky fifty-one-year-old man being interviewed had recently welcomed his new "bride-to-be" from Russia. She had been in the United States only a few days and spoke very little English. Nevertheless, this soft-spoken man declared that they were madly in love: "We fell in love almost the moment we first laid eyes on each other," he exclaimed. He went on to announce that they were to be promptly married within the next week. The young, diminutive Russian woman, nicely dressed in a black goose-down coat, nodded her head in complete agreement. The reporter's crisp, sharp style was a striking contrast to the awkward manner of this couple. She ended her story on a somewhat hopeful note by observing that, although this couple knew each other for only a few days, they were still prepared to take a leap of faith and propel themselves into married life.

It must surely be obvious to most reasonable persons that no matter how sincere this couple may be, they have no idea what romantic love actually means. They are still virtual strangers to each other after such a short time together. The language barrier alone is a major impediment to learning about each other's needs, preferences, and deepest aspirations. There is clearly a sensual attraction at work that often masquerades as love. There may even be the beginnings of a fervent emotional bonding that encourages some people to confidently proclaim that their passionate love "is not just physical." But sensuality and amorous sentimentality are not the same as love. And marriage that is not well founded on real love has the dimmest prospect for success. Unless a man and woman are committed soul mates they cannot achieve the authentic fulfillment that comes from belonging to each other. Without love and deep moral commitment, relationships remain shallow beneath the surface glitter, and too often they eventually become impaired by jealousy, spite, and bitterness.

Regrettably, many other people make the same foolish mistake as this couple being interviewed in the midst of snowy New York. They reduce marital love to the psychological state of sensuality and affectivity that is so prevalent during the early stages of a romantic relationship. They are caught up in an erotic entanglement and overwhelmed by sexual desire. These couples naively fail to realize that their intense emotions will inevitably subside, leaving their relationship suspended in a void. Yet they prefer to listen to the "promptings of sensuality" rather than rely on the surer guidance of reason and good conscience (LR 144).

But what is true love? Many people cannot give a reasonable answer to this question. They persistently sentimentalize romantic love or even reduce it to the satisfaction of concupiscence or sexual desire. There is a tendency today to resist the question or to regard love as "liquid" and fragile. Young people who see so many relationships collapse around them are skeptical about the durability of love. Thus, love is frequently misunderstood. But is the love between a man and a woman so inscrutably opaque that we can't possibly fathom it or explain it? Or are we unwilling to face the reality of love because it will make certain demands on us?

Before he became Pope John Paul II, Karol Wojtyła, the philosopher, set out to unravel the wondrous mystery of love in his book, *Love and Responsibility*. Wojtyła patiently unfolds love's most essential elements and explains how romantic love is both a passion and a virtue. We do not find a similar exposition in any of his papal writings. Hence, if we want to get back to fundamentals in order to grasp the truth about marriage and family, we must review the discourse on love presented in this book.

Wojtyła is primarily concerned with the love between a man and a woman, or what is commonly called romantic love. He first works out a "metaphysical" analysis of love by dissecting its most fundamental elements, which are included in every form of love. This opens the way for his psychological analysis: how love is formed within the psyche of both persons and linked to their sexuality. Finally, he treats love's ethical character. Mature love is always virtuous, since it involves a committed and altruistic relationship between two persons. The Pope has said many times that we cannot understand the dynamic of marital unity without knowing the essential characteristics of love. In this chapter, therefore, our aim is to present a faithful portrait of love with the help of *Love and Responsibility*.[1]

Love's Common Traits

FONDNESS. The first feature of love is fondness or attraction. A woman enters a man's field of vision or sphere of interest as a good to be valued, and a man enters a woman's orbit in the same way. One person is attracted to another person, usually because that individual embodies certain characteristics such as a charming or engaging personality, moral sensitivity, and sheer physical beauty. In the case of a person of the opposite sex, this attraction is due in part to the dynamics of the sexual drive. Thanks to that drive, we are naturally oriented toward certain characteristics of a person of the opposite sex. Wojtyła describes these characteristics as the "sexual values" of a person. Fondness begins to elevate the sexual drive to a personal level. When this fondness is mutual, the barriers between two persons begin to evaporate as they are drawn closer to each other.

Fondness is shaped primarily by our affections or passions, so it is something that happens to us. In the *Jeweler's Shop*, Andrew explains that when his wife Theresa first became the focus of his attention he "*had* to be interested in her" (JS 1:1). Love at this stage commences with our experience of values like beauty, charm, and gracefulness. The "emotional-affective reaction" to these values is the linchpin for the development of fondness toward that person (LR 60). Because Theresa uniquely embodied such attractive qualities, she moved Andrew in some way, and she entered into his world "as a good that has awakened fondness" (LR 60). This awakening or affective reaction is the beginning of love between two persons, and this is why "fondness is already love, even though love is not just fondness" (LR 60).

1 I have discussed Pope John Paul II's description of love as presented in *Love and Responsibility* in my book *Understanding Love and Responsibility*, and I have drawn from that material, but the expression of those ideas in this chapter is new.

Since fondness represents the passionate side of love, the emotions are often in control. However, the predominance of these sub-rational emotions can quickly lead to difficulties. Feelings arise so spontaneously and forcefully that they can easily overwhelm reason and falsify fondness. This could occur if someone perceives values in another that do not exist. This experience can be a source of profound disillusionment for a person who is in the early stages of love. What begins as uncomplicated affection for Mary ends in an acknowledgment that her boyfriend does not possess the values that she thought he had.

Thus, fondness is awakened by spiritual and sexual values perceived in another person. A man is moved by a woman's attractive qualities and this sparks an affective reaction to her that draws her into his orbit. For example, Jim is drawn to Jane because of her loveliness and youthful beauty along with her compassion and high moral character. The values Jim experiences in Jane elevate her in his mind and make her beautiful, compassionate, and upright as a whole person, and *this person* is the object of his love. For fondness "has for its object a person, and always proceeds from the whole person" (LR 60). Love, therefore, has its roots in this emotional response to this particular individual, who stands before me as one who possesses certain qualities that make manifest her unique preciousness as a person. The affective admiration for this individual personality, disclosed through his or her sexual values and other qualities, leads to desire for that person, which is the next stage of love.[2]

DESIRE. Fondness begets desire, as the person seeks to possess the object of his or her attraction. Like fondness, "desire belongs to the essence of love, and sometimes is manifested in love most strongly" (LR 64). What lies behind the force of desire is the human person's otherness or lack of self-sufficiency. Every human being is either a man or a woman, and our existence as a sexual being represents a limitation, a "certain one-sidedness" (LR 64). This limitation suggests our contingency and our dependency upon the person of the opposite sex. As the Pope explained in *Mulieris Dignitatem*, the person "can only exist as a 'unity of the two,' and therefore in relation to another human person" (MD 7). Man needs a woman to

---

2 Seifert, *True Love*, 16–20.

complement his own being, and a woman needs a man in the same way. This objective need for the other is made manifest through the sexual drive and "grows on the substratum of this drive" (LR 64). The experience of this lack or need gives birth to "love of desire," which can ultimately call forth the mutual gift of self through which each person finds herself. Thus love is based on both limit and possibility. The love of desire is different from sensual desire, "for it proceeds from a need and aims at finding the missing good" (LR 64). That good is a person of the opposite sex.[3]

Love of desire (versus desire), therefore, represents a real objective need for the other person who is good for me. This is a person I value and admire, and so I seek to possess him or her in the proper sense. Love of desire is never experienced as mere sensual feeling, an urge to satisfy one's sexual needs. Rather this form of love always includes a *"longing for the good for oneself"* (LR 65). A man longs for a certain woman because he knows that "possessing" her in the right way and sharing his life with her will perfect him and fulfill his hopes and dreams. If love of desire is reciprocal, it can ultimately draw two people into an authentic interpersonal communion. Thanks to their sexual differentiation, they can become a "unity of the two" and find fulfillment. Although this longing for the other goes beyond sexual desire, that desire "remains...in its shadow" (LR 65). The loving person is conscious of its presence, but does not allow it to overpower true love of desire.

All love has this character of desire or longing as well as fondness. But in the transition to desire, the person more actively transcends himself toward the other. He esteems the other not just for the values she embodies but because solidarity with her will fulfill and perfect him. A man is struck by a woman's sexual values and personal qualities, and he actively seeks her out as a friend and maybe even as a spouse. Love of desire does not capture the essence of love, but it is a tangible sign of our destiny "to live in a communion of love" (MD 7).

BENEVOLENCE. While desire is an aspect of love, true love always surpasses longing and desire for the other. Desire that has been awakened by those resplendent values that draw me to another person does not exhaust the substance of love, as some people are wont to believe. Love is

3 Scola, *Nuptial Mystery*, 25–26, 122.

more than a desire for a person as a "good for oneself" (LR 66). It is also essential to desire what is good for that person. Love must involve caring about the welfare of the beloved and a concern about what will make her happy and fulfilled. Wojtyła refers to this aspect of love as benevolence: "Love of one person for another must be benevolent," he says, "otherwise it will not be true" (LR 66).

Love as benevolence is concisely expressed in St. Thomas Aquinas's classic definition of love: "To love is to will the good of another."[4] This form of altruistic love orients the will toward a generous concern for the other and an affirmation of the person for his or her own sake. Benevolence moves me beyond my own interests and desires, beyond merely seeking what is beneficial for me. I now also want what is truly good for this person, what will help her flourish as a person. Benevolence evokes a sincere willing for another person's objective good and a rejoicing in her realization of that good which makes her happy.

The love between a man and a woman would be woefully incomplete if it did not transcend love of desire or longing. Without benevolence, love quickly devolves into egoism. Love as benevolence is a disinterested, selfless love, and it approximates the pure essence of love. As Josef Pieper points out, true love or benevolence never seeks out its own advantage.[5] The truth about benevolent love was beautifully captured by St. Paul, who extolls the virtue of love and describes love as "patient," "kind," never "self-seeking" (1 Cor 13:4–8). "Such love," writes Wojtyła, "perfects its object the most; it develops most fully both his existence and the existence of the person to whom it turns" (LR 67).

Romantic love between a man and a woman will always be shaped by love of desire with its overtones of sexual desire. But it should advance in the direction of a more complete and zealous benevolence. The true love of benevolence must coexist with desire to ensure that this desire does not consume a sexual relationship.

RECIPROCITY. When benevolence and love of desire is mutual between a man and a woman, we have the conditions for reciprocity, which

---

4 Thomas Aquinas, *Summa Theologiae*, I-II, q. 26, a. 4.
5 Josef Pieper, *Faith, Hope, and Love* (San Francisco: Ignatius Press, 1997), 163.

is also necessary for love. Love is not "something in a man and something in a woman," since in that case there would be two loves (LR 68). Rather, love is always a joining together of the two and therefore something that exists *between* a man and a woman. There is a single objective whole or unity in which two persons are involved. The path from "I" to "we" leads through the free will of both persons toward a mutual commitment.

Love that is unilateral or one-sided is unrequited love. But love by nature must be requited, because love is always an interpersonal self-giving and receiving. Love is "closely linked with the force of joining and uniting, and by its nature opposes dividing and isolating" (LR 68). When love is shared between two persons, a single "we" magnificently comes forth from two separate "I's." This reciprocal love produces a whole that is greater than the sum of its parts. Reciprocal love and caring is seen first in the relation of Adam and Eve, where there is a "reciprocity of gift" and a "true balance…in a mutual, two-sided exchange" (TB 261).

If reciprocity is rooted in both benevolence and love of desire, it can be genuine and sincere without the false note of selfishness. In this case, the two persons become co-creators in love: each desires the other and each wills the other's true good. Both persons must contribute their personal love to a relationship or there will be no authentic reciprocity and a union of persons. However, if egoism, utility, or mutual pleasure determines reciprocity, there will be something shallow and unstable about the relationship. True reciprocity cannot arise on the back of two egoisms, nor can it survive if it is based only on desire or on a "consumer attitude" (LR 71). Real reciprocity, on the other hand, unifies persons as it introduces confidence and reliability into a relationship. There is great joy and solace that comes from being loved and affirmed by someone and loving that person in return.

LOVE AS UNION: SYMPATHY AND FRIENDSHIP. Reciprocity leads to an attachment or union between two persons whose lives become dependent on each other. Wojtyła first deals with sympathy, which builds on mutual fondness by creating an emotional bond between two people who become united as they enjoy and experience things together. Sympathy represents a "we," but a tenuous "we" that depends predominantly on these coinciding emotions. Nevertheless, there is a sharp joy of togetherness in this shared action and experience. Sympathy is an affective form of love where the person's will and free choice do not play a significant role. "At best," writes Wojtyła, "the will consents to the fact of sympathy and its direction" (LR 72).

By pulling two people into the same orbit of affection, sympathy brings those two individuals closer together and leads to a delightful co-presence or emotional union. When I am fond of a person who is agreeable to me, she enters my field of vision with a "positive affective overtone" (LR 72). This happens in such a way that I want to be with her frequently and maybe even all the time. Consider the non-sexual summer fling of Sam and Helen. Both their families spend summer at the shore, where they make many friends. But after a few weeks there is a definite attraction between them as they come to enjoy each other's company. They revel in their common likes and dislikes, laugh at each other's jokes, and experience a real exhilaration in being together. There is an incipient friendship, but there is not yet any commitment or altruistic care for the other. There is simply a great delight taken in spending time together.

The weakness of sympathy lies in the way it takes possession of a person's affection and even his will. Consequently, the objective value of the other person is often overlooked. Yet the subjective force of sympathy makes people affectively attuned to each other and thereby draws them closer together. Two lives become closely intertwined: "One lives in the circle of the other, at the same time finding him at every step in one's own" (LR 73). Thanks to sympathy, people deeply feel their own reciprocal love and when sympathy fades, love seems to end as well.

Since sympathy is based on emotion, it can only join people together in a subjective way. Hence this union is usually temporary and insecure. In order to overcome the instability of sympathy, there must be an evolution into friendship where there is mutual benevolence or charity. With friendship, the role of the will becomes more prominent. If I am your friend, "I want the good for you as much as I want it for myself, for my own 'I'" (LR 73). Friendship represents a moral unity between two people who commit themselves to each other. With friendship, there is a "doubling of the 'I,'" where "the will relates to both with equal favor" (LR 74) As the Pope explains elsewhere, "the term 'friend' indicates what is always essential for love, which puts *the second 'I' beside one's own 'I'*"

(TB 562). The stable, moral harmony of friendship differs from the weaker and more superficial union based solely on sympathy. In friendship, unlike sympathy, the will actively commits itself, so there is a decisive choice of the other person, who is also affirmed for his or her own sake.

Love, therefore, must seek to bring about the transformation of sympathy into a more settled friendship. Love cannot be merely a matter of sympathy, because sympathy lacks benevolence and the firm commitment of the will. But friendship also needs the emotional vibrancy of sympathy, without which it will tend to be too formal or reserved. Sympathy is usually strong and vivid at the inception of a friendship when it is still in its earliest stages. A couple must build on the affection and emotional warmth produced by sympathy by working diligently towards a committed relationship that will survive once that sympathy begins to dissipate.

We should now realize that Wojtyła's discussion on love not only captures its essential features but also the path of its evolution. Love as fondness, a fruit of the sexual drive, precedes desire. A person reacts with delight to the other, who touches him in some way. This affection inspires an active seeking and even longing for the other as a source of one's self-perfection or fulfillment. Love matures into benevolence as the person further transcends herself to go beyond such longing to willing the other's good. Desire now coexists with an authentic, affirming love of the other. When reciprocity is present, love further matures into the mutual moral commitment and durable unity of friendship, which is enriched by the emotional warmth of sympathy. These aspects of love are woven together, and they are found to some degree in all types of love. Love always implies a "striving" for the other's good and a "uniting of persons," which perfects both the lover and the beloved (LR 78). The transition from "I" to "We" is just as important as the self-transcendence that enables the willing of another's good. Love can also be described as an interpersonal "synchronization of fondness, desire, and benevolence" (LR 78).

Spousal Love

Spousal love introduces a new dimension to these aspects of love, such as fondness and benevolence. The essence of this spousal love is "giving one's own person...giving one's 'I'" (LR 78). This giving of the self to the other surpasses willing the other's good. No other forms of love quite exceed the depth of spousal love. When a relationship is elevated to spousal love, there is something more than friendship: the reciprocal and total self-giving of two persons. As the Pope explains in *Man and Woman He Created Them*, spousal love "not only unites the two subjects, but allows them to interpenetrate each other, belonging spiritually to one another" (TB 485). This self-donation represents love's highest expression. In spousal love, declares von Hildebrand, we enthrone the beloved person and make him or her the "king" or "queen" of our personal life.[6]

Spousal love can occur between a person and God, but the most common form is marriage. When spousal love "enters into [an] inter-personal relationship," it leads to reciprocal self-giving that is permanent and exclusive (LR 79). But how can a person, who is incommunicable, give herself fully to another in this way? Doesn't the nature of the person resist such self-giving that results in possession by another? In the order of nature there is no self-giving, especially in the physical sense. Self-donation is simply impossible among impersonal creatures that are submerged in matter. Unlike animals, however, the person consciously possesses herself through self-knowledge and self-determination so that she can give herself *freely* to another. She recognizes the value of giving and chooses to make an exclusive and total gift of herself to another, and when that gift is reciprocated there is a mutual belonging. This transcendent bond is made possible with the help of the will "capable of committing itself in this way" (LR 80). In accordance with the inner "law of the gift," the person aims at a higher level of generosity and self-sacrifice than friendship. This ultimate generosity, which involves an exclusive devotion to one other person, is aptly called spousal love. Spousal love creates that "unity of the two" that finally overcomes the limit or "one-sidedness" which engenders love of desire.

Paradoxically, by giving my inalienable self to another I am not impoverished or compromised in any way. On the contrary, reciprocal self-donation enables both persons in this relationship to thrive and flourish: "This 'I' is not in the least destroyed or devalued, but, on the contrary, is

---

6 Dietrich von Hildebrand, *The Nature of Love*, trans. John Crosby (South Bend, IN: St. Augustine's Press, 2009), 66. See also Seifert, *True Love*, 19–24.

developed and enriched" (LR 80). The person achieves a depth of self-possession, affirmation, and self-confidence when he or she enters into this
permanent union of persons. Also, by loving someone in this way I have
greater confidence in my own creative, spiritual powers. By giving myself
to another person, I know that I am capable of making this gift, capable
of creating this lasting interpersonal union of self-sharing and receiving.
Spousal love, therefore, gives the person "a sense of interior richness, of
interior fertility and creativity" (LR 120).

In spousal love, a man and a woman commit to share their lives on every
level of their being. Hence this mutual self-gift has a sexual nature, because
it involves the whole self, including the body with its fertility and sexual
powers. This form of love is made possible by the body's "spousal character,"
which enables a couple to express and experience their love in its fullest
dimension: a total self-giving of their minds, bodies, and hearts (TB 259).
The two sexes, masculine and feminine, "meet in marriage, on the basis of
reciprocity,...and 'compose' the mature totality of reciprocal self-giving"
(LR 81). The corporeal nature of spousal love strongly reinforces its totality
and exclusivity. A man might share his gifts of wisdom and compassion with
many other people, but he gives his whole bodily self only to one woman. The
"sexual moment" is critical for spousal love, which gains "specific intensity"
through the unifying powers of sexual intercourse (LR 81).[7]

However, spousal love should never be reduced to self-giving at a purely
physical or bodily level. Rather, spousal love, "formed in the interiority
of the person" and "bound with benevolence and friendship," creates
an authentic and permanent union of persons based on their mutual
self-gift (LR 83). Sexual relations apart from such a union of persons is
not a true self-giving because it ignores the demands and the totality of
spousal love. Thus, if the sexual act is to embody and signify this exclusive
self-surrender or self-donation, it can only take place within the context
of deeply committed conjugal love.

Spousal love is depicted in Genesis as the pathway out of original
solitude. Affirming the other person and "welcoming the gift...creates
the communion of persons," which builds itself from within (TB 188).
As we intimated in chapter three, spousal love is the means to live out

---

7 Lopez, "Marriage's Indissolubility," 282–83.

the vocation of complete rational self-giving that lies deep within every
personal being. As the Pope explains, there are "two specific ways of real-
izing the vocation of the human person, in its entirety, to love: marriage
and virginity or celibacy" (FC 11). Either a person gives her whole self to
another in a way that leads to marriage or she gives herself to God. But
the person who attempts to reduce the richness of spousal love to an
experience of pleasure or exuberant feelings will remain a prisoner of his
narrow self-seeking tendencies.

The Psychology of Love

After explaining the components of love and demonstrating why spousal
love is exemplary, Wojtyła treats the psychology of love, or love in its "subjective profile" (LR 98). Saint Thomas Aquinas tells us that love is both a
passion and a virtue, and this insight is reflected in Wojtyła's exposition
on love. Love is surely something that happens to us or comes over us in
some way. We often hear from the lips of a young lover: "I'm just crazy
about that woman and I think I have fallen in love with her!" But love is
incomplete without virtues like benevolence or charity that more explicitly
involve the will. Wojtyła prefers to speak about the psychology of love
to capture the essence of love as passion in more contemporary terms.

"Human love begins with an impression," explains Wojtyła, and "everything in this love must be based in some way on this impression…accom-
panied by emotion" (LR 86). The experience of a person of the opposite
sex can easily make a potent impression on someone because of the sexual
drive. He refers to this physical component of love based on this sensory
image or impression as "sensuality." Sensuality is an experience of sexual
values connected with the body of a person of the opposite sex. For example, a man might have a spontaneous and emotionally vivid experience
of woman's sexual properties (or values) such as her neat black hair, her
petite figure, and her beautiful violet eyes. This experience represents
sensuality. Sensuality isolated from the other aspects of love has a consumer orientation, since it is directed at the body and only superficially at
the other as a person. Sensuality tends to sidestep the person in favor of
the body and the immediacy of its striking sexual values. A relationship
based on sensuality alone may have an erotic charge, but it has little else.

Sensuality is not love and could easily become the opposite of love: the use of another person for pleasure. To be sure, fondness and love of desire flow through sensuality, which is the raw material of romantic love. Sensuality, therefore, must always be complemented and elevated by the altruistic aspects of love, such as friendship and benevolence. Unless such integration occurs, one's inflamed passions can easily escalate into sinful love.

Although sensitive to the perils of unintegrated sensuality, Wojtyła never advocates sexual indifference. He acknowledges that "sensual excitability" is "an innate, natural property of a concrete person," and not something to be repressed or scorned (LR 91). Indeed, this "excitability," as long as it is acted upon within the context of marriage, can enrich a person's life and greatly enhance a marital relationship.

Affectivity must be clearly distinguished from sensuality. Direct contact between a man and woman involves an impression often accompanied by emotions, but those emotions need not be associated with the body's sexual values. In the case of affectivity, the object of a person's emotional experiences are the sexual values connected to the whole person of the opposite sex. A man's virility might make a vivid impression on a woman, and a woman's femininity might make a similarly strong impression on a man. For example, a man may not only be drawn to a woman's sensuous appearance, but also moved by her beguiling charm along with her feminine sensitivity. When a man is inspired by these qualities, which are uniquely embodied in this woman, he will delight in her presence. This affectivity is the source of affective love, which differs from sensuality because it does not dwell on the body and its sexual values. On the contrary, affectivity involves "longing for drawing near, for closeness, and at the same time for exclusivity or intimacy" (LR 93). Unlike sensuality, therefore, affectivity is not hobbled by a crude consumer orientation.

Affective love creates a bond between two people by uniting them emotionally even if they are physically far apart. However, like sensuality, affectivity is a subjective experience focused more on the *feelings* that come from being with another than on the person's actual qualities. A woman absorbed in the euphoria of affective love sometimes allows those feelings to shade the truth about the man she loves and the nature of their relationship. As a result, this love is often immature, based only on a vague understanding of another person's character.

Love seeks closeness to the beloved, but affective love "finds itself at a distance from the person, for it does not live on his true value, but…on those values to which the subject himself clings as to his ideal" (LR 95). This can lead to great disillusionment when those "true values" finally surface. Despite many warning signs, Mary cannot discern that Tom's passionate declarations of love and his signs of affection conceal a manipulation of her emotions out of a desire for sexual gratification. There is a great gap between the Tom of Mary's hopes and dreams and the "real Tom."

Thus, if a relationship is defined by sensual love, affectionate love, or their combination, it is destined to be superficial and incomplete. Despite the surface emotions, there will be no authentic intimacy or personal union. A couple in a relationship that feeds exclusively off these two psychological forces will actually be "separated from each other, although it may seem that they are quite close to each other" (LR 96). This psychological state of love represents love's "subjective profile," which falls far short of love in its full richness. Benevolence and friendship are either feeble or completely missing from such immature relationships. Their absence creates a void that can never be filled by sensuality or affection. However, one can sometimes build on these emotions by striving for benevolence and moral harmony that can eventually lead to the mutual gift of self.

Love's Ethical Character

The psychological energies or passions described by Wojtyła "cannot be ultimate concerning the structure of sexual love" (LR 102). The passions must be accompanied by true freedom and a virtuous disposition toward the other. Otherwise, there will be no authentic union of persons, which is the essence of spousal love. Wojtyła admits that it is difficult to capture the essence of love as virtue because it is a spiritual reality. We have already seen that love involves the virtues of benevolence (or charity) and friendship. Now he wants to go further and analyze more precisely how spousal love can be lived out in a virtuous manner. What are the specific ethical requirements of spousal love that will ensure the personalistic norm is realized within the depths of *eros*?

The first and most fundamental requirement is the affirmation of the value of the person. Every person must be affirmed for his or her own sake, as a *someone* who is never suitable for instrumental use. This affirmation is consistent with the "spiritual perfection" of the person who can never be "treated on par with a thing" (LR 104). Sexual values, therefore, must be subordinate to the value of the person. Every person must be esteemed for her own sake and can never be treated as a sexual object. The problem is that we sometimes forget we are dealing with a person. Wojtyła explains that someone in the throes of passion might "miss" the person. What does he mean? An attractive individual makes a powerful impression and appears only as a human being of the opposite sex or as a body for use. Personhood is not part of that impression because it cannot be conveyed by our senses. But human reason reaches "the truth that the 'human being of the other sex' is a person, is a somebody, and is different from anything" (LR 105). This truth calls for the need to integrate sexuality with affirmation of the value of the person, which at the very least means respect for the personalistic norm.

On the other hand, when love is not permeated with this steady affirmation of the value of the person, it can only be a disintegrated love. Romantic love must rise to the level of a committed mutual self-giving that exceeds the passionate feelings evoked by sensuality and affectivity. Love as virtue is not something that happens to us, but something that springs from the will. It is through the will guided by reason that I affirm a person and freely commit myself to him or her. There is no need to repress sexual values within the context of spousal love, but only to bind these values firmly to the value of the person.

An example might help to clarify Wojtyła's meaning. When Steve first meets Kate on a blind date she makes a strong impression that grows stronger and more vivid during the early stages of their relationship. He is soon convinced that his romantic feelings are genuine and mutual, and he asks for her hand in marriage even though they have only dated for several months. He is eager to sleep with her, but he is willing to wait until they are man and wife. The problem is that he knows Kate primarily through the prism of her sexual values, with which he is obsessed. He cares little about Kate's dream of having a big family. Nor does he take much notice of her sincere Christian faith, her deep-seated moral convictions, and her insecurity resulting from several failed relationships. These personal qualities of Kate don't interest him very much because his "passionate love" for her is purely sexual and emotional. However, Kate is not just an amalgam of sexual values. Steve must appreciate the full beauty and depth of Kate's personality and see her as a unique person who must be affirmed for her own sake and not regarded as a sexual object. She will overcome her insecurity, realize her dreams, and grow in spiritual perfection with the support of her soul mate's sacrificial love focused on her true good and happiness. Steve's superficial, self-indulgent "love" is not the way to such perfection. As Wojtyła explains, "Affirmation of the value of the person in which the full truth about the object of love finds its reflection, must itself gain ground among the erotic lived-experiences, the most immediate subject of which is either man's sensuality or affectivity" (LR 107). Love always affirms the other as a whole person who is loveable and beautiful not only because of her innate dignity but also because of those virtues and values that manifest this dignity in such a unique way.

The second ethical requirement is derived directly from the nature of spousal love. Spousal love means that two persons are willing to become the exclusive possession of each other. This form of love, accompanied by sensuality and affectivity, commits the will in a particularly thorough way because "one must 'give the soul'" (LR 108). This reciprocal self-giving and receiving creates a union of persons, a real mutual belonging that is lived out in a lifelong marriage. Sexual relations express and renew that love. Thus, there must first be a union of persons achieved by spiritual, selfless love, and "then sexual intercourse between them can be an expression of this mature union" (LR 109). Some people think it's fitting to reverse this sequence, but that attitude is grossly misguided. Any reversal represents an ethical transgression because love is replaced by mutual self-gratification. Sex without the commitment of spousal love and a union of persons is disposed only to pleasure.

When there is no such personal union or total sharing derived from the whole wealth of a person's being, sexual relations have only an erotic meaning. Sensuality and affectivity must be integrated with authentic spousal love, which is always a gift of one's whole self. Wojtyła's principal argument is that sexual activity itself is not a principle or source of union between two persons. Communion is created only through the mutual self-gift and dedication that binds two people together for a lifetime. Once that personal union is established, sexual relations can become a sign and a means of that couple's total self-giving. But sexual relations without personal union is only hedonism and mutual egoism, not love. If spousal love is deprived of "the depth of self-giving and thoroughness of personal commitment, then whatever is left will be its complete denial and contradiction" (LR 111). At the very least, there is a counterfeit union that lacks any foundation in sincere mutuality and friendship. This is why the sequence of events is so important. It's not just about the superficial advice we hear sometimes, "Just wait until marriage before having sex." It's about first becoming a personal union, belonging to each other through mutual self-giving, so that this love can be nurtured and intensified through the intimacy of sexual relations.[8]

Third, spousal love demands that each person must assume full responsibility for his or her love. That love must be mature and thorough enough to warrant the beloved's trust and hopes for the future. The hope engendered by love is the hope that a person does not lose her soul by giving herself to another, but rather "finds the greater fullness of [her] existence" (LR 112). Responsibility for love is always responsibility for the other person, for her objective good and her spiritual welfare. The magnitude of this responsibility is lost on someone who suffers from infatuation and wants only a romantic attachment. Such an individual confuses love with eroticism in a way that will hopelessly complicate his life as well as the lives of others. But "the 'flavor' of love," explains Wojtyła, "is bound with the sense of responsibility for the person [which] implies concern for the true good of the person" (LR 112). The expansive generosity of reciprocal, altruistic love deeply enriches both members of a couple.

Responsible love begins with the prudent and conscientious choice of a spouse. Choosing another person is equivalent to choosing "another 'I,' as though one were choosing oneself in the other and the other in oneself" (LR 113). Persons belong together only if it is objectively good and sensible for them to be together. A man must be able to find himself in his wife, and she must be able to find herself in him. Authentic spousal love is impossible, therefore, for two individuals who are so incompatible or who share so little in common that they will inevitably lead disconnected and

---

8 Rhonheimer, *Ethics of Procreation*, 113–14; see also Kupczak, *Gift and Communion*, 100.

unengaged lives. There must be spiritual kinship as well as enough physical attraction to sustain spousal love. There are no precise rules for making the right choice of a spouse, but psychological factors, temperament, and character would seem to play a vital role. A man and woman must make sure that they share similar preferences that bear on everyday life. This will help provide the suitable conditions for a true union of persons. Jill and Pete might have different tastes in music, but they are both mature, well-organized, conscientious about money, and fervent in their religious beliefs. Their compatibility and mutual affection lay the groundwork for a successful marriage.

It follows that the sexual values cannot play the overriding role in the choice of another person. Those values can motivate the choice to some extent, because spousal love certainly has sexual overtones. But everyone who chooses another must be fully aware that he or she chooses a person. A person's sexual properties will change over time, but the fundamental value of the person remains the same. We must bear in mind that we are not choosing a *thing* to be owned but a *person* to be loved, someone created to grow in wisdom and love and made for intimate communion with others. The designation "trophy wife" usually implies that a woman is chosen almost exclusively for her youthful beauty and glamour. Such motivation, however, cannot be the basis for a long-lasting relationship. True love is "interiorly full" only when a person is chosen for his or her own sake: "A man chooses a woman and a woman a man not merely as a 'partner' for sexual life, but as a person to whom he or she wants to give his or her life" (LR 115). Moreover, a responsible lover accepts and chooses the other person as she truly is, with all her virtues and vices. He does not love an inflated image of his beloved, but the real person.

The fourth and final ethical quality is freedom. Spousal love requires a *free* commitment to the other. Love as total self-giving seems to be a limitation of one's freedom for the sake of another person. Such constraints on freedom are ordinarily unpleasant and negative. But love makes them positive, joyful, and creative. Spousal love, therefore, is not a limitation or abolition of freedom but the perfection of freedom, since "freedom is for love" (LR 117). Authentic freedom allows a person to give him or herself in love, and this "fills freedom with the good" (LR 117). When I'm free enough to give myself to another and that gift is reciprocated, a communion is formed that satisfies the will, which, by its nature, always seeks what is good.

Freedom always depends on truth, on choosing the true good, which is discerned by reason that is not distracted by sub-rational emotions. Freedom from self-centeredness and purely emotional attachments creates the capacity for self-donation. Freedom is lost or diminished, however, whenever sexual values besiege the will. A person moved merely by sensual appetite does not strive for the true good of the other but only for his own pleasure. Moreover, the free commitment to another depends on knowing the truth about that person, and the prevalence of sexual values sometimes clouds that truth. Love must be based on the true vision of the beloved person, but someone captive to sensual passion is often deprived of that vision. Thus, when a person's will is thoroughly enthralled by sexual values, freedom is easily forfeited.

Benevolence, however, can rescue us from those forces of selfish desire that impede the will from making the gift of spousal love. The disinterested love of benevolence, caring about the other for his or her own sake, has a liberating effect because it brings the person beyond himself, beyond the selfish impulses that can accompany sensuality and affectivity. When this altruistic love begins to inform a relationship, the person can more clearly recognize the needs and gifts of the beloved. Benevolence creates an atmosphere of giving in which a person can also perceive the spousal meaning of the body, which is not a source of self-seeking pleasure but part of the gift of self. The body and its sexual drive can become the means to personal communion and the gift of new life, both goods that will fulfill another person and make her happy. Of course, there is often lingering tension between love and the sexual drive: "The drive wants above all to take, to make use of the other person, whereas love wants to give, to create the good, to make happy" (LR 119).

Let's go back to Steve and Kate. Without the help of benevolence, Steve will not be able to dedicate himself to Kate, because he is not free enough to actively care about her personal needs and aspirations. Under the spell of Kate's sexual qualities, he is unprepared for the sacrifices required of a husband and a father. Their marriage will be only a romantic attachment (at least on his part). But if he begins to care about Kate for her own sake, he will be able to commit himself to the pursuit of what is truly good for her. He will accommodate her religious beliefs and generously support those projects that make her happy and fulfilled. This disinterested love will temper his sexual desires and free him to make a true gift of himself to Kate. Sexuality will become a part of that gift. It will be a means and a sign of a total and lasting personal union that can overcome Kate's insecurity and lead to the transmission of new life, so that she can realize her dreams of motherhood.

Freedom and love, therefore, are interdependent. A person can give herself to another only if she is free from the undue influence of sexual values. But achieving freedom from sexual values and sensual desire depends on cultivating the altruistic side of love: benevolence and friendship. Benevolence balances the love of desire and emancipates this love from a utilitarian attitude. When a man and woman truly care for each other and will the other's good, the body and its sexual powers can be properly conceived as part of the human self that can be given to the other for his or her own good. Thanks to the "interior freedom of the gift," a man and woman can make a true gift of love to each other in the fullness of their bodily-spiritual personhood (TB 652).[9]

In summary, the ethical character of love is reflected in these four criteria: love permeated with an affirmation of the value of the person; the priority of mature personal union and mutual belonging over sexual union; responsibility for the maturity of one's love so that it deserves the hope and trust of the beloved; and a free commitment, based on a true vision of the beloved and unencumbered by sexual values.

Conclusions

Many books about love and marriage flatter and charm their readers. They offer facile advice but all too often fail to convey the sobering truth about marital love. Wojtyła's writings, on the other hand, challenge and inspire. His extensive treatment of love obviously has implications for an accurate appreciation of the high calling of marriage. First, while fondness and desire can happen quickly, benevolence and friendship take much more time to evolve. Yet the need for these altruistic and spiritual aspects

9 Rhonheimer, *Ethics of Procreation*, 114–15.

of love is beyond dispute. Any marriage without a mature caring for the other person is destined for a traumatic future. However, marriage has the greatest chance of success when people marry their best friend to whom they are also sexually attracted. Second, many couples make the same mistake as our mail-order bride from Russia and her American sponsor. They reduce romantic love to its lowest common denominator: the psychological forces of sensuality and affectivity. They assume that love is all about biological compulsion and the exalted emotions of romantic attraction. But, as we have seen, these potent energies are not love, but only the raw material for a lasting spousal love. They cannot create the personal union that is the foundation of marriage. That personal union can only be formed by commitment, caring, and, most of all, interpersonal self-giving and receiving. Third, couples can sometimes mistake mutual self-interest for the genuine reciprocity that is based on care for the other's true good. A couple will never get beyond the synchronization of their two egos if their togetherness is all about the joint pursuit of pleasure. When a relationship is driven by sensuality and affectivity, sexual intimacy can create the impression of a stable personal union. In this case, the subjective experience of pleasure becomes confused with love. But, despite such appearances, this experience is a form of mutual self-gratification that is the precise opposite of love. Authentic romantic love requires an "ethical completeness and fullness" where there is no trace of hedonistic tendencies (LR 151). Couples must affirm the other person for his or her own sake and respond to that person as a whole without the idealization or obscurity that comes from the predominance of sexual values.

Thus, Wojtyła's account of love might sound somewhat theoretical, but it has great practical import that is reflected in questions that help a couple assess the quality of their love: Does this couple merely experience love's psychological conditions, such as sensuality and affectivity, or is their love mature and shaped by benevolence and close friendship? Is there a real personal union rooted in a committed interpersonal sharing, or is there just a superficial togetherness based on strong emotions and sexual attraction? Can each member of a couple assume his or her share of responsibility for the hopes and dreams of the other person, and can this relationship achieve a sincere mutual belonging so that each truly leads a fuller life thanks to the other? Can a person find himself in his prospective spouse so that she brings out the best in him, or is he apt to lose himself in her? Is this a free commitment of the will based on a true vision of the beloved? Finally, are sexual obsessions or other coercive forces at work to undermine the freedom of that commitment? Sincerely addressing all of these questions will help a couple to know whether there is an authentic experience of spousal love at work that will deepen and mature over time. If so, they are ready to embark on the journey of a lifelong and fruitful marriage.

~

IN THESE LAST THREE CHAPTERS, WE HAVE CARE-fully explored the basic concepts of personhood, freedom, and love. We have shown that interpersonal self-giving and receiving is the natural way of life for the human person, who can achieve fulfillment only in union or solidarity with others. Therefore, "man and woman were created for marriage," because every person has a vocation to spousal love, and marriage is the primary way of living out that vocation (TB 201). We have also uncovered the unique character of spousal love, this mutual belonging or personal communion, which is created by the free and total bodily gift of self. That total self-gift is not present in other forms of love, such as friendship or parental love. Sexual relations are appropriate only for spousal love, where sexual union is the sign and means of this authentic union of persons. But self-donation depends on freedom from the bondage of unintegrated sensuality or affectivity. A couple must strive to overcome any residue of sensual egoism, which interferes with making a true gift of love to each other.

With these ideas clarified, we can move on to consider the interrelated topics of sexual ethics and marriage. The choices a person makes in the area of sexual relations affect the good of marital communion even if one is not married or never will be married. Therefore, individuals and couples must be well-disposed toward sexual morality before they enter marriage. And this disposition requires help from the virtue of chastity.

SIX

Sexual Morality and Chastity: A Personalist Approach

O N AUGUST 6, 1978 THE WORLD AWOKE TO THE news that Pope Paul VI had passed away at the papal summer residence in Castel Gandolfo. The frail Pontiff had gone there to escape from Rome's severe summer heat, but he would never return to the Vatican. His death was not a great surprise to Cardinal Karol Wojtyła, who was now Archbishop of Krakow, but it deeply distressed him. He admired Paul VI and saw in this saintly man a true father and pastor. On August 8, accompanied by his secretary and companion Father Dziswisz, he departed for Rome. The other Cardinals, many returning abruptly from summer sojourns, made the same trip. After the funeral, they participated in the conclave that elected Cardinal Albino Luciano, who took the name Pope John Paul I. Luciano was elected swiftly on the fourth ballot, making this one of the fastest conclaves in papal history. After the summer election, the Cardinals dispersed, but Wojtyła remained in Rome for a short time. On August 30 he met with the new Pope, and a few days later he and Dziswisz set out for Krakow.

The Cardinal resumed his busy schedule and had no plans to return to Rome for quite some time. But on the fateful night of September 29, Pope John Paul I passed away in his sleep. Cardinal Wojtyła received the surprising news by a phone call that interrupted his breakfast. He was quite shocked and murmured, "This is unheard of, unprecedented…" He immediately went to his room and then to the chapel for several hours of prayer and meditation.[1]

---

1 Stanisław Dziwisz, "From Krakow to Rome to the Glory of the Altars," in *Stories*

Now it was back to Rome for Cardinal Wojtyła and Father Dziswisz for yet another conclave. Before departing, the Cardinal preached at a memorial mass for the deceased Pope and took care of urgent business. He met with a few friends, including Wanda Półtawska and her husband. While bidding farewell, Wanda asked Wojtyła, "What name will you choose as Pope?" The Cardinal remained silent, but her husband answered, "Obviously, John Paul II!" Perhaps Cardinal Wojtyła had some intimation of what was to happen, but he never said so. He and Dziswisz boarded the plane for Rome, ready to face whatever lay ahead.[2]

People massed outside Saint Peter's Basilica as the new conclave began on the morning of October 15. Vatican experts confidently predicted the election of yet another Italian Cardinal, and proffered their views on the various men who were "*papabile.*" But there was an impassible stalemate among the main Italian candidates. To the world's surprise, the Polish Cardinal, Karol Wojtyła, was elected on the fourth ballot on October 16 at 5:15 p.m. He took the name John Paul II, as Wanda's husband had predicted just several weeks earlier.

The spirited crowd in Saint Peter's Square had been waiting impatiently for some news about the latest ballot. It was a lovely, clear October evening in Rome, and a bright moon shone in a darkening sky. When white smoke appeared, everyone in the Square knew that the Church had a new Pope in this unprecedented year of three Popes. When John Paul II addressed the Roman crowd, he put them at ease by referring to himself as the "man from a far country," whose Italian was not very good. He confessed his fears, but also his total confidence in Jesus Christ and "in His Mother, the most holy Madonna." The response of the Italians and other Catholics to this non-Italian Pope was overwhelmingly favorable. John Paul II settled into his new residence next to St. Peter's Basilica, where he would remain for the rest of his life.

Pope John Paul II accomplished much during his first year in the papacy. He released his inaugural encyclical, *Redemptor Hominis*, in March 1979. There was a trip to Mexico in winter, and then a more momentous trip to Poland in June 1979 that set in motion a chain of events leading to the

---

about St. John Paul II, ed. Włodzimierz Rędzioch (San Francisco: Ignatius Press, 2015), 28.

2 Wanda Półtawska, "Story of a Spiritual Friendship," in *Stories about St. John Paul II*, 78.

downfall of the Soviet Union. There were numerous pastoral visits, and a consistory that created fourteen new Cardinals.

But during this inaugural year, the Pope also began a series of short instructions on September 5, 1979, that will surely be the centerpiece of his legacy as Pope of the Family. These 133 catechetical talks, delivered during his Wednesday general audiences at the Vatican, span five years and are published as *Man and Woman He Created Them: A Theology of the Body*. Pope John Paul II, ardent defender of love and marriage during his ministry in Poland, now took his message to the world stage. He spoke in a prophetic voice and spelled out in great detail his elaborate theology of the human body. The Pope's timing was quite deliberate. There were preparations under way for a Synod on the Family that was to take place in the following year. John Paul II explained that the Wednesday catechesis was to accompany "from afar the work in preparation for the Synod… by turning attention to the deep roots from which this topic springs" (TB 133). The Pope's decision to begin these talks so early in his papacy suggests the high priority he gave to the issue of marriage and family. The final published work has undoubtedly helped to topple the reign of the old marriage manuals with their emphasis on rights and duties in favor of a richer theological vision of human sexuality.[3]

The Pope's extensive catechesis supplements his primer on sexual morality, *Love and Responsibility*, with a deeper Scriptural and theological exploration of love and sexuality. Both works deal extensively with the primary themes of sexual morality such as concupiscence and chastity, and both expose the great dangers of casual sex. Prior to the cultural shift of the 1960s, the prohibition against pre-marital sexual relations was a widely accepted moral norm. Supported by a matrix of traditional values, the vast majority of couples wisely chose to defer sexual relations until marriage. They appreciated the connection between romantic love, sexual relations, and procreation, and they wanted to be sure that their children were raised in a stable environment. But that has all changed. Recreational sex, which is wedded to a deep-seated contraceptive mentality, is now seen as normative. Many people follow their instincts along whatever sexual path

3 Tracey Rowland, "The Culture Wars," in *God and Eros: The Ethos of the Nuptial Mystery*, eds. Colin Patterson and Conor Sweeney (Eugene, Oregon: Wipf and Stock, 2015), 25.

makes them feel content. In a culture that now celebrates the anarchy of
sexual desire, only the thin veneer of consent separates right from wrong.

However, there are severe moral problems associated with non-marital
sex or even sex for pleasure alone within a marriage. Foremost among
them is a pattern of depersonalization that defies the personalistic norm.
Love must be infused with an affirmation of the person for his or her
own sake, and this implies that he or she can never be treated as a sexual
object. Sexual objectification corrodes even the most stable relationship.
In addition, people will have a more difficult time living up to the vocation
of marriage if they are sexually indulgent before marriage. A young college
male with multiple sexual partners cannot simply turn on a switch that
will suddenly spark an awareness of the body's spousal meaning.

Thus, any appreciation of marriage must include a sound theory of
sexual morality that explains why sexual relations open to procreation
are appropriate only within a heterosexual marriage. Sex as an expression
and sign of mutual belonging cannot be absent before two sexually active
people get married and then simply grafted on to the sexual relationship
once marriage occurs.[4] At the root of all these problems is concupiscence,
and so we begin this chapter with a close look at the Pope's sensitive
treatment of this topic.

Sexual Desire and Concupiscence

Although the body can be a means of expressing love, it can also be the
source of errant desires that destroy love. When the era of original innocence ends, the "man of concupiscence" emerges. The communion of
persons created by mutual self-gift is now vulnerable to being replaced "by
a relationship *of possession* of the other as an object of one's own desire"
(TB 254). As we have seen, John Paul II often refers to a threefold concupiscence that contaminates the human spirit: desires of the flesh, desires
of the eyes, and the pride of life (1 Jn 2:16–17). Concupiscence suggests the
"subjective intensity of tending toward the [person] due to [her] sexual
character" (TB 317). When those desires unleashed by concupiscence

---

4 John Piderit, *Sexual Morality: A Natural Law Approach to Intimate Relationships*
(New York: Oxford University Press, 2012), 148–49.

are not prudently restrained, the body loses its "personal meaning" and becomes a "terrain of appropriation" (TB 261).[5]

The Pope provides a careful description of how concupiscence evolves and how it impairs the relationship between a man and a woman if it is left unchecked. First, we must consider how concupiscence can lead to sinful love. Sensuality is a reaction to the bodily sexual values of another person. At this stage there is merely a passive interest in those values that directs us to another person based on his or her physical appearance. That interest, however, can rapidly transform itself into desire, as something in a person begins to "cling to" or "gravitate" toward those sexual properties (LR 130). At the level of desire, the person moved by these sexual values more actively seeks out the object of those desires in some fashion. Jerry the stockbroker might refrain from seeking a sexual relationship with his married co-worker, but thanks to his strong attraction to her he is often found in this woman's company. This illicit sexual desire is different from love of desire because it is motivated purely by another's bodily sexual values. If this desire is not controlled and gains sway over a person's reason and will, the result is carnal or bodily love, which "aims directly toward one and only one end as its precise object: *to satisfy only the body's sexual urge*" (TB 288). The progression of concupiscence underscores the power of the sexual appetite, which often conceals itself behind affection.

Thus, concupiscence of the flesh can quickly pass from interest to desire, and from desire to willingness, as a person yields to his desires and deliberately seeks to satisfy them through carnal pleasure. In this final stage, when passion is not subjected to right reason, there is a failure of the will, which results in a lack of resistance to sexual pleasure purely for its own sake. Jerry yields to his lust and attempts to begin an illicit affair with his attractive colleague. He does not approach this woman as a gift, "someone unique and unrepeatable, someone chosen by eternal Love," but as an object of use (TB 188). Sex in this situation does not serve or enrich a communion of persons but represents the satisfaction of the powerful sexual impulse.

When untamed concupiscence draws someone toward a person of the opposite sex, that person seeks only the satisfaction of his or her sexual

---

5　Kupczak, *Gift and Communion*, 126–30.

desire. Once these carnal energies are satisfied, the relationship abruptly ceases. Love looks forward to a future together. But the temporal dimension of sensuality is not the future but the present. This type of unbridled bodily love substitutes a sexually attractive body for the whole person. Sexual values displace personal values and "crystallize the whole lived experience between these two people" (LR 133). In this experience, the body loses its spousal meaning, and so it is no longer the means of giving to another. It is no longer a medium for expressing love and commitment or contributing to the other's good. As a result, "the personal relations of man and woman are one-sidedly and reductively tied to the body and sex, in the sense that these relations become almost incapable of welcoming the reciprocal gift of the person" (TB 259).

Neither sensuality nor concupiscence is a sin in itself. Sensuality is a reaction to bodily sexual values, while concupiscence is the constant inclination to desires that are aroused by that reaction. But concupiscence is aptly described by Wojtyła as the "hotbed of sin" (LR 143). Sin itself goes beyond interest and desire and proceeds from the will. There must be a voluntary or intentional choice to use another by acting in some way on those desires. The will leads us into sin when it is badly disposed or poorly guided by reason's misconception of love.

Sexual shame is a sign of concupiscence. The person who experiences concupiscence often feels some sense of shame, however remote. He senses the great difficulty of controlling his sexual impulses. The appearance of shame in the relationship between Adam and Eve came about abruptly after the fall. It marked a certain deterioration of their harmonious relationship. Both of them realized that their bodies were no longer just a means of achieving a communion of persons. In the *Radiation of Fatherhood*, Wojtyła explains how the descendants of Adam live in "inner darkness" because they are alienated from their own bodies, which they could not fully control (RF 361).[6] We are plagued by that "concupiscent look" that shades our vision of a person of the opposite sex (TB 281). Like Jerry, one comes to see in a woman only an attractive body isolated from the richness of her personhood. When the

---

6 See Carl Anderson and José Granados, *Called to Love: Approaching John Paul II's Theology of the Body* (New York: Random House, 2009), 111–12.

passions become inflamed, we are inclined to reduce "the wealth of the perennial call to the communion of persons...to the mere satisfaction of the body's sexual 'urge'" (TB 298).

Concupiscence may seem harmless to some, particularly to single men and women who are sexually vigorous. But the man of concupiscence cannot fully control his body, and so he can easily forfeit his freedom. In the words of Aquinas, when reason becomes a slave of the passions, freedom is "not genuine but apparent."[7] However, as we have observed, freedom is a necessary condition of love and self-donation. Also, sexual relations apart from a free mutual self-gift have no power to create or strengthen a communion of persons. Rather, the experience of concupiscence reveals that the sensual appetite has a purely self-gratifying character that fosters isolation rather than communion. Without spousal love, man seeks through the sexual drive "only *libido* alone" (LR 47).[8]

Sexual Morality and the Futility of Hedonism

Thanks to concupiscence, a person's whole approach to another can become shaped by this desire to use. The current moral milieu, captive to the utilitarian mentality, provides little rationale to quell erotic or emotional excesses. Such use, of course, is forbidden by the personalistic norm, which demands that every person be respected for his or her own sake. The use of another's body merely for pleasure has a depersonalizing quality that deeply concerns the Pope. The personalistic norm, which stands at the core of his theory of sexual and conjugal morality, implies that anything that damages the integrity of spousal love and personal communion is a retreat from moral responsibility. In order to appreciate the Pope's views on sexual morality more thoroughly, we must examine why using someone for pleasure is so damaging to marriage, even if this using takes place before individuals get married.

The personalistic norm forbids the use of another's body merely for pleasure, but what precisely does this mean? We can illustrate Wojtyła's

---

7 Thomas Aquinas, "Commentary on the Epistle to the Romans," in *S. Thomae Aquinatis Super Epistolas S. Pauli Lectura*, ed. Raphael Cai (Turin: Marietti, 1951), ch. 6, lectio 4, ad 2, v. 20.

8 Rhonheimer, *Ethics of Procreation*, 112.

principle with the help of a fictional couple, Joe and Gail, who represent any man and woman. According to the personalistic norm, it is wrong for Joe to intentionally have sex with Gail solely for the sake of his sexual satisfaction such that Gail's body becomes merely a source of an agreeable experience for him. This couple does not have sex for the purpose of expressing and strengthening their marital union, that is, to unite themselves as two free bodily-spiritual persons in an act that includes the possibility of procreation. Sexual intercourse is not the consummation of spousal love, the reciprocal self-giving of two persons who serve the transmission of human life. The sole motive for sex is the achievement of mutual self-gratification. In this experience, "the subjectivity of the person gives way in some sense to the objectivity of the body" (TB 259). But what are the specific reasons why such sexual permissiveness is so damaging to an unmarried man and woman, even when there is mutual gratification and the sexual act is consensual?

First, when the entwined procreative and unitive purposes of the sexual drive are rejected, the will "imparts to the drive a purely egocentric meaning" focused on pleasure (LR 50). There is no striving for the other's good, no commitment or selfless caring, and no formation of a union of persons. There is only a quest for the momentary and mutual satisfaction of sexual impulse. A cohabitating couple might think that an active sex life before marriage will create a bond that can inspire enough confidence to take their wedding vows. But they suffer from a serious delusion, because sex alone cannot bind two people together. "Instead of being 'together with the other' — a subject in unity, or better, in the sacramental 'unity of the body' — man becomes an object for man, the female for the male, and vice versa" (TB 259). This false sense of union can be damaging for a couple and lead to discord and severe anxiety when the relationship collapses. Human relationships must always be based on truth and not illusion.

Second, a misappropriation of the sexual drive by the unmarried pleasure-seeker has implications for achieving romantic intimacy and conjugal communion in the future. Wojtyła is not persuaded that a person can easily reverse his or her subjective perception of the sexual drive as a source of selfish pleasure. Nor can someone overcome the negative self-image associated with using another or allowing oneself to be used as a tool.[9] This confusion over the true meaning of the body, its spousal nature as a means of creating a union of persons in marriage, will linger even after these sexual activities come to an end. And because the spiritual life is so entangled with the body, the confusion caused by "utilitarianism in sexual ethics" will affect "the whole spiritual situation of man" (LR 50).

To appreciate the dangers of this confusion, let us return to our two acquaintances, Joe and Gail. They freely engage in consensual sex and allow their bodies to be "used" by each other for mutual satisfaction. In the sexual act, Joe does not relate to Gail as a spouse or even as a person but as a body to be manipulated for his immediate gratification. By yielding to concupiscence, Gail is not present to Joe as a gift, as a *person* of the other sex, but as a sexually attractive body. In choosing to use the body for pleasure, Joe contributes to an attitude of self-alienation from the body. For both Gail and Joe, the body is treated, experienced, and perceived as non-personal, an object separate from the conscious mind (or soul) for which it provides this experience of pleasure. By choosing to fornicate, this couple does not choose an act that fulfills them as unified bodily persons. On the contrary, the purpose of the conjugal act that flows from spousal love is a bodily communion of persons. But for Gail and Joe, the body is not part of the whole for whose sake the act is done, but only a means to achieve a pleasurable sensation. If men like Joe do not regard Gail's body as part of her subjectivity or personal reality, she too will come to think of her body in the same way. Yet "the body is an integral part of the person and thus it cannot be separated from the totality of the person" without disrupting one's well-being (LR 90). The objectified body is also stripped of its "beatifying meaning" (TB 149). It no longer makes manifest the person's spirituality or dignity "in relation to his or her own body" (TB 349).[10]

The damage caused by licentiousness, therefore, is twofold. First, it reinforces a negative or inferior image of the body, which is not regarded as an expression of the person's inner beauty. When the body is assimilated by a sexual partner, it is no longer "a sign of the person" but instead is

---

9 Even the person who uses another sees himself as an instrument. According to Wojtyła, "I must treat myself as a means and a tool since for my own sake I treat the other that way" (LR 24).

10 Grisez, *Living a Christian Life*, 640–55.

reduced to a mere object (TB 361–62). Failure to acknowledge the truth about the body and its vocation as a gift for the other can open the way to further humiliations and indignities.

Second, objectifying the body can easily create an impediment to the basic human good of self-integration, which represents the dynamic harmony among all parts of a person. Self-integration affected by sex for pleasure is the unity of a person's consciousness and spirituality with his or her body. By repeated instrumental use of the body, a person comes to see herself as a non-bodily or "spiritual" person who simply occupies a material body. There is a form of self-alienation and a loss of identity that accompanies this detachment from love. In *Man and Woman He Created Them*, John Paul II explains that concupiscence and sinful love (or lust) "brings with it an almost constitutive difficulty of identifying oneself with one's own body…in the sphere of one's own subjectivity" (TB 248).[11]

Without this aspect of self-integration, the sincere gift of one's whole bodily self to the other faces an obstacle, because the person has a disintegrated view of the self that does not include his or her body. As a result, damage to the good of self-integration impairs the person's capacity to make a full bodily gift of his or her whole self to another. When Gail gets married, she is still apt to regard the sexual act as a mere bodily act that is not infused by spiritual love but only represents a gratification of her sensual appetite. Her body, with its generative and spousal meaning, is not part of the gift of self that is acted out through these sexual relations. In her mind, marital love is something purely "spiritual": it springs only from her conscious, spiritual self and is disassociated (or only loosely connected) with bodily expression. When the body is so alienated and objectified, it is deprived of its spousal meaning. The body loses its capacity to serve the communion of persons and to make the fullness of that communion a reality. Thus, sinful love before marriage can deprive married persons of being together "in the sacramental 'unity of the body'" long after their sexual escapades have ended (TB 259). The objectified body becomes subject to manipulation through contraception and deviant forms of sexual behavior. But, as the Pope points out, it is "through the body [that] the human person is 'husband' and 'wife,'" and through

11 Ibid., 650–51.

the body that this husband and wife become an authentic communion of persons (TB 211).[12]

The hedonistic life, of course, is one of complete futility because it is based on a misapprehension of the sexual drive as the "drive to delight" (LR 46). The narcissistic hedonist simply cannot appreciate the spousal and parental values embedded in the gift of the body as a sacramental expression of the whole person. The pursuit of sexual pleasure for its own sake represents uncaring self-centeredness that leads to isolation and self-enclosure rather than personal communion and the joy of togetherness. Thus, licentious behavior deserves moral censure not only because it involves selfish using, but also because it is self-defeating, since the hedonist's individualism stifles the possibility of "living in a communion of love" (MD 7). The human person is made for interpersonal self-giving and receiving and will not find fulfillment in self-centered acts of pleasure.[13]

Chastity

How can we cope with the persistent threat of concupiscence and the reality that sexuality has become "an obstacle in man's personal relationship with woman" (TB 249)? How can we regard the other as a precious gift to be prized rather than an object to be used? The inclination to vice must be conquered by virtue. Chastity is the virtue that enables us to effectively deal with concupiscence and errant sexual desire. Chastity, however, is often misunderstood and maligned in this hyper-sexualized culture. In a culture that regards uninhibited sexual expression as the key to emotional health and happiness, chastity will be seen as a perverse form of sexual restraint. Chastity is disparaged so harshly because it collides with the priority of sexual desire.

But this virtue must be reassessed and enthusiastically embraced. The motivation for impugning chastity is often associated with resentment, an attitude that distorts our perception of moral values. Resentment proceeds from the vice of sloth, which induces people to shun pursuit of the good

12 John Crosby, "The Personalism of John Paul II as the Basis of His Approach to the Teaching of *Humanae Vitae*," in *Why Humanae Vitae Was Right*, ed. Janet Smith (San Francisco: Ignatius Press, 1993), 217–18.

13 Scola, *Nuptial Mystery*, 130, 220.

because it is too difficult. Resentment deprecates what a person should esteem so that he or she is not required to measure up to the true good. With the image of a true good like marital fidelity falsified, a person can acknowledge as "good" only what suits her arbitrary desires. A voluptuous married woman might conclude that fidelity to her spouse is an antiquated ideal. This is because she cannot resist the illicit passions of other men. So she easily succumbs to several passionate affairs, and tells herself that "free love" is just as good as being a faithful wife.

The Pope aims to revitalize the virtue of chastity by first cutting through the confusion about the nature of love. This was his mission in *Love and Responsibility*. As we observed in the previous chapter, people often reduce love to sensuality and affectivity. When they make this mistake, chastity is regarded as a repressive force aligned against the sexual expression of "love" and intimacy. Yet love is far more than an amorous experience. True love includes benevolence and friendship, and reaches its fullest expression in spousal love, the reciprocal self-giving of two persons of different sexes. This love binds people together and creates a durable union of persons. But if we see another through the lens of sensuality and affectivity as a sexual partner, we will not be able to approach that individual as a person to create such a union. Chastity provides the transparency that allows spousal love to flourish in all its ethical depth without smothering love's sensual overtones.

Thus, the virtue of chastity must be reinvigorated because of the natural affinity between chastity and love. Chastity is not just about moderation and self-control. Chastity must not only control concupiscence of the flesh, but also contend with "those interior centers in man from which the attitude to use emerges and spreads" (LR 154). What Wojtyła has in mind is that the utilitarian attitude so dangerous to marriage springs from subjectivism or egoism. Both can distort our reasoning and seize control of the will. Subjectivism can take two forms. Subjectivism of affection implies that the person who "falls in love" is merely caught up in the vortex of sensuality and affectivity that are the raw material of romantic love. The objective profile of love, which includes benevolence and friendship, is faintly present or completely missing. A person is so absorbed in the emotions that accompany sensuality and affectivity that he or she loses sight of the beloved, the real person who lies beyond superficial sexual values.

This form of subjectivism leads directly to a "subjectivism of value" which enthrones pleasure as the highest good. Pleasure becomes the "interior measure of all human acts" (LR 138). Subjectivism typically gives birth to sensual egoism: a person strives not for benevolent love and durable union but simply for an erotic experience linked with sexual activity.

A person must be liberated from the tyranny of pleasure and sensual egoism in order to rediscover the proper place of sexuality. This liberation opens the way for the virtue of love to take root, directed by reason and prudence and aimed at affirming the other for his or her own sake. The virtue of chastity makes this liberation possible and allows love to "possess its ethical completeness" (LR 151). With chastity's help, one can live up to the ethical requirements of love enumerated in the previous chapter of this book. Chastity combats subjectivism and sensual egoism so that love's creative powers can be unleashed.

Chastity, therefore, is a necessary condition of love. The primary meaning of chastity is a "'transparency' of interiority" without which love cannot be itself (LR 154). What does Wojtyła want to convey with this elliptical phrase? Chastity allows us to foster a transparent and direct relationship with another person that is not burdened by subjectivism, egoism, or any trace of a utilitarian attitude. We perceive the preciousness of the other person with great clarity. The achievement of this transparency, however, does not demand the suppression of sexual values or the denial of their potency. Chastity should not be understood in a Freudian way as the repression of sensual forces that will eventually erupt into a person's conscious life.

Rather, the essence of chastity consists in the habitual readiness to affirm the value of the person in every context and to elevate to the personal level all sensual or affective reactions. Chastity is above all a saying "yes," a positive reaction to the unqualified dignity and value of another person. Love is threatened when someone prioritizes pleasure at the expense of that person's true good. The person's intrinsic worth is discounted thanks to the power of his or her sexual values. But chastity guards against such tendencies. The true nature of chastity lies exactly "in this 'keeping up' with the value of the person in every situation" (LR 155). Chastity allows us to recognize the beauty, inner depths, and spiritual reality of the person who is made manifest to others in and through his or her body. In his commentary on the *Song of Songs*, John Paul II describes how the body is properly seen as transparent to the dignity and spiritual values of the person. Chastity allows us to experience the other person's beauty, which "focuses on what is visible, although at the same time it involves the entire person" (TB 554). Perceiving the other person with such transparency is the way Adam first saw the naked Eve before the Fall. One sees the person with "an original depth [that] affirms what is inherent in the person, that is, what is 'visibly' feminine and masculine, through which the 'personal intimacy' of reciprocal communication is constituted in all its radical simplicity and purity" (TB 176).[14]

The virtue of chastity is cultivated with the help of a healthy sense of shame. A woman tends to experience "relative" shame as she tries to protect herself from a man's predatory gaze. As a defense mechanism, she tries to conceal or mollify her sexual properties. A man, on the other hand, is more apt to experience "immanent shame" as he recoils at the "concupiscent look" he fails to control. A man who experiences such shame often has a difficult time identifying with his own body. He detects that "his body has ceased drawing on the power of the spirit, which raised him to the level of God" (TB 244). The Pope concludes that immanent shame is evidence of a certain rupture within our fallen humanity, "a breakup, as it were, of man's original spiritual and somatic [bodily] unity" (TB 243–44).

To a certain extent, sexual shame "charts the direction of all sexual morality" (LR 162). The experience of shame represents a fitting springboard to reflect on sexual ethics. Shame confirms that the person belongs to herself and naturally resists being callously used by others. The presence of shame instinctively tells a person to avoid any relationship to another person "that fails to correspond…to the very 'personhood' of his being" (LR 163). Thus, shame can rescue two people from relating to each other in a way that virtually annuls their personhood so that they become for each other mere objects for use rather than persons to be loved. Regrettably, many people are anaesthetized to the natural reaction of shame in our toxic culture that celebrates uninhibited sex and eroticism.

Sexual shame, therefore, is by no means a flight from love but rather an opening to love. The value of the person often stands behind his or

14 Kupczak, *Gift and Communion*, 54, 189.

her sexual characteristics, which make such a strong initial impression. Shame manifests that value not in an abstract way but in a way that is vivid and concrete. A man tempted by concupiscence, for example, pulls back because he has a deep experience of a woman's value and inviolability. He says to himself: "I must not touch her even with the interior will to use; she may not be an object of use" (LR 164). In this way, shame leads to the affirmation of the value of the person, which is an essential aspect of love's ethical character.

Chastity is impossible without the virtue of moderation or temperance, which can also be expressed in terms of self-mastery. The life of a chaste person is marked by mature self-possession and self-control. The virtue of moderation implies a settled habit of finding the right balance or "measure" for dealing with both sensual excitability and affective sensibility. The moderate person avoids the extremes of excess and defect, both of which detract from the ability to love. Moderation, therefore, is "the ability to maintain equilibrium among the concupiscence of the flesh" (LR 180). Anyone who has not attained moderation cannot be properly self-possessed or chaste.

The method for achieving moderation through self-mastery is continence, or the habit of restraining concupiscence of the flesh. "Mastery," the Pope explains, is "a virtue that concerns continence in all desires of the senses, above all, in the sexual sphere" (TB 341). Someone with this virtue abstains from fornication and restrains the sexual impulse. Continence is not easy and it does not function in isolation, but always in connection with other virtues, such as prudence and fortitude. However, continence or chastity must have priority in the order of operation, since sensual egoism can undercut a virtue like prudence. As Aquinas observed, "pleasure above all corrupts the estimate of prudence, and chiefly sexual pleasure which absorbs the mind and draws it to sensible delight."[15]

However, continence cannot be an end in itself. Continence blindly carried out for its own sake is not really a virtue. But when continence is relied upon to protect the integrity and value of another person, it is not blind anymore. Continence becomes an established virtue only when a

---

15 Thomas Aquinas, *Summa Theologiae*, II-II, q. 53, a. 6. See also Reinhard Hütter, "Chastity and the Scourge of Pornography," *The Thomist* 77 (2013): 12–13.

person restrains the advance of concupiscence for the sake of the value of
the person, who must never be an object of use. If Joe restrains his sexual
impulses because he is afraid of offending his parents, he is not acting
virtuously. But if he restrains those impulses out of respect for another's
dignity, virtue is present in this noble action. Temperance and self-mastery
are "indispensable in order for man to be able to 'give himself,' in order
for him to become a gift, in order for him to be able to 'find himself fully'
through a 'sincere gift of self'" (TB 186).

Conclusions

Men and women must resist the desire for sexual gratification stirred up
by concupiscence and rely on the personalistic norm as a measure of their
actions. That norm forbids using another for pleasure. Sex for pleasure
has the character of depersonalization that is incompatible with a person's innate dignity. It is also counterproductive, because it obstructs the
fulfilling goods of personal communion, family, and parenthood. Since
hedonism thrives on the instrumental use of the body, it is also frequently
the source of self-alienation: an inability to recognize the body as part of
one's personal reality. This deformed vision of the spiritual self separated
from the body "deprives man of the subjectivity proper to him" and turns
the body into an "object of manipulation" (TB 631). When the body is no
longer seen as part of the human "I," part of the gift of self, a couple will
not be able to "encounter each other and give themselves reciprocally in
the fullness of their subjectivity" (TB 201).

   Chastity, in conjunction with other virtues, allows a person to overcome
the seductive power of concupiscence. With the help of this virtue one can
always transparently see the other as a person in all her inner depth and
spiritual richness that is made manifest through the body. Only the chaste
person is capable of spousal love and the gift of self that creates communion.
Thanks to chastity, the body will not be an impediment in the personal
relationship between man and a woman but a means of self-giving. The
gift between man and woman who become "one flesh" has a sexual nature,
and so it must be purified of any trace of a utilitarian attitude. For the
chaste man and woman, the body in its masculinity and femininity is an
"expression of the spirit that tends toward personal communion" (TB 257).

It should be apparent that Wojtyła's personalist approach provides sound normative reasoning to support the Church's doctrinal statements on sexual morality. A mature person should recoil at being the victim of another person's untamed egoism. Nor should a person want to compromise the fullness of the gift of self, which is the basis for a sound marriage. Thus, Wojtyła's dichotomy between love and use remains apposite even in the midst of the moral chaos of this libertine culture. Hedonists may be unlikely to read *Love and Responsibility* or the Pope's work on theology of the body. But if they do, they should realize that Wojtyła is not the voice of the enemy, but the voice of a man who realizes that human dignity is always endangered by sinful love and contempt for traditional virtues such as chastity.

SEVEN

Marriage: The "Great Mystery"

T
HE VILLAGE OF NIEGOWIĆ IN POLAND IS A
long way from Rome. Within weeks of his ordination, Wojtyła
was sent off to Rome for the first time in his life. Cardinal Sapieha,
Archbishop of Krakow, had chosen him to pursue a doctorate in theology
at the Angelicum, a pontifical university operated by the Dominicans.
Upon his arrival in Rome, Wojtyła took up residence in the Belgian
College, which provided lodging for the Polish seminarians. Wojtyła had
the privilege of studying with one of the great Thomists of his day, Father
Garrigou-Lagrange. He finished his degree in just two years, writing his
doctoral thesis on the mystical theology of St. John of the Cross.

Shortly after his return to Poland in 1948, Father Wojtyła was appointed
as assistant pastor at the Assumption of the Blessed Virgin parish church
in the town of Niegowić. This small village was located near Gdów, at the
foot of the Carpathian Mountains. After many isolated hours consumed
by his theological studies, Wojtyła could now enjoy the companionship
and social activities provided by parish life.

The morning of July 28 marked the beginning of a pleasant summer
day as Father Wojtyła departed for his first assignment. He carried a small
suitcase, filled mostly with his books. After a long bus ride to Gdów, a one-
horse carriage rumbling across the rough terrain took him to a village called
Marszowic, where he went the rest of the way on foot. Crops about to be
harvested hazed the landscape and waved gently in the summer breeze as
Wojtyła hiked through the fields. After a short time, full of anticipation, the
young priest caught his first glimpse of the simple church. "When I finally
reached the territory of Niegowić parish," he said, "I knelt down and kissed the
ground. It was a gesture I learned from Saint John Mary Vianney" (GM 62).

Father Wojtyła was a gifted intellectual who later wrote prodigiously on philosophy and theology. But he also had a great talent for pastoral work. His natural warmth and obvious spirituality created immediate respect and affection. Father Wojtyła directed much of his energies toward helping the youth of this poor parish, and he assumed responsibility for its five elementary schools. Many families and children were still suffering the effects of the brutal Nazi occupation and welcomed the young priest's compassion and solicitude.

Eleven months later, Wojtyła was transferred to Saint Florian's parish in the busy city of Krakow, where he would later be appointed Archbishop. This parish was in close proximity to the Jagiellonian University and not too far from the cathedral, which towers above the city on Wawel Hill. The parish had an active youth ministry, which especially suited Wojtyła's pastoral gifts. Along with Saint Ann's, Saint Florian's provided chaplaincy services for the university. Wojtyła gave frequent talks to university students. "I would speak to them," he said, "about fundamental problems concerning the existence of God and the spiritual nature of the human soul" (GM 63–64).

The youth of the parish welcomed Father Wojtyła with great enthusiasm. They appreciated his mentorship and guidance. They were attracted to the young priest's charisma and impressive intellect. They also admired the unquestionable integrity that fortified his battle against the grim face of communism. Father Wojtyła's popularity grew immensely in a short span of time. One of his first priorities was the initiation of a marriage preparation program. This was a complete novelty in Poland at the time and reflected the young priest's instinct for the future, which would be a mark of his papacy. Father Wojtyła spoke candidly about marriage and sexuality, and he spoke in a language that young people could easily comprehend. One thing is surely clear about Wojtyła's early pastoral work: an unwavering commitment to strengthen marriage and family life. He sought to vigorously promote these Christian institutions, which were threatened by the militant atheism introduced by the Communists.[1]

This chapter considers some of the Pope's later reflections on marriage, which no doubt were influenced by his early years in the priesthood. It

---

1 Renzo Allegri, *John Paul II: A Life of Grace* (Cincinnati: Servant Books, 2005), 124–26.

seeks to explain in simple and concrete terms the permanent features of the sacred and unbreakable marital bond. John Paul II offers profound wisdom about marriage in many sources, including apostolic exhortations or letters such as *Familiaris Consortio, Letter to Families,* and *Mulieris Dignitatem.* In all those meditations, the Pope underscores the spiritual significance and sacramental nature of marriage. He speaks confidently about the "grandeur" of marriage, a notion often brushed aside in our casual culture, which prefers to think about married life in more pedestrian terms.

Most people still have an accurate, intuitive sense about the idea of marriage. They believe in the ideal of monogamy and sincerely hope that their marriage will last a lifetime. They are unconvinced by fashionable arguments for polygamy or polyamory, and they regard children as a blessing. As we have argued in this book, however, we cannot fully understand the eternal truth about marriage without laying the proper foundation. We have done this by exploring the meaning of personhood and freedom along with reviewing Wojtyła's extended explanation of love, including spousal love. With this background in mind, we can now concentrate on the theme of marriage. In the pages ahead we will unfold the truth about marriage, following the Pope's lead by probing in some depth God's original design for marriage and family. We begin with the Pope's instructive reflections on the importance of sound marriage preparation.

Preparing for Marriage

The need for extensive marriage preparation, which was discerned by Father Wojtyła at Saint Florian's, is certainly beyond dispute. Years earlier, Pope Leo XIII wrote that men and women should enter the married state "with proper dispositions [and] right ideas of the duties of marriage and its noble purpose" (ADS 41). Suitable preparation is more urgently needed in a culture where there is ambiguity about the nature of marriage. Moral and theological illiteracy has also become a major problem within the Church. Engaged couples must come to appreciate the sacramental character of marriage, and this requires some instruction in sacramental theology. Couples must also take the opportunity to reflect seriously upon their duties and expectations as husband and wife. It is vital to bear in mind that God uses indissoluble marriage to *"realize his creative and salvific plan* in the history of mankind" (LR 277).

Given his unusual dedication to this task as a young curate, it is no surprise that John Paul II thoughtfully addresses the matter of marriage preparation in his writings. In *Familiaris Consortio*, the Pope envisions marriage preparation evolving in three stages. Preparation for marriage actually begins in childhood, which the Pope calls the "remote stage." During this time, esteem for human values and interpersonal relationships is instilled by the child's parents. Parents and others begin to shape a child's character as they teach the importance of chastity and self-control. At this stage, children should begin to appreciate that marriage is a fundamental way of living out the vocation to love. Even at an early age a child can begin to discern a vocation to marriage.

The remote stage is followed by more "proximate preparation," which should take place as part of the religious formation of young people. This preparation should be largely focused on the meaning and Christological significance of the sacraments. The sacraments, which represent the acts of the Risen Lord within the Church, must be approached with the proper moral and spiritual disposition.[2] The sacraments accomplish in the human person the mysterious work of God, Who calls each one of us to holiness in Christ. The sacramental sign "always 'makes visible' the supernatural mystery that is at work under its veil" (TB 490). The sacrament of marriage is an encounter with Christ, who remains within the marriage as a source of grace and spiritual strength. In addition to this focus on the sacraments, marriage will be presented as a profound interpersonal relationship between a man and a woman that must be continually renewed and developed. This formation will also concentrate on the "nature of conjugal sexuality and responsible parenthood" (FC 66). Now is the right occasion to introduce Natural Family Planning (NFP) and the responsibilities of raising a family. The Pope stresses that a proper vision of the family apostolate and fraternal solidarity should be presented at this time. Young people should come to appreciate the great value of a "well-ordered family life," which can serve the Church's global mission (FC 66).

---

2 Carlo Rocchetta, *Sacramentaria Fondamentale* (Bologna: EDB, 1989), 380.

Finally, there is the step of "immediate preparation," which occurs in the months or weeks leading up to the wedding ceremony. A more intense format should be designed for engaged couples, especially for those who are unfamiliar with Church doctrine about marriage and the sacraments. This is the last opportunity before marriage for acquiring "a deeper knowledge of Christ and the church" (FC 66). Couples should receive additional instruction about the Church, which is not just another worldly institution. Rather, the Church possesses a certain "sacramentality," which is "constituted by all the sacraments through which she fulfills her sanctifying mission" (TB 491). The Church proclaims the mystery of salvation, and our eternal salvation is achieved with the help of the sacraments. Marriage, "the most ancient sacrament," has participated in this mystery from the beginning (TB 491).

During this final phase of preparation, couples should be reminded of the invaluable graces that flow from the sacrament of marriage. There should also be a close concentration on the responsibilities entailed by Christian marriage. Every couple must now prepare themselves spiritually for reception of the sacrament of marriage. A short contemplative retreat would be a perfect way to ready oneself for entrance into this new and permanent state of life.

In keeping with John Paul II's reflections in *Letter to Families* and the theme of this book, the last stage of marriage preparation might also include some candid consideration of the fundamentals. In a permissive and secularized culture that leaves little room for self-giving, there must be better formation grounded in the truth about the human person. There is a special need for catechesis on love to counteract the immense confusion that results from tendencies to reduce love to its psychological state. Young people poised for marriage must discover anew how delight in another person's sensuality can be combined with the Gospel love of *agape*.

It also seems fitting that sound marriage preparation, especially in the later stages, should include a careful consideration of the theme of marriage in the Bible. This reflection should commence with God's plan for marriage articulated in the opening chapters of Genesis. Since Jesus Christ reveals the "truth of marriage, the truth of the beginning," special attention should be given to His unequivocal teaching in passages such as Matthew 19 and Mark 10, where we learn that marriage is an exclusive and perpetual commitment (FC 13). This instruction should be supplemented with reflection on Ephesians 5, where St. Paul compares marriage to the spousal love between Christ and His Church. Along the way, several questions should be carefully pondered. What is marriage according to Sacred Scripture and what are its defining characteristics? Why is it so significant to think about marriage as a "covenant" rather than a contract? Why is marriage possible only between one man and one woman? What do we mean when we say that the marriage bond cannot be provisional and must last forever? Why is openness to life a necessary condition of marital unity? And why is marriage called the "primordial sacrament"? We turn to the Pope's answers to these questions in the remainder of this chapter.

Defining Marriage

Every couple looks forward with great anticipation to their wedding day. In the *Jeweler's Shop*, Wojtyła poignantly describes how Christopher and Monica eagerly awaited their marriage ceremony and celebration. Christopher recognized that on the day of his wedding, he and his bride would stand on the threshold of happiness. Such happiness is neither spontaneous nor unspoiled by difficulties. Marriage brings with it "the new pain of love" and the "pain of a new birth" (JS III:3). Yet despite its occasional travails, married life lived out with virtue and commitment remains the key to personal fulfillment and moral growth for many people.

So what is marriage? There has been some tendency over the centuries, even within the Church, to conceive marriage in legalistic terms. It is easy to lose sight of the personalistic dimension when marriage is reduced to a contractual arrangement that springs forth from the free will of a man and a woman. But the Second Vatican Council has strongly emphasized that marriage is an "intimate communion" (GS 48). John Paul II fully concurs: "Marriage is a unique communion of persons, and it is on the basis of this communion that the family is called to become a community of persons" (LF 10).

The Council Fathers also define marriage as a "covenant" (GS 48). Cardinal Wojtyła explains that this term is more "theological and personalistic" than a contract, "although the legal aspect is not lost" (PC 323).

The covenantal marriage bond is formed by the irrevocable personal consent of husband and wife that is found at the heart of the marriage liturgy. The marriage vow is different from an ordinary promise because it is a permanent and perpetually binding commitment. This "sacramental word" or exchange of vows gives an intentional expression "on the level of consciousness and will" to the reality of a couple's spousal love and devotion (TB 532–33). But the spoken language of the vows is incomplete. Those words can only be fulfilled when man and woman become a one-flesh union according to the eternal truth established in the mystery of creation. The "language of the body" confirms the words of consent and "expresses in this sign the reciprocal gift of masculinity and femininity as the foundation of the conjugal communion of persons" (TB 533). Without this consummation, marriage does not yet exist in its full reality.

This spousal covenant between man and woman mirrors the unique communion of life and love that God sought to establish with humanity. Just as there is a permanent mutual belonging between God and His people (Jer 7:23), so there is also such a mutual belonging or indwelling between man and wife. Marriage is not about the willpower to honor the terms of a contract but about participating in a sacred reality that transcends the spouses' individual wills.[3]

This marital communion grows out of spousal love as a man and woman give themselves to each other in a manner proper to the marriage covenant. As the Pope explains, marriage fulfills the "desire born in the atmosphere of spousal love whereby the woman's 'sincere gift of self' is responded to and matched by a corresponding 'gift' on the part of the husband" (MD 10). The complex reality of spousal love, including desire, the mystery of reciprocity, friendship, the giving of one's whole self to the other, begins to disclose what the marital relationship is all about. The vocation to spousal love fulfilled in marriage with the help of grace is based on the "law of the gift" inscribed in every person. "Marriage proceeds from the very 'interiority' of this love, for the shape of the reciprocal self-giving of a man and woman demands it" (LR 293).

---

3 Carlo Rocchetta, *Il Sacramento Della Coppia* (Bologna: EDB, 1996), 164. See also Ouellet, *Mystery and Sacrament of Love*, 31–32.

Marriage is also a social (and legal) institution, for it is "the only 'place' in which this self-giving in its whole truth is made possible" (FC 11). The institution of marriage provides the appropriate framework and support for the living out of spousal love. Marriage "justifies" sexual relations between a man and woman within society at large. Married men and women need not experience any shame or stigma for living together and expressing their conjugal love. For this reason, the marriage ceremony is a public act that takes place before society and the Church. The public vows that finalize the marital bond bear witness to the maturity of the interpersonal union between a man and a woman. And, thanks to the sacrament of marriage, this sexual relationship is sanctified by the Creator as well as justified in the eyes of society.

In summary, marriage has "three dimensions which imply one another": *institution, covenant, and communion* (PC 323). As an institution, marriage provides the proper framework and support for spousal love. Marriage, rooted in sexual reciprocity, is also a covenantal communion between man and woman, mirroring the irrevocable covenant between God and His people or Christ and His Church. Hence it is far more than a contractual or open-ended arrangement.

Unfortunately, those who perceive marriage solely through the prism of psychology and romance fail to grasp what marriage is all about. Think about a real couple we'll call Patty and Don, who have been married for over forty years. They were two mature individuals who fell in love in college and decided that they wanted to spend their lives together. During the liturgy of marriage, they declared their perpetual vows and have been faithful to those vows every day. Despite their generous openness to new life, they were not blessed with the gift of children. But thanks to their commitment and mutual self-giving, they enjoy a deep personal communion renewed many times through the conjugal act. They experience the confidence, security, and joy of permanent togetherness. Anyone who knows them knows that they belong to each other and live for the other in a way that is uniquely precious. Just as one cannot imagine God abandoning His people, so one cannot imagine Patty or Don abandoning their spousal covenant. If love is the meaning of being alive, spousal or married love is being most fully alive.

The Properties of Marriage

Three essential properties follow from the covenantal view of marriage and the logic of spousal love: *real unity, absolute fidelity, and fruitfulness.* A number of Scriptural sources confirm this conception of marriage as a natural institution defined by unity, fidelity, and fruitfulness. These properties are also obliged by the unique nature of spousal love and the personalistic norm, which governs all sexual relationships. Also, given these three indispensable features of married life, we can deduce that marriage must always be heterosexual, indissoluble, monogamous, and open to new life. Attempts to define marriage aside from these norms, for example, "outside strict monogamy (which implicates indissolubility), are incompatible with the personalistic norm" (LR 195). They are also incompatible with the Word of God. By exploring the different norms of marriage, we can go a long way in unveiling the hidden plenitude of the nuptial mystery.[4]

First, marriage is always a heterosexual union. In *Mulieris Dignitatem*, John Paul II explains that a careful reading of Genesis reveals two ways in which a human person images the Creator. Each individual person has a rational nature, and so he or she is created in God's image as a rational free being. But the Genesis text, "male and female He created *them*" (Gn 1:27) also means "that man and woman, created as a 'unity of the two' in their common humanity, are called to live in a communion of love, and in this way to mirror in the world the communion of love that is in God, through which the Three Persons love each other in the intimate mystery of the one divine life" (MD 7). Thus, man and woman form a conjugal communion and, through that communion, image the Trinity. Just as the Trinitarian union of interpersonal love is real and substantial, so is this conjugal communion, which is created by the total self-giving and receiving of spousal love.[5]

This conjugal union, rooted in sexual difference, which is essential to marriage, transforms each member of a couple as one becomes "husband" or "wife." They "are no longer two," says Jesus (Mk 10:8), but form a higher

---

4 Ouellet, *Mystery and Sacrament of Love,* 68–75.
5 Ibid., 33.

and more complete unity with a new center of action that can generate new life. "Together," writes the Pope, "they thus become one single subject, as it were, of that act and that experience" (TB 207). This "real union of persons" goes beyond the procreative capacities that are enabled when their bodies are joined together (PC 323). The two retain their identity but still become a single unified presence that transcends their individuality and shapes their whole being. There is a "reciprocal permeation so that the persons can live in and by each other" (LR 113). As St. Paul declares, "The one who loves his wife, loves himself" (Eph 5:28).[6]

This spousal love, which creates a permanent union of persons, requires sexual complementarity. According to the Pope, "This conjugal communion sinks its roots in the natural complementarity that exists between man and woman" (FC 19). Only a man and a woman can give their whole bodily self to the other, including their fertility and potential motherhood or fatherhood, which is an essential part of their personal identity. By natural design, only a man and a woman can become one flesh so that each becomes a complete gift for the other in a way that "fulfills the very meaning of being and existence" (TB 186).

Since only a man and woman can create a full, fruitful communion consistent with the total sharing of spousal love, marriage is by nature heterosexual. Two people of the same sex are simply incapable of the totality and fruitfulness that characterizes the gift of spousal love. A same-sex couple cannot form a transformative union that preserves the identity of each spouse but is still greater than the sum of its parts because of its procreative potential. There is no possibility of the complete mutual self-giving of spousal love because there is no sexual duality, which is always a prerequisite of such love. On the contrary, homosexual relations flout the natural language and procreative meaning of the body along with the "inner order of conjugal communion" (TB 637). Sexual complementarity, however, opens man and woman to the complete gift of self, which allows each one to grow in self-awareness and find him or herself in the *other*: the spouse as well as the child who is welcomed as the fruit of their love. A man, for example, discovers his masculine

6 David Schindler, "The Crisis of Marriage as a Crisis of Meaning," *Communio* 41 (2014): 346–48.

qualities by seeing himself in the light of the feminine other within the intimacy of marital union.[7]

Thus, the impossibility of same-sex marriage is a logical consequence of the immutable nature of spousal love, which is based on this sexual reciprocity. We must face up to the "consequences of the decision of the Creator" (MD 1). He made man male and female, this dual unity, or "unity of the two," in order to form a personal communion that has a sexual nature. In the reciprocal relationship of these two persons who become a "one flesh" union, "sex expresses an ever-new surpassing of the limits of man's solitude" (TB 167). In addition, many New Testament passages (e.g., Mt 19:3–9) touch directly on the heterosexual nature of marriage by reminding us of the unitive and generative nature of spousal love. According to John Paul II, "if someone chooses marriage, he must choose it exactly as it was instituted by the Creator 'from the beginning'" (TB 434). By creating the natural order in a certain way, God has made the rules about marriage, and as His faithful servants, we are obliged to obey.

The second permanent feature of marriage is indissolubility and absolute fidelity. This quality of marriage follows logically from the nature of spousal love. The marriage vow, which ratifies, proclaims, and sanctifies a couple's spousal love, is not just an ordinary promise, but a binding and irrevocable commitment. The interpersonal giving and receiving characteristic of spousal love entails a totality and permanence that is absent from other forms of love.

There is certainly adequate Scriptural warrant for indissolubility. In the First Letter to the Corinthians, written shortly after Paul's sojourn to Corinth in AD 51–52, there is a clear prohibition of divorce with reference to Jesus's own teaching on the matter (1 Cor 7:10). When Jesus is questioned about divorce by the Pharisees, he refers his questioners to the opening chapters of Genesis. This arrangement was the original plan of the Creator and therefore part of the "*ethos* of creation" (MD 12). "Male and female He created them" (Gn 1:27), Jesus reminds his audience, and when a man is joined to his wife "the two shall become one flesh" (Mt 19:6). And "therefore what God has joined together let not man put asunder" (Mt 19:6). Moses allowed for divorce as a concession to our

7 Scola, *Nuptial Mystery*, 102–3.

fallen human nature and hardened hearts. But we must return to the way it was in the beginning. This sounds like a difficult teaching, but Jesus goes on to explain that marriage is not for everyone. Marriage is a gift, with abundant graces, for those who have been called to this way of life: "He who is able to receive this, let him receive it" (Mt 19:12).

In the simplest terms, marriage is indissoluble because if love is truly based on the value of the person, it will endure forever. For the gift of self to be total and unconditional, it cannot have temporal boundaries. Nor can that gift be withdrawn without losing its character as a complete gift of self. As the Pope explains, "if the person were to withhold something or reserve the possibility of deciding otherwise in the future, by this very fact he or she would not be giving totally" (FC 11). Thus, indissolubility necessarily flows from the nature of the gift of one person to another, which must be "lasting and irrevocable" (LF 11). A tentative or conditional union would be equivalent to two people "loaning" themselves to each other rather than making a total gift of themselves.

Hence, when two people become a one-flesh union, they must strive for "fidelity to marriage's promise of total mutual self-giving" (FC 19). Unless the marital union is permanent and exclusive, it cannot provide the security, inner peace, and joy of togetherness that flow from spousal love. Without marital permanence, a husband and wife cannot have confidence that their spouse will always support them through life's difficult trials and challenges. A marital union cannot be dependent on love's "subjective profile," especially sensual attraction, which usually recedes over time. To base such a profound interpersonal union on these unstable and shifting grounds will put any marriage at great risk. What's required is the will of a husband and wife, fortified by grace and undistracted by emotion, to embrace and renew their perpetual marriage bond. A change of heart or loss of affection cannot abolish the ontological reality that a married couple who have had conjugal relations are forever united to each other as spouses, since they "are no longer two" (Mk 10:8).[8]

---

8 Some of the material in the last few paragraphs and on the sacramentality of marriage has been adapted from a previously published article. See Richard A. Spinello, "The Logic of the Gift: Spousal Love and Marriage in the Thought of Karol Wojtyła/ John Paul II," in *Woman as Prophet in the Home and the World*, ed. Mary Lemmons (Lanham, MD: Lexington Books, 2016), 177–95.

This permanent exclusivity is also a potent symbol of Christ's abiding love for His Church. Just as Jesus is a faithful witness to God's promise to care for His Church, so too is a married couple called to everlasting fidelity during their life together on earth. According to the Pope, indissolubility is the *"fruit, sign and requirement"* of this couple's exclusive and perpetual self-donation that reflects Christ's enduring dedication to His holy Church (FC 20).[9]

Dissent on the issue of indissolubility, however, remains a source of tension in the Church. Some theologians propose a more contractual conception of marriage. They regard the marital union as simply a moral bond that is contingent on the good will of the two spouses. Breaking that bond might be a sinful act on the part of one or both members of a married couple, but that bond is sustained only through their ongoing consent. This conception of marriage is consistent with secular anthropology, which gives priority to the spouses' individual freedom. They have the ability to make and break commitments, and this includes the solemn commitment that creates the marriage bond. However, according to the covenantal view, which is faithful to the character of spousal love, when two people freely and consciously give themselves to each other there is a lasting communion of life and love that cannot be broken. The freedom of the spouses must be limited by the truth of marital permanence, "rooted in the personal and total self-giving of the couple" (FC 20). Indissolubility is demanded by the totality of this gift, which implies offering to another person one's whole self for life while also forsaking the possibility of reclaiming that gift.[10]

Third, marital love must also be monogamous or exclusive because the union of man and woman is a full and complete union based on the gift of one's whole self. According to the Pope, marital communion is "radically contradicted by polygamy" (FC 19). When a married couple is truly committed to mutual self-giving and total union, there is no possibility for a simultaneous union of the same kind. Spousal love, the love of mutual self-giving, "commits the will in a particularly thorough way" (LR 108). Polygamy, therefore, is not truly marriage. It is a pale imitation of

9 Nicholas Healy, "The Merciful Gift of Indissolubility and the Question of Pastoral Care for Civilly Divorced and Remarried Catholics," *Communio* 41 (2014): 323.

10 Lopez, "Marriage's Indissolubility," 276, 284.

spousal love, and it denies the equal personal dignity of men and women. In polygamous relationships men too often regard their multiple wives as objects that represent only a variety of sexual values or a means of reproduction. There are many other moral arguments against polygamy, such as the way it causes fractured relations between siblings and half-siblings.[11]

Monogamy, on the other hand, underscores the value and uniqueness of the chosen person as the central and exclusive focus of marital love. In true spousal love someone chooses one special person to whom he or she wants to give his or her entire life. Marriage is about covenantal communion or mutual belonging, and this I-Thou relationship is possible only between two people.

In addition, the fact that the gift of self is corporeal as well as spiritual strongly reinforces its monogamous character. If it were not exclusive of other sexual relations, the conjugal union would be severely defective. It would not be a union of two equal persons and it would not be consistent with spousal love, which is the total gift of self and total reception of the other.[12] If marriage is to be a sacramental sign of the union between Christ and His Church based on His "unconditional faithfulness," there is no room for polygamy or other sexual partners (FC 20).

The final requirement of marriage is fruitfulness. Since the time of original innocence, the unity of man and woman has been endowed with fruitfulness (Gen 1:28). The gift of fruitfulness allows the sexual act to achieve its full potential. Man and woman who answer the call to become "one flesh" must acknowledge that this union "has itself been blessed from the beginning with the blessing of fruitfulness" (TB 526). A married couple discover not only the spousal meaning of the body but its generative and paternal meaning as well, as they enter into the "cosmic current" that carries on the work of bringing forth new life (LR 38). With God's cooperation, they are capable of the greatest possible gift: a new human person who comes into being as a result of their love for each other. Spouses have a direct share in the "great mystery of eternal generation" (MD 18).

Also, when a child is born, man and woman take a further step along their journey of self-discovery and self-enrichment. Thanks to the birth

---

11 John Finnis, "Marriage: A Basic and Exigent Good," *The Monist* 91 (2008): 396–414.

12 Lopez, "Marriage's Indissolubility," 283.

of the child, "*the mystery of femininity reveals itself in its full depth through motherhood*" (TB 210). Both man and woman "*know each other reciprocally in the 'third' originated by both*" (TB 211). They find not only their physical likeness but also their identity in this child. Every person is a social being who comes to know him or herself through the other, and this self-knowledge happens in a special way through children. The person exists most fully as a "we," not an "I." Marriage, blessed with the gift of new life, expands the "we" into a family community.

A couple cannot obstruct this potential fruitfulness of marital communion, since such action is incompatible with the gift of one's whole self that liberates love's creative energies. Spousal love creates fulfilling goods, such as conjugal communion and new life. Contraceptive intercourse, however, means that a man and woman do not give their whole bodily-spiritual personhood to each other. There is a missing element in the marital union of their shared lives as a whole, since they hold back their fertility from each other. As the Pope explains, "the logic of the sincere gift of self requires that a communion of persons...becomes a communion of parents" (LF 11). Every married couple must have an attitude of openness to new life, a gift of the Creator. When a husband and wife freely choose sexual intercourse, they engage in an act of loving bodily union that, by its nature, serves the purpose of procreation.[13]

There is (or should be) an important link between fruitfulness and indissolubility. This gift of life, a newborn child, witnesses to the inseparability of spousal union, conception, and birth. Husband and wife become embodied in the person of their child, who carries within herself what belongs to both parents. Marital unity is thereby reinforced as this husband and wife *forever* become mother and father to the same child. As a sign of their spousal communion, the child always reminds parents that they participate in a love that is far greater than what they can comprehend.[14]

Responsible conjugal love, therefore, is completely tethered to responsibility for procreation. A willingness for parenthood, concludes Wojtyła, "constitutes a necessary condition of love," because without it a married couple's comprehensive union is disrupted (LR 223). If sexual intercourse

---

13 Rhonheimer, *Ethics of Procreation*, 83–84.

14 Lopez, "Marriage's Indissolubility," 289. See also Fabrizio Meroni, "Pastoral Care of Marriage: Affirming the Unity of Mercy and Truth," *Communio* 41 (2014): 446.

is not generative, it cannot be unitive. Without the interior attitude of parental readiness, a couple is saying "I refuse to be a father," and "I refuse to be a mother," even though I engage in this generous act whose primary purpose is procreative. This refusal to share their fertility is a living contradiction to a full one-flesh union that can strike at the heart of the marriage covenant.

This interior attitude of readiness for parenthood achieves the right equilibrium between overemphasis on procreation and its positive exclusion. In marriage, one strives for interpersonal union along with the other's true good, which includes the goods of parenthood and family. Those goods should not be explicitly excluded in the sexual act. However, spouses should not be required to actively will procreation in every act of sexual intercourse. This position is too demanding and deflects the spouses' attentions from their love for each other expressed in the conjugal act. It is sufficient for a married couple to accept the possibility of conception even if they do not wish it to happen in a particular instance.

The Sacramental Character of Marriage

How can one possibly live up to this high calling of marriage? How can married couples keep their union permanent, fruitful, and exclusive as traditional sexual ethics unravels? Fortunately, marriage is not just a human or legal institution; it is also a sacrament. Marriage is "the most ancient sacrament" because it was established by the Creator at the moment He created in His image the first man and woman as gifts for each other (TB 491). In the words of Genesis, "Therefore a man leaves his father and his mother and cleaves to his wife, and they become one flesh" (Gn 2:24). Marriage reflects the Creator's plan for man and woman to live in a communion of life and love. In the state of man's original innocence, we find the unity of the couple, man and woman, as part of the mystery of creation. Marriage was instituted as part of the "sacrament of creation," in order to "extend the work of creation or procreation...to further generations of human beings" (TB 506). Indeed, writes the Pope, marriage represents the "central point" of this sacrament of creation, and in this respect we can call it the "primordial sacrament," which "draws its efficaciousness from the 'beloved Son'" (TB 506).

Thus, marriage is a sacred institution, since man and woman are joined together for the purpose of cooperating with God to create new life. Marriage was instituted in the beginning to further the work of God's creation, and also "to extend the same sacrament of creation to future generations of human beings" (TB 506). Marriage became unsettled, however, by original sin and man's fallen sexuality. Marriage was deprived of the full supernatural help it relied upon prior to the fall. Nonetheless, marriage never ceased to be a sacrament and "the platform for the realization of God's eternal plans" (TB 507). As the original sacrament, marriage has remained a sign of the mystery of salvation already at work in God's creation.

The theme of sacramental marriage also occupies an important place in the teaching of Jesus Christ. Christ not only confirmed the existence of marriage instituted by the Creator (MT 19), but he also included marriage "as an integral part of the new sacramental economy" (TB 511). Christ institutes marriage as one of the seven sacraments, which are all signs and instruments of graces in the economy of salvation. The aim of this new sacrament is to aid man after the fall, because he is now burdened by the threefold concupiscence. Christ "*opens* marriage to the salvific action of God, to the powers flowing from the '*redemption of the body*'" (TB 518). The "sacrament of creation" becomes the "sacrament of redemption," since marriage becomes not only a source of supernatural graces but also a sign of Christ the Redeemer's gift of Himself to His Church. Thanks to this sacrament of redemption, the "'language of the body' can be reread in the truth" so that the body can retrieve and preserve its spousal meaning (TB 538).

Thus, marriage is a sacrament in a dual sense. Marriage is "sacred" because it was instituted by the Creator in order to sanctify man and woman as His collaborators in the creation of new life. In this regard, marriage is aptly called the "primordial sacrament." Marriage is also something "holy," one of the seven sacraments that provide sanctifying grace to spouses as a way of helping them faithfully live out this challenging vocation. These sanctifying graces continue for the life of the marriage: "The gift of Jesus Christ is not exhausted in the actual celebration of the sacrament of marriage, but rather accompanies the married couple throughout their lives" (FC 56).[15]

---

15 Ouellet, *Mystery and Sacrament of Love*, 57.

Husband and wife are the ministers who confer this sacrament on one another by their words of consent, through which the marriage comes into being. These words formalize the permanent covenant of mutual self-giving and thereby objectify spousal love into the form of marriage. But marriage as a personal communion becomes a reality only through the marital unity of the conjugal act. According to the Pope, "without this consummation," marriage does not yet exist "in its full reality" (TB 532). Each time a married couple sincerely engages in the marital act, they renew the sacramental reality of their marriage.[16]

The sacramental character of marriage is often overlooked as a couple's wedding day gradually fades into history. But many faithful Christian couples, like our happily married couple Don and Patty, will readily admit that the real source of their successful marriage is its "sacramental power." That power preserves marital unity, which doesn't just depend on the married couple's will power but is a gift from God. The sacred bond of marriage is put into the hands of Christ Himself, Who always stands ready to bestow His sanctifying graces. Those graces heal the wounds of sin and help the couple cope with the daily tribulations of married life. They also perfect both persons within this conjugal union so that they can grow in virtue and holiness. Reception of the Eucharist and Eucharistic adoration as a couple are powerful means for fortifying a marriage with supernatural help. John Paul II explains that thanks to the graces of marriage, natural conjugal love takes on "a new significance which not only purifies and strengthens them, but raises them to the extent of making them the expression of specifically Christian values" (FC 13).

Finally, it is important to underscore why marriage stands out in the sacramental order. In addition to being the "sacrament of creation," marriage is also a *prototype* of all the Church's sacraments. According to the Pope, "all the sacraments of the New Covenant find their prototype in some way in marriage as the primordial sacrament" (TB 511). The spousal union of husband and wife mirrors Christ's union with His Church (Eph 5:22–33). Marriage is blessed from the beginning with natural and supernatural fruitfulness flowing from the unifying powers of spousal love. Similarly, all the sacraments of the Church have a spousal dimension

16 Schu, *The Splendor of Love*, 140–42.

because they draw their power and efficacy from Christ's spousal love for His Church. In addition, the sacraments unite Christ (the Bridegroom) with members of His Church (the Bride). Each of the seven sacraments, such as baptism and the Eucharist, infuse us with divine life. Thus, the sacrament of marriage is a prototype because it most fully expresses and exemplifies the spousal love between Christ and His Church to which all of the other sacraments are related.[17]

Conclusions

The mutual self-donation of spousal love is elevated to the level of marriage when a couple takes their wedding vows and expresses their total fidelity to each other. This permanent communion of persons is a covenant rather than a contract, and it mirrors the faithful relationship between Christ and His Church. Marriage is also a natural and civil institution that provides a framework for the living out of spousal love. But, above all, marriage is a "sacred and sacramental reality rooted in the dimensions of the covenant and of grace" (TB 614). The Word of God and the nature of spousal love are the foundation for this covenantal conception of marriage, which always implies real unity, absolute fidelity, and fruitfulness. Therefore, marriage must always be heterosexual, indissoluble, monogamous and open to new life.

Marriage is heterosexual because only a man and woman can give their whole bodily self to the other in accordance with the unifying fruitfulness of their spousal bodies. It is precisely "through being man and woman [that] each of them is 'given' to the other" (TB 205). When man and woman commit themselves to each other in marriage, there is a higher and more complete bodily unity that cannot be broken by an exercise of the will. Thus, marriage is by nature indissoluble and monogamous because spousal love always implies permanence and exclusivity. Indissolubility is *the fruit, the sign, and the requirement* of all spousal love. The monogamous character of marriage is also demanded by the nature of spousal love and reinforced by the bodily nature of this total gift of self.

---

17 Ouellet, *Mystery and Sacrament of Love*, 142–49. See also Christopher West, *The Theology of the Body Explained* (Boston: Pauline Books & Media, 2003), 361–62.

Finally, marriage requires fruitfulness, since from the beginning conjugal union has been connected "with the blessing of fruitfulness pronounced by God" (TB 389).[18]

Since marriage is a bodily communion of persons ordered to procreation and the raising of children, it is a vocation to parenthood as well as to spousal love. All married life is a mutual gift, but this becomes most pronounced when a couple becomes one flesh and new life is made possible. A married couple discovers their identity and vocation in their marital union *and* in the children whom they conceive. While parents should not become preoccupied with procreation, the moral attitude of parental readiness is appropriate.

Marriage embodies the mystery of creation and redemption. Marriage is the original sacrament, since it was instituted by the Creator at the beginning. Although the whole original order of creation was destabilized by original sin, marriage remained a "platform" for the realization of God's divine plan. Christ confirms the existence of marriage from the beginning and also makes marriage *"an integral part of the new sacramental economy,"* which is directed toward fallen man and draws its fruitfulness from the abundant graces of Christ the Redeemer (TB 511). Marriage is also the prototype of the sacraments because it most fully expresses and symbolizes the spousal love of Christ for His Church.

18 Meroni, "Pastoral Care of Marriage," 443.

EIGHT

Defending Humanae Vitae

OR MOST OF HUMAN HISTORY, POSITIVE CON-
traception was viewed as morally and culturally unacceptable.[1]
Large families were normal, and married couples found natural
ways, such as abstinence, to avoid frequent pregnancy. However, traditional attitudes about marriage and family life began to change in the late
eighteenth century. An anti-family sentiment seemed to be a byproduct
of the emerging rationalism that broke away from Europe's Christian
past. As humanity supposedly advanced into the bright light of reason,
people began to rethink the wisdom of large families. One result was an
appreciable decline in the birth rate in France, the center of the European
Enlightenment. Most experts believe that this decline can be attributed
to the clandestine use of contraception. By 1850, France was failing to
reproduce itself. At the same time, a movement advocating contraception
had begun in England. Its leaders proclaimed that contraception was
the optimal solution to the miseries of widespread destitution because it
eliminated unwanted children.

Another motivating force behind the escalation of this contraceptive
mentality was the 1798 publication of Thomas Malthus's book, *An Essay on
the Principle of Population*. Malthus presented evidence of an impending
population explosion. He argued that food supplies could not keep pace
with his projections of population growth at a geometric rate. His extrav-
agant claims persuaded social and political leaders about the urgency of

---

1 Positive contraception means that in the sexual act one or both partners have
intentionally prevented that act from resulting in reproduction. See Alexander Pruss,
One Body: An Essay in Christian Sexual Ethics (Notre Dame: University of Notre
Dame Press, 2013), 263.

population control. Even today Malthusians remain committed to the idea that overpopulation is at the root of society's most severe problems. Paul Ehrlich's 1968 book, *The Population Bomb*, continued to propagate the myth that millions of people would perish from starvation if we didn't quickly contain population growth. These dire warnings inspired misguided government policies such as China's repressive one-child mandate. The Chinese, however, have recently conceded that restricting families to only one child has been a disaster for the country's future.

Greater confidence in science and technology also inclined people to believe that life and birth could finally be controlled by perfecting medical techniques. As Western societies gradually began to cast aside the bonds of religious dogma and history in favor of rationalism and moral innovation, birth control began to sound much more palatable. There was widespread conviction that the adoption of effective birth control methods could remove the scourge of poverty and social chaos from the planet. According to the new politics of reproduction, it was finally time for emancipation from the primitive theological prejudices of the past that cast such a long shadow on progressive thinking. Advocates welcomed new birth control methods as the perfect tool for social engineering with little thought about the costly trade-offs. Today the most effective methods appear to be hormonal implants (tiny rods inserted under the skin) and intrauterine devices (IUDs).

In the early twentieth century, the inchoate birth control movement rapidly gained international momentum. International congresses promoting birth control were held in a number of cities from New York to Paris. And in 1927, supporters of birth control organized the World Conference on Population in Geneva, which provided the basis for population studies to confirm the suspicion that birth control intervention was desperately needed in many countries. Perhaps most consequential was the dramatic shift in position by the Anglican Church. At its 1930 Lambeth Conference, the Anglican Bishops approved the use of contraception for morally valid reasons. Prior to this Lambeth event, the teaching forbidding use of contraception had been universally accepted throughout Christianity. But the Anglican Church was now open to new ideas and new norms. The surprising Anglican decision was a watershed moment in the history of Christianity. The bishops of the one Church that had the greatest theological affinity with Catholicism no longer adhered to an absolute prohibition of positive contraception.[2]

Also, as Mary Eberstadt points out, the road to the Anglican Church's embrace of homosexuality and irregular sexual unions effectively begins at this fateful Lambeth conference. As a former Archbishop of Canterbury proclaimed, once you admit that sexual activity for pleasure or sheer delight is pleasing to God, on what basis can you exclude homosexuals from engaging in same-sex expression?[3]

Soon after Lambeth, other protestant churches followed the precedent set by the Anglicans. They were supported by eminent theologians such as Karl Barth and Reinhold Niebuhr, who both gave their assent to the moral validity of birth control. Many people expected the Catholic Church to change its position either during or after the Second Vatican Council (1962–65), but that was not to be. The Council Fathers deferred taking an explicit position on new methods of "artificial" birth control, but they never articulated any modification in Church teaching. Pope Paul VI's 1968 encyclical, *Humanae Vitae*, reaffirmed Catholic doctrine on the moral unacceptability of all forms of birth control and shocked many progressive voices who had predicted that change was on the horizon. Opposition in the United States and Europe was strong and swift, though often misinformed. Theologians at Catholic University of America and elsewhere signed a "Statement of Dissent," signaling their refusal to teach this settled doctrine. While most others in the Church avoided the high drama of these theology professors, they still registered their disapproval. Within the Church hierarchy, support for the encyclical was often muted and half-hearted. A number of Bishops, exhausted by the endless theological debates of the 1960s, hoped the issued would just fade away.

Yet *Humanae Vitae* was a striking sign of defiance in the early stages of the culture wars that now run so deep. As the sexual revolution intensified, the world more boldly discredited traditional sexual morality. It also relied on instrumental reason to frame and resolve most moral issues. In this turbulent milieu, many Catholics could no longer perceive any difficulty with the use of birth control methods within marriage.

2 John Noonan, *Contraception* (New York: New American Library, 1965), 461–83.
3 Mary Eberstadt, "Christianity Light," *First Things*, February 2010, 24.

The moral reasoning of the encyclical was sound, but it was ultimately unconvincing.

On June 28, 1978, shortly before Paul VI passed away, he said: "You will thank God and me for *Humanae Vitae*."[4] As many know, Pope Paul VI was vilified for this visionary encyclical, which proclaimed in unequivocal terms the indissoluble connection between conjugal sexuality and procreation. He also predicted that if that link were broken there would soon be calamitous social consequences. Artificial birth control could not become normalized without changing the meaning of the conjugal act. And by changing the meaning of the conjugal act the pathway is cleared for the redefinition of marriage. In addition, the endorsement of contraception also makes it easier to rationalize the need for abortion under some circumstances. There is a common legal argument that in the name of equality and sexual freedom, both men and women have a right to sex without consequences. Since contraception is not always effective, abortion is therefore sometimes necessary to ensure that result.

In recent years, Pope Paul VI's successors have come to his defense and expressed their gratitude for his heroic reaffirmation of an essential Church doctrine. According to Pope Benedict XVI, the encyclical not only expresses an "unchanged truth," but it also reveals Paul VI's inspired "farsightedness." "The truth expressed in *Humanae Vitae*," declares Pope Benedict, "does not change; on the contrary, precisely in the light of the new scientific discoveries its teaching becomes more timely and elicits reflection on the intrinsic value it possesses."[5] However, *Humanae Vitae* is fifty years old, and it remains a lingering source of contention and division within the Catholic Church. The secular culture has welcomed artificial birth control with open arms, and lamentably many Catholics have chosen to stand with the culture.

The moral issues related to contraception are complex, and they defy a simple formulation. However, to understand the whole truth about

4 See "Cardinal Caffarra Expresses Serious Concerns about Family Synod Debates," *Zenit*, March 24, 2014, accessed August 18, 2016, https://zenit.org/articles/cardinal-caffarra-expresses-serious-concerns-about-family-synod-debates/.
5 Pope Benedict XVI, "Address to International Congress Organized by the Pontifical Lateran University on the 40th Anniversary of the Encyclical *Humanae Vitae*" (Clementine Hall, Rome, May 10, 2008).

marriage, it is imperative to explore the enlightened wisdom of this papal document. In John Paul II's view, the moral principles expressed in this encyclical defend in a compelling way the integrity of the conjugal act and the marital relationship. Those who support contraceptive intercourse tacitly endorse a mechanistic view of the body. Accordingly, they tend to regard human sexuality "as an area for manipulation and exploration," rather than a "primordial wonder," which is the means for the union of persons in marriage (LF 19).

Birth Control and Catholic Doctrine

Despite the secular triumph of rationalism and pragmatism, the Catholic Church has never wavered in its teaching on the moral unacceptability of contraception. The Church did not react aggressively when the birth control movement first got underway in the nineteenth century. But the renewal of Thomism under Pope Leo XIII gave his capable successors the necessary theological tools to more effectively address the moral implications of birth control.

In response to the Lambeth Conference and calls for reform among Catholic dissenters, Pope Pius XI issued the encyclical *Casti Connubii* in December 1930. Pius XI contended that positive contraception was an act "against nature" and therefore it was "intrinsically indecent" (CC 559). The prohibition against contraception was also reaffirmed in a number of allocutions by Pope Pius XII. In 1951 he declared that any act of spouses directly "impeding the procreation of new life" is immoral.[6] In *Gaudium et Spes,* the Council Fathers reaffirmed that the conjugal act must "preserve the full meaning of the mutual self-donation and human procreation in the context of true love — which cannot be done without fully cultivating the virtue of married chastity" (GS 51). The Council Fathers never mention "contraception," but there is little doubt where they stood and little doubt about the close affinity between *Gaudium et Spes* and *Humanae Vitae.*

The issue facing Pope Paul VI was whether or not the newly-invented birth control pill fell into the same category as other forms of contraception

---

6 Pope Pius XII, "Address to Italian Catholic Union of Midwives," October 29, 1951, *Acta Apostolicae Sedis* 43:823.

that had been condemned by the Church. Since the pill left the act of sexual intercourse intact, it might appear that its use lacked the moral character of contraception. But in *Humanae Vitae*, the Pope came to the inescapable conclusion that the pill was no different from other types of contraception when viewed from a moral perspective. There must be a rejection of all direct attempts to "impede procreation," including the use of the birth control pill (HV 14). Quite simply, a man and woman cannot have sexual intercourse and deliberately prevent that act from resulting in procreation.[7]

This moral conclusion was brusquely dismissed by a number of moral theologians at the time. They claimed that contraception could be used by married couples under certain circumstances. The common argument was that as long as a married couple was open to procreation in the "totality of married life," it was not necessary for every conjugal act to manifest such openness. There is something disingenuous about this argument, however, because it focuses on the totality of acts rather than the moral quality of the act itself. Is judging the propriety of a single moral act in light of the totality of such acts in a person's life a valid means of moral reasoning? It seems to assume that a particular act cannot be wrong if it were part of a pattern of morally appropriate actions. Could a married man say that his occasional adultery was acceptable because when his marriage was looked at in its totality he was faithful to his wife? Could we imagine any self-respecting wife accepting this rationalization from her husband: "Well look, Jane, why are you so upset about my short affair with your best friend? I've been faithful to you throughout our whole marriage. Why don't you focus on the 'totality,' rather than this isolated indiscretion?"

Humanae Vitae was also attacked for its alleged obsession with the physical reality of reproduction and its failure to uphold "personalist values," which might sometimes justify the choice to employ contraception. According to this line of reasoning, persons have the right to make choices using their conscience as a guide and the right to freely exercise responsibility over their marital affairs. This includes the right to make decisions about family size and the spacing of children with the assistance of modern reproductive technologies like the pill. To oppose the broad

---

7 John Finnis, "On Retranslating *Humanae Vitae*," 346–48.

rights of conscience in these matters is to fail to give proper recognition to each person's moral autonomy and dignity.

In the post-conciliar Church, *Humanae Vitae's* defense of the tradition was also undermined by a growing consensus among dissident theologians that even established moral doctrine could be modified. Citing the shifting attitude of many Roman Catholics and presuming the historical evolution of human nature, they maintained that the teaching on birth control had to be adapted to the modern era. It was time, reasoned some of the Church's star theologians, to cast aside a static view of human nature in favor of one that is more dynamic and more supportive of doctrinal development. People and cultures change, and so, too, must Church doctrine. Such an approach, however, runs the risk of transforming theology into something purely subjective, driven by the winds of cultural and social change. Moreover, there is no evidence of any evolution of human nature when it comes to the basic possibilities of human flourishing. The fundamental goods of life and health, knowledge of truth, and aesthetic appreciation of beauty, marriage and friendship, remain the primary forms of human fulfillment in which every person wishes to share.[8]

Humanae Vitae has had many staunch supporters who have punctured the fallacious arguments of its opponents. Natural law theologians have persuasively demonstrated that contraception is wrong because it directly interferes with the procreative purpose of the sexual act. While sensitive to this obvious argument, John Paul II embarks on a somewhat different line of defense. In various writings, John Paul II sought to demonstrate the personalist anthropological vision implicit in the encyclical, which serves as a foundation for its normative conclusions. He also presents his case that sexual relations become depersonalized when contraception interferes with spousal self-donation.

John Paul II's Defense of Humanae Vitae

Saint John Paul II was one of the most ardent supporters of this encyclical's principles throughout his long career as scholar, bishop, and Pope. In *Man*

---

8 John Finnis, *Historical Consciousness* (Toronto: University of Toronto Press, 1990), 22–28.

and Woman He Created Them and in numerous essays, he articulated the "inseparable connection" between the unitive and procreative significance of the marital act that was the focal point of the entire encyclical. When *Humanae Vitae* appeared in 1968, Wojtyła had been a Cardinal for only about a year. He was appointed by Paul VI to the Papal Commission organized to study this issue, but was unable to attend the meetings in Rome due to passport problems. However, in 1966 he assembled a group of theologians in Krakow to review the issues being debated by that Commission. The Krakow Commission guided by Cardinal Wojtyła finished its work in 1968 and issued its own report called "The Foundations of the Church's Doctrine on the Principles of Conjugal Life." Its summary conclusions were prepared by the Cardinal and sent along to Pope Paul VI. The principles articulated in the Krakow Document were based to a great extent on Wojtyła's reflections in *Love and Responsibility*, which are anchored in a personalist approach to conjugal morality. As we have seen, a personalist perspective contends that undermining the procreative purpose of the sexual act means that it is no longer a marital act which expresses total spousal unity. The dignity of the husband and wife is impaired because the sexual act is reduced to self-gratification. As a result, they begin to become instruments of use for each other. While *Humanae Vitae* does not have such an overt personalist tone, the Commission's reflections were quite influential on Paul VI as he composed the final draft of his encyclical.[9]

After *Humanae Vitae* was released, Cardinal Wojtyła hastened to explicitly defend Pope Paul's encyclical along these same lines because he saw that it was both widely misunderstood and misrepresented. The encyclical's basic ideas and premises were often crudely distorted by the secular media and even by some prominent theologians within the Church, who were reluctant to go against the tide of secular culture. Those theologians questioned the argument that contraception was somehow contrary to nature, as popes such as Pius XI had supposed. They were quite skeptical that artificial contraception caused any harm to either member of a married couple. Why was intentionally sterilized sexual intercourse not also a sign of love and respect, as long as the couple were faithfully married?

9 Janet Smith, "The Krakow Document," *Nova et Vetera* 10 (2012): 361–81.

In the midst of this crescendo of protest and dissent, Wojtyła offered his own unequivocal support for *Humanae Vitae*. There are many fruitful avenues for providing a justification of the encyclical's key arguments, such as the use of natural law reasoning. Wojtyła never discredited this line of reasoning, but he chose to defend *Humanae Vitae* by relying primarily on the appealing logic of personalism. In this way, he demonstrated the hollowness of arguments put forth by those critics who condemned this encyclical precisely because of its lack of personalist credentials. Some theologians falsely claimed that the encyclical was flawed because of its failure to take into account the dignity and moral autonomy of the free human person. For John Paul II, however, the principal argument of the encyclical addresses that very question: "What corresponds to the dignity of man and woman when one is dealing with the important problem of the transmission of life in conjugal life?" (TB 630). Thus, if we appreciate who the person is and how his or her dignity is sullied through contraception, we will better grasp the theological merits of *Humanae Vitae*.

Earlier in this book we reviewed the Pope's vision of the human person as a harmonious unity of body and soul: "The body (matter) and spirit (the soul)...have from the beginning constituted man's very essence" (TB 330). The soul informs the material body and together they become a unified, acting subject. The body is not an appendage or an instrument of the human self, but a vital part of our personal reality. Each of us lives out the moral life as a bodily-spiritual person. A married couple, therefore, cannot regard the body and its fertility or biological rhythms as something sub-personal that can be manipulated for pleasure or other reasons. Rather, the body and its sexuality is "constitutive of the person" (TB 166).

Spousal love has a distinctive character because it is a permanent and exclusive mutual self-gift. This spousal love has a sexual nature, since it is fully actualized when man and woman become one flesh. When married couples choose to engage in sexual relations, they must have this intention of total self-giving, of becoming a complete gift of love for the other. Otherwise, this is not a marital act that expresses total union, fidelity, and fruitfulness. This mutual self-giving must involve the *whole* self, body and soul, including a person's masculinity or femininity, which is ordered to the communion of persons. In this one-flesh union the pro-creative meaning of the sexual act becomes transparent, since this act can bear fruit in the form of new life. Therefore, the procreative and unitive meanings of the sexual act are distinct but inseparable. According to the encyclical, there is an "indissoluble connection between the unitive and procreative meanings" of the conjugal act (HV 12). That connection is part of nature — it has been established by God, and human persons have no moral right to sever it.

Thanks to the soul, every person is a free human subject with an inner life. Every person is present to herself from within through self-aware-ness. Moreover, the human subject has the capacity to think and make free choices based on certain desires and intentions. There are limits to freedom, however. No one has the liberty or capacity to arbitrarily change the meaning of the natural order designed by the Creator. Spouses do not have the freedom to alter the meaning of the conjugal act and to behave as if it has nothing to do with procreation. They can't pretend with impunity that sex is all about their "pleasure" or self-gratification. This subjective interpretation "imparts to the [sexual] drive a purely egocentric mean-ing" (LR 50). It ignores the objective end of sexual engagement, which is always procreation and the creation of a total, personal union. Our sexual powers exist for the sake of union and procreation, not pleasure, and when a man and woman join in sexual intercourse the result is often a child if the woman is fertile. No one can alter the natural reality that makes the unitive and procreative meanings of the sexual act inseparably connected.

According to Wojtyła, if we begin to look at contraception and pro-creation through the lens of "meaning," we can recognize the implicit personalist argument in *Humanae Vitae*. Paul VI emphasized "the twofold meaning of the conjugal act: the intended meaning of union and the intended meaning of parenthood" (HV 12). According to John Paul II, by appealing to the precise meaning of the conjugal act, Paul VI is using a "theology of the person" to make his case against contraception (PC 308).

In commenting on this section of *Humanae Vitae*, Wojtyła explains that there must be "a harmony between what the conjugal act objectively 'signifies' and the 'meaning' that the spouses confer on it" (AV 125). Wojtyła's point is that, in addition to the objective meaning of the act, there is also a subjective one. The objective meaning is clear enough: the conjugal act is a sign and a means of total and mutual self-giving, a bodily-spiritual union that is by its very nature open to procreation. Embedded in the natural language of sexual engagement is a union of two persons who become a "single subject" in a way that makes procreation possible (TB 207). But the conjugal act also has a subjective meaning, that is, the meaning a man and woman attribute to this act. What is their intention in having sexual intercourse? Two college students who get together one afternoon to have sex for "fun" are not truly engaged in a marital act, since there is no intention of total and mutual self-giving. "Love cannot be simply identified with the conjugal act, but must be sought in the persons, in their awareness, choice, decision, and moral responsibility" (PC 309). This fun-loving couple cannot negate the objective meaning of the conjugal act, since their behavior doesn't affect how others perceive and perform this act. They simply disguise the conjugal act with their own subjective meaning (pleasure). In this case, "a real bodily union is brought about, but it does not correspond to the inner truth and dignity of personal communion" (TB 633).

What happens when married couples engage in contraceptive intercourse? Let's assume that a couple wants nothing to do with procreation, at least for the time being. Their *subjective intention* is to have sex just for pleasurable intimacy, and so the woman takes contraceptive medication. In this case, they too no longer intend what the act *objectively means*: a total gift of self in their bodily-spiritual personhood that serves procreation. There is no total self-donation or comprehensive union, since their fertility, their full masculinity and femininity, is held back in the very act of giving themselves to each other. However, only when the objective meaning is preserved in their minds and hearts can the sexual act be an authentic marital act that expresses spousal love, a love that is total, faithful, exclusive, and fruitful. To perform a marital act that expresses fruitful spousal love, spouses must relate to each other as husband and wife, and as a potential mother or father. But contraceptive intercourse changes the whole meaning of the act by stripping away the possibility of procreation. The conjugal act objectively "means not only love but potential fruitfulness," but without the latter, the act is *"deprived of its inner truth"* and falls short of a full personal communion (TB 632–33).[10]

10 Stephan Kampowski and David Crawford, "The Wisdom of *Humanae Vitae* and the Pastoral Care of the Family," *Catholic World Report*, October 20, 2015, accessed January 10, 2016, http://insightscoop.typepad.com/2004/2015/10/the-wisdom-of-humanae-vitae-and-the-pastoral-care-of-the-family.html.

To be honest and sincere, a married couple should have the proper intentions and honor the unitive and procreative meaning of the conjugal act, since this is what the act signifies in the objective order. In this way the sexual act is truly a marital act that expresses and fortifies their personal communion. When the objective and subjective meanings coincide, the conjugal act signifies a "special union of persons and fecundity," and so it is *"intrinsically true and free of falsification"* (PC 309). However, if a couple engages in contraceptive intercourse, they obscure the objective meaning of the sexual act, which becomes "intrinsically dishonest" (HV 14). Therefore, a married couple must always intend the objective meaning of the conjugal act: a complete union of persons with the possibility of procreation.[11]

The problem with contraceptive intercourse is this deliberate holding back of fertility and potential parenthood. Contraception substantially limits the spousal self-giving of conjugal communion by its refusal to give to the other the whole innate goodness of femininity and masculinity. When a couple severs the connection between the unitive and procreative meanings of the marital act, that act cannot have the unitive significance the couple seeks — it cannot express or reinforce the total bodily union of the married state.[12] Through recourse to contraception a husband and wife "degrade human sexuality and with it themselves...by altering the value of 'total' self-giving" (FC 32). If the conjugal act stops short of full communion, the couple cannot claim that they are engaging in this act to express and actualize their marital union. They must have a more self-centered motive, such as mutual self-gratification. They end up treating each other as sexual partners rather than spouses, in violation of the personalist norm. When a married couple's sexual relations are devoid of any procreative or unitive meaning, "what is left in the conjugal act is sexual use alone" (LR 225). This couple cannot have a "right conscience," nor can they be "faithful interpreters" of the objective moral order established by the Creator (HV 10).

Thus, John Paul II claims that deep within *Humanae Vitae* we find this subtle personalist justification for the ancient moral norm that forbids

11 See Thomas Petri, *Aquinas and the Theology of the Body* (Washington, DC: Catholic University of America Press, 2016), 157.

12 Elizabeth Anscombe, "On *Humanae Vitae*," in *Faith in a Hard Ground*, eds. Mary Geach and Luke Gormally (Exeter, UK: Imprint Academic, 2008), 192–97. See also Finnis, "On Retranslating *Humanae Vitae*," 355.

contraception. Paul VI was not obsessed with the biology of reproduction, as his critics contend. On the contrary, he was quite sensitive to the subjective dimension of the conjugal act and the preservation of human dignity in conjugal life. When a married couple conscientiously preserves in their sexual behavior the unitive and procreative meaning of the sexual act, they live out married life in the truth. Their bodily union corresponds "*to the innermost truth of the conjugal act*" (TB 633). Only an honest, personal love is true to the nature of the person and the "inner order of conjugal communion" (TB 633). Falsification, disingenuousness, and pursuit of self-gratification contradict love and union, and are more consistent with using rather than loving. Pope Paul VI's encyclical "answers the question about man's true good as a person" (TB 630). The duplicity and depersonalization caused by contraception is the source of personal harm that cannot serve the good of any person.

John Paul II's argument is further clarified by examining the whole issue from a slightly different perspective: the language of the body. The body has its own "innate language," and so each person speaks through his or her body (FC 32). A person reveals his or her whole self through the language of the body, which has a profound interpersonal meaning. In the language of the body, man and woman continue the dialogue that began on the day of their creation. This "language" is subject to the same demands for truth as any other language. Therefore, the body should express the "*truth of the sacrament of marriage*" as a communion of persons (TB 631). When contraception is used, a couple's bodily union *means* something other than the complete mutual self-gift that it should mean. According to the Pope, the body's language that "expresses the total reciprocal self-giving of husband and wife is overlaid, through contraception, by an objectively contradictory language, namely, that of not giving oneself totally to the other" (FC 32). One speaks a lie by contradicting the generative and parental meaning forever embedded in sexual union. Spousal love, however, cannot be based on such an illusion where conjugal union fails "to express the mysterious '*language*' *of their bodies in all the truth that properly belongs to it*" (TB 632).

Contraception fits well with secular anthropology, which denies the body-soul unity and perceives the body in purely biological terms. That anthropology also exaggerates human freedom and consequently inflates

134   *The Splendor of Marriage*

our moral prerogative over human sexuality. The effort to dominate procreation reflects the "utopian drift" of our activities under the conditions
of modern technology, whether it works on nonhuman or human nature.[13]
Medical technology supplies the magic formula that emancipates the sexual drive from the "burden" of pregnancy. However, as Wojtyła explains,
humanity cannot conquer nature by violating it, "but only through adapting
to its immanent finality" (LR 216). We achieve "mastery" over our sexual
nature only by taking advantage of the possibilities for human flourishing,
which it provides through the goods of authentic conjugal communion
and new life. Thus we can remain faithful to the person in the order of
love only if we are faithful to nature.

Christian anthropology, on the other hand, gives priority to permanence of the gift over human freedom. It also insists that the body is not
sub-personal in any way but part of our personal reality and moral subjectivity. Spouses must give themselves in their totality as bodily-spiritual
beings, or the conjugal act that exemplifies spousal love falls short. But
contraception "*breaks* the constitutive dimension of the person, deprives
man of the subjectivity proper to him, and turns him into *an object of
manipulation*" (TB 631). Like recreational sex, contraception tends to
alienate a person from his or her body, which becomes the adversary of
freedom rather than the subject of free choice. Authentic freedom is always
subject to the truth of the Creator's plan for life and human sexuality. Man
does not have dominion over life. Rather, his task is to serve life "with
reverence for the laws of the generative process" (HV 13).[14]

Conjugal Abstinence and Natural Family Planning

Contraceptive intercourse is always morally wrong because it alters the
nature of the marital act. But this does not imply that a married couple
should be preoccupied with procreation. The purpose of the conjugal act
is not the transmission of life but total mutual self-giving, which may or
may not be fruitful. As we have discussed, the suitable parental attitude
for married couples is parental readiness, a willingness to conceive and

13 Hans Jonas, *Philosophical Essays: From Ancient Creed to Technological Man*
(New York: Atropos Press, 2010), 17.
14 Rhonheimer, *Ethics of Procreation*, 129.

accept the gift of new life. It is not necessary to directly will or intend procreation in every sexual act. Nor is it necessary that all married couples have large families. Sometimes personal circumstances such as ill-health make this a formidable hardship. But contraception should not be the means for limiting family size.

Couples who seek to avoid pregnancy for a morally valid reason should depend upon the "natural regulation of fertility" (TB 629). Instead of relying on contraceptive pills or devices, they must practice "conjugal chastity." Unlike contraception, marital continence can sustain the "inner order of conjugal life" (TB 653). In rare situations, where major health issues are at stake, conjugal abstinence may need to be permanent. But in most cases only periodic continence is necessary. This type of periodic continence means that a married couple must abstain from sexual relations during a woman's fertile period. Conjugal abstinence is particularly difficult, since married couples become easily accustomed to regular sexual relations. But sometimes continence is the only way to demonstrate "reverence for the twofold meaning of the conjugal act in marriage" (TB 654). This honorable means of regulating birth builds upon the moral maturity of two spouses, and, at the same time, strengthens that maturity.

Periodic continence should be based on the reliable natural family planning method (NFP), which requires that a couple refrain from sexual activity during a woman's fertile periods if they want to avoid pregnancy. NFP helps a couple achieve *"responsible fatherhood and motherhood"* (TB 633). Unlike contraception, NFP is not imposed against nature. The sacrifice called for does not injure conjugal love but actually "confers on it a higher human value" (TB 634). For example, Tom makes the sacrifice of continence during his wife's fertile days because he knows that bearing another child is a risk due to his wife's fragile health. His wife appreciates his care and benevolence and their marital love is enriched by his self-sacrifice. Also, when the practice of periodic abstinence integrates the sexual drive with the good of marriage, marital intercourse becomes a deeper expression of the love between a husband and wife. Continence must not be practiced as a technique, but cultivated as a virtue. This means that family size should be regulated for valid ethical reasons.[15]

---

15 Grisez, *Living a Christian Life*, 687–88.

NFP is morally superior to positive contraception for several reasons. With NFP, there is no intention to deliberately impede the birth of a child. When a couple chooses NFP they are not engaging in an act that prevents a baby form being born. NFP regulates conception by taking advantage of infertile periods when conception cannot occur and by abstaining from sexual relations during those periods. It reconciles human dignity with the natural rhythms of fertility, "which has its own meaning for the truth of the 'mutual language of the body' in conjugal life" (TB 655). In contrast to contraception, NFP fully preserves the natural and generative end of the conjugal act. Use of this method does not overlay the objective meaning of that act with a different meaning by rendering the body sterile. NFP respects a woman's God-given fertility cycles while artificial contraception does not. In *Familiaris Consortio*, John Paul II declares that "the choice of the natural rhythms involves accepting the cycle of the person, that is the woman, and thereby accepting dialogue, reciprocal respect, shared responsibility and self-control" (FC 32). NFP protects and promotes the full self-giving that sexual relations express at the heart of marital love.

Natural family planning, however, should not be regarded simply as a means to the end of avoiding pregnancy for any reason. While married couples must be allowed to regulate the size of their families, they should avoid a "minimalistic attitude" that might support "the principle of convenient life" (LR 229). A married couple who deliberately limits the size of their family for the sake of a luxurious house and other material comforts would be guilty of such an attitude. There are circumstances, such as physical or mental health, that demand the sacrifice of parenthood for the family's own common good. To be sure, there will be some ambiguity in certain situations about the proper size of a family. But NFP must be practiced with the help of the Holy Spirit so that it remains "interiorly true and authentic" (TB 655).

In modern society, the problem is that many families are having too few children even when they possess adequate resources to support a large family. To some extent, this reflects the tendency, influenced by technology, to dispense with the mystery of conjugal sexuality and subject all human phenomena, including the family, to tight control and planning. There is also a certain posture of indifference about the value of adding to the family community. And in some cases there is an unwillingness to sacrifice much of one's personal preferences and freedom for the sake of a child. Sometimes the grip of materialism interferes with good judgment about the right family size. The tragic result is that "families today have too little human life" (LF 11). To overcome this problem, Catholics must confront the ongoing challenge of individualism and the ethic of material success.

Conclusions

While Christian churches have capitulated to the demands for birth control, the Catholic Church has remained steadfast in its opposition to positive contraception on moral grounds. Pope John Paul II followed the lead of his predecessors and strongly defended that doctrine re-promulgated in *Humanae Vitae*. As Pope and philosopher, John Paul II defended *Humanae Vitae* by emphasizing its subtle appeal to personalistic values.

In keeping with Church tradition, John Paul II insists that contraceptive intercourse cannot be an expression of total, faithful, and fruitful marital love. There is no full and complete gift of self when the generative purpose of the conjugal act is deliberately frustrated. If we are attentive to the language of the body, we recognize that the "conjugal act 'means' not only love but potential fruitfulness," and it should not be deprived of its proper meaning through artificial intervention (TB 632).

Sensitive to the personalist approach championed by Cardinal Wojtyła, *Humanae Vitae* suggests that there must be a harmony between the objective and subjective meanings of the conjugal act, which is by nature generative and unitive. People cannot deprive the conjugal act of its inner truth by superimposing a different meaning upon that act with the help of contraception. Contracepting spouses do not give themselves in their totality to one another. Since fertility is withheld, there is a substantial limitation imposed on the gift of love. Contraceptive intercourse might involve a real bodily union, but it is not a communion of persons. And without personal communion, what remains is only shared sexual use. Two spouses relate to each other not so much as husband and wife, or as the potential mother and father of their child, but more so as sexual partners. This is the underlying personalist message conveyed in Pope Paul VI's encyclical. *Humanae Vitae* uses "the measure of the person" and what is consonant with her essential dignity to evaluate the moral character of sexual activity (TB 612). Natural methods like NFP measure up to that dignity, since they respect the natural rhythms of fertility along with the procreative finality of the sexual drive.

NINE

The Family

ON A WARM SUNDAY AFTERNOON IN APRIL, Pope John Paul II made a pastoral visit to Santa Maria Madre dell'Ospitalità parish on the outskirts of Rome. The papal motorcade proceeded smoothly along broad streets lined with patches of trees and ancient stone buildings. The Pope arrived in good spirits to greet the many parishioners who gathered to hear his brief speech. Just a week before, on April 8, 1994, he had celebrated mass in the Sistine Chapel to commemorate the restoration of its famous ceiling frescoes. Perhaps this accounted for why the Pope seemed to be in such a jubilant mood. He spoke to the faithful parishioners about many things and told them how their little parish had enriched the Church of Rome. "I greet you heartily," he said, "and I wish you also a Basilica. Maybe you could take one of the old Basilicas in Rome and move it here!" But towards its conclusion the Pope's speech lost its amiable tone as his mood suddenly shifted. He told the crowd that he would be returning to the Vatican to pray the Regina Coeli but also "to combat a program, a project of the United Nations, which wants to destroy the family." In an anguished voice, the Pope went on: "My God! The United Nations! I say simply, reassess your position and convert! If you are the United Nations, you cannot divide and destroy."[1]

How was the United Nations trying to divide and destroy the family? The Pope was referring to the upcoming World Conference on Population and Development to be held in Cairo in September. With the backing of the United Nations, the world governments were on the brink of defining a new set of international rights, including a universal right to abortion.

---

1 John Paul II, "Speech to Parish of Santa Maria Madre dell'Ospitalità," Rome, April 17, 1994.

Organizers were emboldened by the enthusiastic support of the Clinton Administration, which catapulted the United States to the frontlines of population control efforts. John Paul II had good reason to be apprehensive. The original draft of the Cairo Conference document said nothing about the importance of families based on stable marriages or the need for both mothers and fathers to care for their children. Sexual activity after puberty was declared to be a basic human right. If parents objected, teenagers could turn to "reproductive health care agencies," which would be designed to help everyone exercise their sexual freedom. The document also favored strong reproductive rights, which included abortion, as a basis for family planning. States were encouraged to intervene to protect these rights and guarantee comprehensive family planning.[2]

John Paul II was keenly aware of the catastrophic implications of this UN initiative for the future of the family. He also recognized that political intimidation would likely be used to ensure that these rights were imposed on developing countries. Silence or neutrality was not an option. Hence the Pope orchestrated a broad campaign to rebuke the most offensive proposals in the Cairo document. In a series of Angelus addresses, he spoke passionately about marriage and family, often drawing from his work on theology of the body. His pleas to modify the Cairo manifesto were woven with principled reasoning about the nature of marriage and the sanctity of life. Meanwhile, other Vatican officials, such as his talented spokesman, Joaquin Navarro-Valls, joined the heated debate.[3]

When the conference began in September, the stage was set for a titanic battle. Would John Paul II and the Vatican stand alone against world powers like the United States? Much of the media watching the unfolding drama thought so. Fortunately, the Vatican had many powerful allies in developing countries whose voices could not be easily silenced by the West. Prime Minister Bhuto of Pakistan, a woman of some international stature, denounced the document because it sought to impose adultery, sex education, and abortion on countries with distinctly different moral values. She was followed by many other speakers who sounded the same alarm. The result was a final report that retreated from the aggressive proposals of the

2 Weigel, *Witness to Hope*, 719–21.
3 Ibid., 723–25.

initial draft and even repudiated the use of abortion for family-planning. It was a dramatic triumph of sorts for the Vatican. More importantly, the whole event was a striking demonstration of a countercultural church productively engaged in a heroic fight to protect the dignity of marriage and family. For John Paul II, this was all part of the larger battle for truth and freedom against the growing presence of the anti-Word.

Despite the Cairo triumph, the prospects for marriage and family have certainly not improved. The sexual offensive unleashed in the 1960s and the cultural disarray left in its path have led to higher levels of promiscuity and marital infidelity, which contribute to the abnormally high divorce rate. Regrettably, there is a close correlation between sexual license and the disintegration of the family. Children born out of wedlock now represent 43 percent of all births. Thanks to divorce and extra-marital sex, over 35 percent of children are in single-parent homes. The negative impact of divorce on both spouses and children is also well-documented. Problems such as psychological distress, poor educational performance, juvenile delinquency, and poverty are statistically linked to those children who have the misfortune to be raised in one-parent families. Committed married couples and their children, on the other hand, enjoy better emotional and physical health.[4]

The family has also been severely battered by the churning whirlwind of cultural change. The culture's acquiescence to same-sex marriage means that children will be subject to the indignity of being deliberately conceived without a mother and a father. And the cavalier push for artificial baby production continues to threaten the integrity of the conjugal act. Society's shifting conventions have displaced the traditional institution of the family where children are begotten by a father and a mother who remain together to care for them. Marriage is no longer seen as a permanent, monogamous union between a man and a woman, but rather as a social convention and a matter of subjective preference. The child is regarded as a "right" of some sort or even a possession, but not as a gift of the Creator.[5]

The distinguished sociologist, Carle Zimmerman, intimated certain aspects of this severe crisis many years ago in his book, *Family and*

4 Paul Johnson, *A History of the American People* (New York: HarperCollins, 1997), 971–72. See also Judith Wallerstein, Julia Lewis, and Sandra Blakeslee, *The Unexpected Legacy of Divorce: A 25 Year Landmark Study* (New York: Hyperion, 2000).

5 Reilly, *Making Gay Okay*, 213–15. See also Scola, *The Nuptial Mystery*, 150.

Civilization. He classifies the families of human civilization into three
basic typologies. The first is the trustee family whose "ideal type" is the
tribe or clan where family members are bound closely by ties of blood
and honor. The second paradigm is the domestic family, the extended or
nuclear family, typified by many children and strong marital fidelity. Unlike
the trustee family, it satisfies the desire for freedom from family bonds,
but also provides enough structure and security for all family members.
Finally, there is the "atomistic" family, a couple of individuals with no
more than one or two children, bound loosely by the marriage contract
and mutual self-interest. In trustee periods the family was sacred, but "in
the atomistic period, the individual becomes sacred."[6]

The "modern family" benignly portrayed in TV shows and movies
represents the atomistic family, with loose ties, a plurality of parental
arrangements, and sometimes no natural kinship. The family is an association, merely a group of "interacting personalities," not much different
from other groups. According to Zimmerman, Western civilization is
now in the late stage of the atomistic family, which tends toward being
no family at all. Its low reproduction rate has portentous ramifications
for a civilization's future survival.[7]

Many people believe that the atomistic family, directly connected to
the modern malaise of individualism, is the new norm for family life.
Just as people are confused about personhood, freedom, and marriage,
they are confused about what it means to be a fully authentic family. But
the Christian family is the antithesis of the atomistic family. The Pope's
writings clearly present a moral vision of the family consistent with the
Creator's divine plan. In this chapter we concentrate our attention on
that plan.

Papal Writings on the Family

The Synod of Bishops was created by Pope Paul VI during the Second
Vatican Council to restore greater collaboration between the Bishops
and the Holy See. Shortly after Cardinal Wojtyła was installed as Pope

6 Carle Zimmerman, *Family and Civilization* (Wilmington, DE: ISI Books, 2008), 31.
7 Ibid., 31–36. See also the essay by James Kurth in this same volume, "Demog-
raphy is Destiny: The Fate of the Western Family and Western Civilization," 305–20.

John Paul II in 1978, he convened a Synod of Bishops on "The Role of the Christian Family in the Modern World." Living under repressive totalitarian regimes for so long, the Pope was no stranger to family problems in Poland and other Soviet countries. The conjunction of technology and power was a lethal combination for family life. But he also sensed a different sort of crisis for the family in democratic societies. He was cognizant of the sexual revolution's extreme effects on stable family life. The 1980 Synod sought to address the new wave of problems afflicting family life along with related topics such as sexual morality. The Synod was convened on September 26, 1980, and lasted for over a month. The Pope attended every general session, listened intently to the Bishops' speeches (or "interventions"), and took copious notes. He presided and preached at the opening and closing masses. During his homily at the closing mass, the Holy Father acknowledged the difficulty of marital chastity, but also reaffirmed the virtue of self-mastery, which liberates a person to give herself.

To mark the completion of a Synod, the Pope usually composes an apostolic exhortation, which reflects the bishops' discussions along with the Pope's conclusions on the issue at hand. Accordingly, a new apostolic exhortation, *Familiaris Consortio* (or Community of the Family) was issued in November, 1981. The Pope later told his papal biographer, George Weigel, that this was one of his favorite documents in his rich treasury of papal teachings.[8]

The Pope was a notable but uncertain presence in the world at this point, and some Catholics might have expected him to make doctrinal adjustments in his exhortation. Laity or clergy with such expectations, however, knew little about the writings of Karol Wojtyła and his herculean efforts to defend traditional Catholic morality along with the discredited teaching of *Humanae Vitae*. *Familiaris Consortio*, addressed especially to the young "who are beginning their journey toward marriage and family life," both reaffirms and amplifies the Church's teachings (FC 1). It focuses on the need for a proper understanding of freedom and personal dignity, and it dissects the essential qualities of marriage and family. The document explored doctrines like marital indissolubility "rooted in the

8 Weigel, *Witness to Hope*, 383–85.

total and personal self-giving of the couple and being required by the good of the children" (FC 20). But its main focus was the role of the Christian family in society.

A number of years later in 1994, the Pope composed a second major teaching document on the family. This was simply called *Letter to Families*. *Familiaris Consortio* offers a theology of marriage and family along with the pastoral implications of the Pope's theology of the body: examining marriage as it was "in the beginning." The *Letter to Families* is a somewhat more pensive work that attempts to expose the roots of the family crisis. This letter also represented a new form of papal pedagogy: a personal reflection addressed primarily to a specific audience. That audience were the attendees of the 1994 "International Year of the Family."[9] Like *Familiaris Consortio*, this letter promotes the dignity of marriage and the family. Each person walks many paths, wrote the Pope, but "the family is the first and the most important," and it is "a path from which man cannot withdraw" (LF 2). John Paul II was particularly concerned with attempts to present irregular family situations as normal and even glamorous. Those situations "contradict 'the truth and love' which should inspire and guide relationships between men and women" (LF 5).

Although written decades ago, these rich documents have lost none of their intellectual force or deep wisdom. They both deal candidly with the challenges to the family that have arisen in our postmodern relativistic culture. And they both seek to discern the genetic makeup of marriage and family, which cannot change no matter what some judge or legislative body may imperiously decide. Hence, they confidently proclaim the truth about marriage and family, not as a normative ideal, but as a livable reality that is the effect of God's creative act.[10] Despite their sober appraisal of the challenges facing the family, they are both cloaked in hopeful realism rather than bleak pessimism.

9 Ibid., 695.
10 Carlo Caffarra, "The Church that Engages in Sociology," *Zenit*, March 24, 2014, accessed April 16, 2016, http://www.zenit.org/en/articles/the-church-that-engages-in-sociology.

What is the Family?

A recent United Nations report provocatively declared that it is no longer possible to define what it means to be a family. On the contrary, claims this report, the family should be understood in the widest possible sense. The family structure is plastic and variable, and there is no necessary connection between family and marriage. A plurality of parental arrangements is possible to care for children. If we accept this proposition, we must dismantle the "myth" that children need both a mother and a father. These views, of course, are consistent with the demise of the traditional family recorded by Zimmerman. But according to the UN, the modern family has become so amorphous that it defies uniform definition.[11]

For John Paul II, of course, this kind of talk would be utter nonsense. There is no ambiguity about what constitutes a family. The "natural foundation" of the family is marriage, a real communion of persons between a man and a woman (PC 339). To this dual unity God has from the beginning entrusted "the work of procreation and family life" (LW 8). The first married couple is immediately told to "be fruitful and multiply" (Gn 1:28). As John Paul II proclaims, "marriage and conjugal love is ordained to the procreation and education of children, in whom it finds its crowning" (FC 14).

Thus, the family first arises through the marital bond, which creates a permanent communion of life and love. This one flesh union of a man and a woman expresses their total lifelong mutual commitment. Sexual relations must be confined to marriage, since "the only 'place' in which this self-giving in its whole truth is made possible is marriage" (FC 11). Marriage is the foundation for stable family life, and only marriage can do justice to all parties concerned, including the Creator. The mother and father of the child need each other for mutual support. As the Pope explains, "Motherhood necessarily implies fatherhood, and, in turn, fatherhood necessarily implies motherhood" (LF 7). In addition, children need to be raised and educated by both parents who witness to a shared union of love and self-sacrifice.[12]

---

11 Stefano Gennarini, "United Nations Report: There is No Definition of the Family," *LifeSite News*, January 27, 2016, accessed March 22, 2016, https://www.lifesitenews.com/news/un-report-there-is-no-definition-of-the-family.

12 Stephan Kampowski, "Why the German Bishops Are Wrong about Abstinence

When a married couple transmits life to a child, "*a new human 'thou'…
becomes a part of the horizon of the 'we' of the spouses*" (LF 11). In this newborn child, the common good of the family is realized. The communion
of husband and wife expands into a family community and eventually
into generations of families. This family community is "pervaded by the
very essence of communion" (LF 7). There are many close interpersonal
(I-Thou) relationships between brother and sister, mother and daughter,
and so forth.

In contrast to prevailing opinion, therefore, the family is not "an 'artificial' or arbitrary society, left entirely up to the human will" (PC 340).
The family is a "natural society" based on marital unity. But the goods
of marital unity and family cannot be properly understood without first
comprehending those familiar categories of "*communio*, person, and gift
each of which have a certain greatness and specific import of their own"
(PC 325). The family is properly conceived as the marital communion
of persons based on spousal love: a *total* mutual self-giving and sharing
that includes openness to the gift of new life. And the gift of self cannot
be fully grasped without knowing "the very being and goodness of the
person," who is made to love and be loved (PC 325). Spousal love requires
self-sacrifice, which prepares a married couple to generously care for their
children. Within the family, the child first satisfies the yearning for love
and learns to become a gift for others.

Thus, far from being amorphous, the family has a certain immutable
form and meaning: the maturation of a married couple through reciprocal
self-giving accompanied by a generous openness to the generation and
formation of children. When the child is born, the couple assumes their
natural and complementary roles as mother and father.[13] The Creator
had only one design in mind for the family, which is exemplified by the
Holy Family of Nazareth. God ensured that his Son was raised by Mary
and Joseph, a mother and a father who brought to this simple family in
Nazareth their complementary gifts. Both were closely involved in the
spiritual parenting of Jesus.

---

for 'Remarried' Catholics," *Catholic World Report*, August 14, 2015, accessed October 22, 2015, http:www.catholicworldreport.com/Item/4099/why_the_german
_bishops_are_wrong_about_abstinence_for_remarried_catholics.

    13   Scola, *Nuptial Mystery*, 143.

This family community constitutes a "single *communal subject*" with its own unique identity and primacy over other social institutions (LR 15). Only by belonging to a family can a person achieve authentic fulfillment and self-knowledge, especially during the early stages of life. It is within the natural family structure that the person first perceives his social nature and discovers his personal identity as boy or girl, brother or sister, son or daughter. These family relations are natural realities that are vital for human identity and mature growth. The natural family tells us who we are and where we have come from. A married couple also grows in self-awareness and in knowledge of each other through their children. In the child, explains the Pope, "man and woman recognize each other, their humanity, their living image" (TB 212).[14]

Education and Service

The newborn child is part of the common good of the family. "Is not every child a 'particle' of that common good without which human communities break down and risk extinction?" asks the Pope (LF 11). This child must be enthusiastically welcomed and valued for his or her own sake. The child is given to parents and siblings as a gift, but also as a task and responsibility. And a major part of that responsibility is education and character formation.[15]

Without the proper education, without being trained in the virtues, the child cannot flourish as a person. By begetting a child in an act of love, parents must assist this person to live a full and fulfilling human life. This role cannot be completely delegated because only parents can provide the irreplaceable love and care, rooted in the bond between parents and child, that makes this education effective. Many sociological studies confirm the child's natural need for special attention from both of his or her parents.[16]

Education is not just about training in the arts or learning skills, but about the wonderful "bestowal of humanity" on a young person (PC 334). As

14 Ibid., 150–51.

15 Anderson and Granados, *Called to Love*, 233–35.

16 See, for example, David Popenoe, *Life without Father: Compelling New Evidence that Fatherhood and Marriage Are Indispensable for the Good of Children and Society* (New York: Free Press, 1996).

the child grows, the family is the place where virtuous habits are developed
that put us in control of our passions and emotions. Each child learns the
essential values of human life and forms a proper attitude toward human
freedom. Through the example of their mothers and fathers, they learn how
to be a man or a woman and come to understand the fulfilling meaning
of marital intercourse. The family is the starting point for a long path of
self-perfection based on self-control and the imitation of mature adults.

John Paul II was especially insistent that parents have the primary
responsibility for educating their children in matters of sexuality. He knew
well that sexuality is a powerful force in every person's life and that improper
care in this area can cause psychological damage. Every person must learn
to cultivate a disciplined approach to erotic or sexual encounters. The Pope
also knew that contemporary sexual education has a bias towards "safe
sex" and often conveys a tolerance for deviant forms of sexual behavior
(LF 13). Vulnerable children should not be subjected to these views until
they are mature enough to process them correctly. Conscientious parents
will seize the initiative for sex education, although they can delegate some
of this responsibility to schools or religious institutions that they trust.[17]

John Paul II observes that in raising and educating children two fundamental truths must always be kept in mind. First, every person is called
to live in truth and love. This means that they must be taught to know
what is true and to distinguish authentic love from its counterfeit forms.
Second, every person achieves fulfillment through the sincere gift of self,
for it is only in giving ourselves that we can find ourselves. Parents and
other educators, who beget in a spiritual sense, must communicate these
truths through their words and deeds.

Perhaps the best way to capture the family's essential pedagogy is to
highlight the difference between socialization and personalization. Public
institutions like schools usually do a good job of socializing individuals,
but only the family community excels at personalization. Unlike other
social structures, the family performs the work of "personalization" by
helping young persons to mature properly and to develop "truly personal
relationships" (PC 341). The child is a person by nature but is awakened

---

17 See Roger Scruton, *On Human Nature* (Princeton: Princeton University Press,
2017), 111–12.

to the exercise of her personhood within a loving family where the journey from potential to actual self-possession begins. Within the family, a child grows into a moral person, however imperfectly. Thanks to greater self-awareness and self-mastery, she achieves a mature self-possession that creates the freedom to sacrifice for others and to give herself. "This freedom presupposes that one is able to direct sensual and emotional reactions in order to allow the *gift* of self to the other 'I,' *on the basis of the* mature *possession* of one's own 'I'" (TB 652).[18]

Parents and mature children, disciplined by self-reflection and virtue, are guided by this "law of the gift." Children learn to live in moral solidarity with others. They are pre-disposed to take some responsibility for the destiny of others, especially the less fortunate. The family, therefore, is also a means for personalizing a society that has become desensitized to personal dignity. "The family," writes John Paul II, "possesses and continues still to release formidable energies capable of taking man out of his anonymity, keeping him conscious of his personal dignity, enriching him with deep humanity, and actively placing him, in his uniqueness and unrepeatability, within the fabric of society" (FC 43).

In summary, the family is a community of persons based on marital communion and complementarity. Its primary mission is to serve life and welcome children, educating those children by shaping their humanity and moral character so they can live out their own vocation to interpersonal communion. A person "cannot exist alone" (MD 7). Every person exists in his or her fullness only as a "we" who reaches out toward others to share his or her gifts and to receive the gifts of others in return. Marriage and family is the paradigmatic form of this "we." Schools and other civic associations facilitate the process of socialization. But only the family performs a "personalistic and communal function" which makes the family a natural and irreplaceable institution (PC 342).

The Domestic Church

The family is referred to as a "domestic church" in *Lumen Gentium*, but there is little elaboration on what this description really means. John Paul II's

---

18 Clarke, *Person and Being*, 59–61.

deeper reflections on this notion represent a major development in the theology of the family. He explains that the family is a domestic church or "church in miniature" because it participates directly in the mystery of Christ and His Church (FC 49). What does this mean? Quite simply, the family is an intimate communion that shares in the saving mission of the Church. The Christian family is not an ordinary social structure nor a self-enclosed unit isolated from doing the work of evangelization. Rather, it is called to play an original and specific role in the Church's mission to save souls.

The Pope clarifies that there is a sacramental grounding for this vision of the family. By virtue of the sacrament of marriage, which "takes up again and makes specific the sanctifying grace of baptism," parents and children receive Christ's love and become a *saved community* (FC 56). But they are also called upon "to communicate Christ's love to their brethren, thus becoming a *saving community*" (FC 49; my emphasis). In this way, the family becomes a "fruit and sign of the supernatural fecundity of the church" (FC 49). The family, therefore, is an essential part of the Church — it is not just an iconic image of Christian fellowship, but an ecclesial reality by virtue of this sacramental foundation.[19]

The family's sharing in the Church's mission should follow a community pattern whereby the family, as a community of one heart and soul, lives out its calling of service to the Church and the world. The family builds up the kingdom of God, not necessarily through extraordinary deeds, but through everyday realities that typify its state in life. The family's openness to life, for example, demonstrates generosity. Also, through faithful love between spouses and between parents and children, lived out in "totality, oneness, fidelity, and fruitfulness," the family participates in the salvific work of Jesus Christ and realizes its sacred mission (FC 50). Love and life therefore constitute the essence of the saving mission of the Christian family.

Many families are simply unaware of their vocation to evangelize and save souls. The Pope exhorts the family "to *become* what you *are*," to live out this vocation more zealously (FC 17). The family must be transformed into the domestic church it is supposed to be by closely following in the steps of Christ, who is prophet, priest, and king. Thus, in emulation of

19   Ouellet, *Mystery and Sacrament of Love*, 100–104. In addition to Cardinal Ouellet's treatment of this issue I am indebted to Owen Vyner, "The Family in the Life and Mission of the Church," in *God and Eros*, 162–76.

Christ, every family must aspire to be "1) a believing and evangelizing community; 2) a community in dialogue with God; 3) a community at the service of man" (FC 50).

The family fulfills its first prophetic role by embracing and announcing the Word of God. Christian spouses and parents must live their lives in the "obedience of faith" (FC 51). Like the whole Church, the family must be constantly evangelized, and this implies an ongoing education in the faith. Parents communicate the faith to their children, but also receive the same Gospel from them. As the whole family matures in the faith, it becomes an evangelizing community. The family plays a pivotal role in the new evangelization by reinvigorating those who have lost the faith. As the Pope explains, "the future of evangelization depends in great part on the church of the home" (FC 52). The family must also stress the importance of ecclesial service. A family open to God's call and a life of service becomes fertile ground for vocations to the priesthood and religious life.

Second, the Christian family is a sanctified community in dialogue with God. Through the sacrament of marriage, the family is constantly vivified and strengthened by Jesus Christ. Through the sacraments and daily prayer, it is also engaged in dialogue with God and thereby fulfills its priestly role. The Eucharist becomes a life-giving and unifying principle for the Christian family. The bonds within and among families are fortified when family members are drawn closer to union with the Body of Christ. "By partaking of the Eucharistic bread," writes the Pope, "the different members of the Christian family become one body, which reveals and shares in the wider unity of the Church" (FC 57). Families must also accept the call to conversion and repentance through frequent use of the sacrament of penance.[20]

Third, the Christian family is a community of service. As a kingly people, it is called "to exercise its 'service' of love toward God and toward its fellow human beings" (FC 63). Inspired by the example of Jesus Christ, the Christian family welcomes, respects, and serves every human being. This respect and service begins within the family but extends to the wider community. The family should be especially sensitive to the poor, the marginalized, and those who suffer. Thus, the Christian family "places

---

20 Vyner, "The Family in the Life and Mission of the Church," 167.

itself at the service of the human person and the world" (FC 64). Families must resist the enticement of secular ideologies like materialism and individualism, which threaten this mission of the domestic church by turning people inward and making them more self-absorbed.

Now that we understand what it means for the family to be a domestic church, we can better comprehend the full mission of the family. In *Familiaris Consortio*, the Pope indicates that this mission includes "forming a community of persons; serving life; participating in the development of society; sharing in the life and mission of the church" (FC 17). The family bears witness to God's great love for humanity and helps to create the "civilization of love" (LF 12).

The Sovereignty of the Family

As a community of life and love, the family is an institution and a "sovereign society" (LF 17). Those who endorse modern society's tendencies to individualism might assert that the individual is the fundamental unit of society. This implies that an individual's welfare supersedes the good of the family. But the Pope insists that the common good of the family takes priority and constitutes the basic cell of society. The family has primacy over the state and the right to pursue its common good without the interference of the state. This sovereign status of the family is based on the permanence of marital unity, which is the effect of spousal love. Love and self-giving at the heart of marriage create permanent bonds and dependencies that cannot be matched by other institutions.

What is implied by the family's sovereignty? First, the family has intrinsic value. This means that its dignity and elevated status are not bestowed or removed by the state. Living in a family is necessary and natural because it is indispensable for achieving those goods and virtues that fulfill us as persons. Each person "flourishes within the sphere of his own family" (RH 14). It also means that parents do not derive their authority from the state. Parental authority is neither delegated nor withdrawn by the state, but exists independent of government authority. Only parents have the knowledge, capacity, and loving disposition to properly care for their children. There is nothing comparable to a mother's nurturing relationship with her child, nor the protective care of a benevolent and wise father.

Second, sovereignty means that the family is the subject of rights. These rights are closely linked to the rights of the person. They are essential for the family and its members to thrive and flourish. In *Familiaris Consortio* John Paul II identifies a thick set of rights that will protect the family from the encroachment of the state, which often seeks to usurp the family's authority. What are some of a family's fundamental rights? Families have the right to exercise responsibility for the transmission of life and education of their children. They have a right of religious liberty, to profess and propagate their faith. And they have the right to raise children according to the family's own traditions along with its religious and cultural values. Along those lines, families have the right to safeguard their children from harmful drugs, pornography, and alcohol. There is also a right to the "intimacy of conjugal and family life," which would seem to include reasonable privacy rights (FC 46). The family has several political and economic rights defended by the Pope, such as the right to property and housing, along with the right to "form associations with other families and institutions" in order to carry out its role in society (FC 46).

The state must respect these rights and abide by the fundamental principle of subsidiarity, a doctrine that has been central to Catholic social teaching. According to that principle, frequently cited by the Pope, every superior society must support and help lower societies, but they should not assume the functions that the lower societies can perform. Thus, education is the fundamental responsibility of the parents, but their educational mission must be supported by the Church and the state. Thanks to the principle of subsidiarity, that assistance finds an "absolute limit" in the "prevailing rights and actual capabilities of parents" (LF 16). Parents have a right to determine how their children will be educated: public school, private school, or home school. That decision will be based on many factors, including the capabilities and background of the parents. The state has no prerogative to insist that all children be educated in its public schools. Nor can the state oppose home schooling if parents have the capability to teach their own children. According to the Pope, "only in those situations where the family is not really self-sufficient does the State have the authority and duty to intervene" (LF 17).

The most persuasive justification for the family's sovereignty lies in the indissolubility of marriage. The stability of the marital union, which anchors the family community, stands in contrast to the transience and unpredictability of political institutions and social agendas. Moreover, the family is uniquely capable of moral formation because it is a communion of love, and love is foremost among the virtues. By word and deed, a mother and father can teach their children the meaning of an intimate communion (I-Thou) in a way that impersonal institutions cannot. Children witness the mutual self-giving of their parents, which can be emulated as they mature into adults. In the family, children form the habit of love, which is then shared with friends, neighbors, and the wider community. The mutual self-giving of husband and wife "is the model and norm" for the family and its relationships (FC 37). Also, parents, who intimately know their children, are far better equipped than the state to define and communicate a vision of the good life. That vision will be based on the needs and temperament of their children and consistent with their cultural and religious traditions. The state can only offer a bland and uniform vision that rarely accommodates cultural and religious diversity.

Unfortunately, the family's sovereignty is under severe duress and its rights are being routinely suppressed. There is enormous pressure to take the moral education of children out of the hands of parents, especially when it comes to matters of sexuality. The state claims that it is filling a vacuum by providing "sex education," but in reality it is only making concessions to powerful pressure groups seeking to press their own social agendas. One such pressure group is same-sex marriage activists. In a relentless drive for social acceptance of same-sex marriage, these activists have been able to push their agenda throughout many public school districts in the name of diversity and tolerance. The end result has been a terrible defeat for family sovereignty.

In Ontario, for example, the government has refused to let parents opt out of those sections of a controversial sex-education program that deal with homosexuality and gender identity. The Canadian Education Act allows for such parental discretion, but it has been overridden by local authorities. The curriculum contains explicit sexual content, including instruction about masturbation and homosexual practices. Elementary school students will be taught that a household with two mothers or two fathers is perfectly normal, and that any criticism of such marital arrangements reflects a lack of tolerance. Nothing is said in the program about chastity or sexual abstinence before marriage. This is an egregious example of how the state, instead of parents, determines the moral beliefs children should have about sexuality.[21]

Such common policies bluntly ignore the sound principles of family sovereignty and subsidiarity. Parents have a right and a duty to resist any instruction that is inconsistent with *"God's own saving pedagogy"* (LF 16). Same-sex marriage is not just a diversity issue, as some courts have blithely proclaimed. It's also a moral and religious issue. Jesus places his own teaching on marriage in the context of a long moral tradition that begins in Genesis: "Have you not read that He who made them from the beginning made them male and female, and said, 'For this reason a man shall leave his father and mother and be joined to his wife, and the two shall become one?' So they are no longer two but one. What therefore God has joined together let no man put asunder" (Mt 19:4–6). Christians, therefore, rightfully believe as a basic tenet of their faith that marriage can only be between a man and a woman and that other sexual relationships cannot be morally valid. Schools and courts may not concur, but they should at least respect a parent's right to teach this belief to shield impressionable young children from contrary views that will confuse and agitate them.

In addition, schools and other public institutions have no qualms about distributing condoms to adolescent children without their parents' knowledge or consent. Those who support these programs contend that this action is necessary in the name of "public health." This policy also grossly interferes with the sovereignty of the family. Children who are taught sexual abstinence by their parents find themselves confronted with a contradictory message, and often they are not yet mature enough to handle this type of conflict. Also, contraception is not health care, since it interferes with the body's normal reproductive function. There are obvious limits to the family sovereignty if real health issues are being ignored by parents. But one would be hard-pressed to justify condom distribution as a health imperative that must be undertaken despite parents' principled objections.[22]

21 Reilly, *Making Gay Okay*, 166–72. See also Pete Baklinski, "Ontario School Board Tells Parents They Cannot Opt-Out of Gay Lessons," *Lifesite News*, September 3, 2015, accessed, January 3, 2016, https://www.lifesitenews.com/news/ontario-school-board-tells-parents-they-cant-opt-out-of-gay-lessons.
22 Germain Grisez, *Difficult Moral Questions* (Quincy, IL: Franciscan Press, 1997), 833–34.

The Mission of Fatherhood and Motherhood

Mothers and fathers have distinct roles to play in the upbringing of their children. Attempts to deconstruct and relativize the family are destined for abject failure because they refuse to acknowledge that these complementary roles, based on the dual unity of humanity, were established by the Creator. Unfortunately, modern society is plagued by fatherlessness, which has led to the family's precipitous decline. Family sociologists like David Popenoe describe the human "carnage" of fatherless families. Children without fathers are far more likely to have emotional and behavioral problems. Nevertheless, some feminists continue to insist that fatherhood is merely a social role that can be replaced. Are fathers really necessary? These feminists answer "no," or at least "maybe not."[23]

However, John Paul II was convinced that the absence of the father causes psychological and moral imbalance within the family. The Pope's perception aligns with abundant sociological evidence. Researchers have demonstrated that family instability caused by detached or absent fathers predisposes young girls to risky sexual behavior. On the other hand, the prolonged presence of a "warm and engaged father" can shield girls against such promiscuous conduct. A biological father's protective instinct and caring concern for his children cannot be simply "transferred" to someone else.[24]

Within the family community, therefore, a man must assume his irreplaceable role as a responsible husband and father. According to the Pope, a man is called "to ensure the harmonious and united development of all members of the family" (FC 25). He performs this task by exercising generous responsibility for the life conceived by the mother of his children, by commitment to education, and by his work, which never divides the family but promotes its unity and stability. He also gives witness to the Christian faith and introduces children to Christ and His Church. The father's ultimate mission is to "reveal and relive on earth the very fatherhood of God" (FC 25). Every child should be able to faintly behold the face of divine paternity in his or her human father.

---

23 Popenoe, *Life Without Father*, 8–19. See also Yenor, *Family Politics*, 203–20.

24 Melvin Konner, "The Link Between Detached Dads, Risk-Taking Girls," *The Wall Street Journal*, June 3, 2017, C2.

The father has a leadership role within the family that demands a unique kind of authority. This authority is not to be confused with domination or control, but is based on service to the family. The father acts for the common good of the family, sometimes making difficult decisions when consensus cannot be reached, in order to ensure the family's harmony and "unified development." The exercise of authority is a "radiation of fatherhood" that reflects God the Father's loving care for His children (RF 341).[25]

John Paul II puts particular emphasis on the role of women in the family and in society. He famously spoke about woman's "feminine genius" and its many manifestations in the world (MD 32). Mary is the highest expression of feminine genius. Mary, the "handmaid of the Lord" (Lk 1:38), graciously accepted her vocation as wife and mother, and through this service "was able to experience in her life a mysterious, but authentic 'reign'" (LW 10). Womanhood "was lived in such a sublime way by Mary," who so thoroughly dedicated her life to others (LW 10).

We can begin to comprehend a woman's feminine genius by reflecting upon motherhood. "*The mystery of femininity,*" writes the Pope, "*manifests and reveals itself in its full depth through motherhood*" (TB 210). Motherhood involves a special communion with the mystery of life as a baby develops within the mother's womb. Pregnancy has been called a "school" of feminine genius, since it enables a woman to develop the habit of welcoming and caring for the other. This unique contact with the new human person developing within her "gives rise to an attitude towards human beings… which profoundly marks the woman's personality" (MD 18).

This attitude that arises in mothers who welcome new life is a poignant unfolding and reinforcement of the feminine genius that can flourish in any woman. Feminine genius means that a woman is more capable of paying attention to persons she encounters, even those "invisible" creatures who have been marginalized by society. She more spontaneously perceives the person as "someone" of inestimable value, always worthy of loving-kindness. According to John Paul II, "Perhaps more than men, women acknowledge the person, because they see persons with their hearts. They see them independently of various ideological or political

---

25 William May, "The Mission of Fatherhood," *Josephinum: Journal of Theology* 9 (2002): 42–55.

systems. They see others in their greatness and limitations; they try to go out to them and help them" (LW 12). This attitude of "feminine genius" is cultivated more easily in women, especially mothers, but it is not confined to women. Also, it is not found in every woman.[26]

Motherhood is a special manifestation of feminine genius. A woman's physical constitution, which enables conception, pregnancy, and birth, is naturally disposed to motherhood. But motherhood is not reducible to biology and psychology. Motherhood must also be understood on the basis of the personal dimension of the gift of self. Through that gift to her husband, she signifies her generous readiness to accept new life within her. That same giving of self becomes especially evident in a mother's selfless devotion to her child, which is not easily matched by the father's love. Mary is the model of motherhood. She freely and generously conceives a child, rejoices in that child's birth, and dutifully cares for that child until he reaches manhood.

Human parenthood is shared by man and woman but is lived out more fully in the woman, especially in the prenatal period. Carrying a child and giving birth consume a woman's energies. In their shared parenthood the husband owes a great debt to his wife. The man "always remains 'outside' the process of pregnancy and the baby's birth; in many ways he has to *learn* his own *'fatherhood' from the mother*" (MD 18). A woman becomes a mother naturally by giving birth, but there is no equivalent natural transformation for the father.

Both parents are indispensable, but the mother's contribution is decisive in laying the foundation for this new human personality. The woman is uniquely disposed to receive new life and to give that life the loving and constant care it requires. Thus, the woman's primary role is to nurture that child, while the father's primary role is to protect and provide for his wife and children. Mothers accept and encourage their children, while fathers challenge and discipline them in order to ensure family harmony. These complementary roles are by no means mutually exclusive, but represent different emphases within the family structure.[27]

In his writings on the family and motherhood, the Pope also reviews the role of women in society. He realizes that some women will have to

26 Susan C. Selner-Wright, "St. John Paul II on the Genius of Woman," in Lemmons, *Woman as Prophet*, 11–18.
27 May, "The Mission of Fatherhood," 49–51.

work outside the home for economic reasons and remarks that they should enjoy the same rights and opportunities as men to perform various public functions. However, even in these situations the husband-father does not abdicate his role as provider and protector. The pope also encourages us to recognize that the work of a woman who devotes herself to a child's upbringing is comparable to other forms of professional work. Ideally, society should be structured so that mothers are not compelled to work because of financial constraints. Moreover, the modern mentality that honors women more for their work outside the home than for their work within the family must be overcome. Society should encourage the creation of conditions conducive to allowing mothers to remain at home to raise their families.

It is especially critical to refute deformed views of freedom, which regard motherhood and child-rearing as a restriction on a woman's autonomy or her opportunities for a career. Even worse is the tendency of some secular feminists to seek liberation from the "tyranny" of their feminine bodies so that they are not constrained by the burdens of pregnancy and motherhood. This effort to negate the generative meaning of the body undermines the great potential of motherhood to develop the feminine personality. Not every woman is called to the vocation of motherhood. But those who are so called can achieve spiritual maturity and find themselves through this vocation of service. The mother shares with the father in the noble task of shaping the life of a human person so that he or she can live life in the manner of a gift. According to the Pope, "being a mother not only endows her feminine personality, directed toward the gift of life, with its full development, but is also an answer of faith to woman's own vocation" (JPSW 292).

Conclusions

The family is based on the marital bond and rooted in the communion and complementarity of man and woman. When spouses mutually give and accept each other in a manner proper to the marriage covenant, they form a communion of persons. This conjugal *communio* is the "*natural* foundation" of the family (PC 339). Thanks to the gift of new life, the marital bond becomes the parental bond, and when a child is born the marital communion becomes a family community.

In addition to serving life in this way, parents have the responsibility to make "a gift of mature humanity to this little person, this gradually developing human being" (PC 334). While social institutions like schools can aid in the process of socialization, the family is essential for the more important task of personalization — helping young people to grow in mature self-possession so that they become moral persons capable of sincere self-donation.

The family is not just an ordinary social organism but also a domestic church, which shares in the mystery of Christ and His Church. Thanks to the sacraments of marriage and baptism it is a saved community, but it must become a saving community. The Christian family emulates Jesus Christ as prophet, priest, and king. Hence, it must be an evangelizing community, a community of prayer and devotion, and a community of service to others.

To accomplish its lofty mission as domestic church and educator of children, the family must enjoy a high degree of sovereign power. Sovereignty, which is grounded in the permanent union of the married couple, implies the priority of the family over the state and civil authorities. It also implies that the family unit is the subject of fundamental rights. The claim of family sovereignty was one of the major innovations in John Paul II's social magisterium that deserves more careful attention.

Every child's upbringing must include contributions from a mother and father, but mothers have a particularly integral role to play. A mother is especially prepared to welcome and nurture new life. Thanks to her maternity and feminine qualities, a woman "has a genius all her own, which is vitally essential to both society and the Church" (JPSW 276). Women who are tempted by secular feminism's trivialization of motherhood should seek inspiration in the life of Mary, who was totally fulfilled by caring for her husband and son.

John Paul II often communicated his apprehension about the escalating attacks on motherhood and family life. Pornography, same-sex unions, cohabitation, and no-fault divorce are evidence of a confused society that "has broken away from the full truth about man" (LF 20). The traditional family is being slowly dismantled with the help of the "father of lies," who "constantly seeks to draw people to broad and easy ways" (LF 23). It is urgent to restore a proper vision of the family, because "the history of mankind, the history of salvation, passes by way of the family" (LF 23).

TEN

Marriage and the Culture of Life

THE 1960S MARKED THE INCEPTION OF A REMARK-
able transformation of American values. John F. Kennedy was
elected President in 1960, in a tight race that brought an abrupt
end to the Republicans' control of the White House. The liberal Kennedy
struggled in some parts of the country, but performed well enough in traditional Democratic enclaves to beat the Republican, Richard M. Nixon,
by a razor-thin margin. The Kennedy people who took over Washington
were young, ambitious, and aggressive. At the time, there was an incipient
impatience with inherited moral norms and traditional pieties, along with
great faith in social progress. Kennedy himself, who always seemed cool
and secure in his beliefs, was a persuasive spokesman of the progressive
creed. His powerful convictions and resolute manner stirred crowds
across the country. In speech after speech, this favorite son of Boston and
Harvard conveyed the pressing need to move the country forward rather
than "lie at anchor and drift."[1] The Kennedy style and eloquence was only
possible in a world that had not yet been corrupted by the vulgarities of
America's partisan politics.

Although born Roman Catholic, President Kennedy was detached
from traditional Catholicism. He had little interest in Catholic doctrine
or tradition. He was generally indifferent to the Church's social teachings and to the distinct scholastic pedigree of its theology. Kennedy felt
some fellowship with the popular Pope John XXIII, who died in 1962,
but this was based more on this great Pope's personal character than on
any theological affinity. Kennedy was not a typical American Catholic,

---

1 Quoted in Arthur Schlesinger, *A Thousand Days: John F. Kennedy in the White
House* (Boston: Houghton Mifflin, 1965), 75.

and he demonstrated to his many Catholic followers that there was no conflict between Catholicism and modernity. In retrospect, we can mark this period as a significant moment in the triumph of modern secularism, with its unshakeable belief in the progressive tendency of history.[2]

Arguably, Kennedy's rather laissez-faire attitude toward the faith, the natural result of his pragmatic and anti-metaphysical intellect, helped to galvanize liberal American Catholicism in the 1960s. That version of Catholicism was open and accommodating rather than dogmatic and self-assured. It was marked by a willingness to compromise fundamental doctrinal principles, even if this meant tolerating moral innovations such as artificial birth control. During this same decade, prominent Catholic leaders suggested that Church history was a living channel of revelation, with the self-revealing *Logos* adaptable to new situations.[3] This new attitude about the faith accounted for the disillusionment of so many American Catholics over the teaching of *Humanae Vitae*. There was dismay about the post-Conciliar Church's lack of resiliency. Liberal theologians confidently assumed that the Church must recognize the current historical moment, when men and women were being invited to assume greater responsibility for their own moral development.

The Kennedy era promised change, and by the later part of this tumultuous decade the cultural landscape was changing at an alarming pace. At the same time, the moral fabric of the country was becoming hopelessly frayed. The echoing sound of collapsing moral certitudes could be heard throughout Western culture. A moral code based on tolerance and pluralism was slowly taking hold. The institution of marriage was beginning to display symptoms of deep distress. The extended family structure was unraveling. The convenient birth control pill helped to suppress the procreative meaning of sexuality in the minds of many couples. Abortion no longer affronted the moral sensibility of the cultural elite, especially those in institutions like universities and the media. When abortion on demand virtually became the law of the land in 1973 thanks to *Roe v. Wade* (and its companion case, *Doe v. Bolton*), most people acquiesced

2 Ibid., 107–10. See also James A. Patrick, "Benedict XVI: Unwinding the Age of Kennedy," in *Essays on Modernity*, ed. James A. Patrick (Fort Worth, TX: Tower Press, 2015), 115–24.
3 Avery Dulles, "The Theology of Revelation," *Theological Studies* 25 (1964), 53–55.

to this exceptional change in the country's moral consciousness. They simply accepted the court's faulty reasoning that the unborn are not "constitutional persons" and therefore have no rights. Even Catholic leaders, committed to the pro-life cause, were skeptical that they could reverse the march to an abortion culture, where there is little regard for the sanctity of life in the womb.

During this chaotic time, the use of contraception grew exponentially. Supporters justified contraceptive intercourse by arguing that there was no necessary connection between sexual union and procreation. People could have sex to procreate, but they could also have sex for the pleasure and intimacy it provides. However, dissolving this connection has led to many disastrous consequences, such as the social acceptance of same-sex marriage. If marriage is not centered on children but on self-fulfillment, why not let same-sex couples "fulfill" themselves in this way? Abortion is another subtle effect of the contraceptive mentality that rejects the pro-creative purpose of sexuality. If contraception fails, will a couple take the next logical step and prevent the unwanted birth by means of abortion?

In this final chapter, we explore in more depth the relationship between contraception and abortion, along with the moral problems associated with artificial procreation. At the center of this moral disorder is man's desire to exercise unrestricted dominion over sexuality and even human life itself. Medical technology now equips us with awesome capabilities that are often deployed in a moral vacuum. As a consequence, modern society's Promethean attitude has created a brittle anti-life, eroticized culture that puts fruitful marriage and family at great risk. Despite rhetoric to the contrary, the family flourishes in a culture of love, and a culture of love can only be a culture of life.

Spousal Love, Sexuality, and Fruitfulness

Consistent with Scripture and the Catholic tradition, John Paul II insists that the marital act must always be generative and unitive and that it cannot be one without the other. Only a unitive act that is generative by nature can express the reciprocal self-giving of spousal love, which is defined by total union, absolute fidelity, and fruitfulness. "Conjugal love," he writes, "involves a totality...[and] aims at a deeply personal unity" (FC 13). Love must be open to life and therefore always potentially fruitful. Otherwise, there cannot be a total bodily and spiritual self-gift that is the essence of marriage.

Both spousal love between a man and a woman and procreation are rooted in the sexual drive. The Pope describes the body and its sexual drive as the "substratum" or foundation for spousal love and the communion of persons (TB 248). Similarly, he explains that "procreation is the proper end of the sexual drive" (LR 39). Thanks to their sexual powers, a couple can fully express their spousal love by becoming a one-flesh union that can beget new life. Thus, there is a deep interconnection between sexuality (based on sexual difference), spousal love, and procreation.

Sexual relations, love, and procreation are so intimately bound together that a person cannot have one apart from the other two without substantially changing the meaning of all three. It's not possible, for example, to segregate procreation from spousal love and human sexuality by technical means without converting procreation into mechanical production. Also, unless two married persons come together as a total one-flesh union that is open to life, their sexual union will not be an expression of spousal love or conjugal communion. Instead, it will begin to resemble selfish self-gratification. And if sexuality and procreation are not mutually implied, spousal love loses its essential meaning, since the "rich content" of sexual difference is negated (TB 292). Yet sexual difference, which is the basis of reciprocal attraction, makes possible the totality of the gift that distinguishes spousal love from all other forms of love.[4]

However, our ambient culture has largely succeeded in obliterating this interconnection for the sake of convenience and utility. In past decades, we have witnessed a willingness to isolate procreation from spousal love. On one hand, children are sometimes conceived, not as the fruit of love between two parents, but as the end product of technologies like in vitro fertilization and gestational surrogates. The routine application of human cloning and gene editing to create children may soon be on the horizon. On the other hand, contraception of all stripes removes potential fruitfulness from spousal love and drives a wedge between the unitive and procreative meanings of the conjugal act. According to the Pope, "when

---

4 Scola, *The Nuptial Mystery*, 125–28.

couples...separate these two meanings that God the Creator has inscribed in the being of man and woman and in the dynamism of their sexual communion,...they 'manipulate' and degrade human sexuality" (FC 32).

In addition, under the banner of the sexual revolution, sexuality has been detached from both spousal love and procreation. Thanks to changing social mores, it is perfectly acceptable to indulge in recreational sex without love, commitment, or the possibility of procreation. Inspired by Freud and his disciples, the sexual drive has been redefined as the drive for pleasure and sexual delight. This false interpretation of human sexuality conceals the real purpose of the drive, its "objective finality linked to procreation" (LR 48). It also nullifies the spousal meaning of the body, which is "the antithesis of the Freudian libido" (TB 312). But what are the adverse consequences of dissolving the interrelationship of sexuality, spousal love, and procreation and how does it affect marriage and family? We address this question in the remainder of the chapter.

Contraception and Abortion

The Catholic Church teaches that in order to preserve the integrity of the marital act, a married couple cannot have sexual relations and deliberately prevent that act from being fruitful. Nonetheless, many Catholics have chosen to engage in contraceptive intercourse, either out of moral indifference or ignorance. Contraceptive intercourse fails to take into account the moral truth about the inseparability of the unitive and generative aspects of the sexual act. Unless a married couple's sexual act is open to procreation, it cannot represent the marital union of their shared lives as a whole. The couple is not relating to each other as husband and wife or as potential mother and father. When the act is sterilized and fertility is withheld, they relate to each other, not as spouses, but more so as sexual partners where each one becomes "a means of pleasure" (LF 12). When the attitude of parental readiness is absent, the sexual act cannot express marital or spousal love.[5]

Contraceptive intercourse violates the natural language of the body by closing off the marital act from the procreation of new persons and

---

5 Kampowski and Crawford, "The Wisdom of *Humanae Vitae*."

the possibility of a marriage's greater fulfillment as a family. Contraception reflects an anti-life attitude, since it always involves the deliberate impeding of a new human life. The new person who might be the fruit of conjugal love is not welcome. The Pope interprets this anti-life attitude as part of the larger antipathy to life that bedevils modern society. Sexual pleasure-seeking and lack of solidarity with potential new life reflects a utilitarian mentality that does not sufficiently value the great gift of life. From a utilitarian perspective, life can be sacrificed for an apparent greater good, such as professional ambitions or the material welfare of a couple. The failure of contraception to prevent the conception of unwanted life, therefore, could easily induce a couple to take further steps, like abortion, for the sake of these objectives. According to the Pope, "If an individual is exclusively concerned with 'use,' he can reach the point of killing love by killing the fruit of love. For the culture of use, the 'blessed fruit of your womb' (Lk 1:24) becomes in a certain sense an 'accursed fruit'" (LF 21).

As Pope Paul VI's encyclical observed, acceptance of contraception tends to foster tolerance for other forms of sexual immorality, including extreme moral turpitude, such as abortion. He even warned about the prospects of forced abortion in some countries. Abortion is an intrinsic evil and an indefensible crime against life. We must recognize that even at conception there is a complete human being with its entire genetic identity. This new human organism has the intrinsic potential to develop into a mature and rational human being. Some make the case that in the early stages of its existence as an embryo and fetus, the body exists without the soul, and, until there is a soul, there is no person. But can a human body come into being and properly develop without the soul? John Paul II, following the philosophical reasoning of Aquinas, makes a compelling case that the body and soul form a harmonious unity, so that there can never be a living human body without a spiritual soul. For Aquinas, the soul makes someone a living human organism and makes its bodily functions human. Hence, the soul must be infused by God at the moment of conception: "When a new human being is conceived, then a new spirit is also conceived, a spirit that is substantially united to the body and whose embryo begins to exist in the womb of the woman-mother" (LR 39).

Thus, the embryo or the fetus in the womb is not a potential person but a person with potential. This living human organism is a person from the moment of conception, with the radical capacities to think and make choices, even if it cannot actually exercise those capacities at this stage of its young life. Animal embryos lack these capacities altogether—a cat will never be able to think or do mathematics. But once a child is born and matures, these capacities become activated. The moral gravity of procured abortion becomes apparent when we face the reality that "the one eliminated is a human being at the very beginning of life" (EV 58). Even the *Roe* court acknowledged that human life might really begin at conception. But it still expanded abortion rights because of the "detriment that the state would impose upon the pregnant woman by denying her" a virtually unrestricted abortion liberty.[6]

This is no place to talk at length about the sinister effects of legalized abortion. But consider just one of the devastating consequences that flow from society's recourse to abortion to solve its problems. During the protracted debates over President Obama's Affordable Care Act, pro-choice advocates insisted that those who oppose abortion on demand and free contraception are engaged in a "war on women." However, the real war on women is not about depriving women of free contraceptives but the unrelenting attack on female babies, particularly in countries like India and China. Predictably, sex selection has become a major reason for aborting a child, since many families regard daughters as a liability. In the past three decades, 163 million female babies have been aborted by parents who preferred to have sons. In India there are 112 boys born for every 100 girls, and in China the ratio is 118 boys for every 100 girls. Sociologists call attention to the fact that these high sex ratios lead to "surplus men," with no hope of marriage or a family of their own. Also, societies with such a surplus have historically been more violent and unstable than societies where the ratio of boys to girls is normal. Manipulating nature has portentous consequences for social cohesion and moral order. This calculated "gendercide" is the tangible legacy of the secular culture's dream of unrestricted abortion.[7]

In *Evangelium Vitae* John Paul II explicitly discussed the tight connection

---

6 *Roe v. Wade* 410 U.S. 113 (1973), 153.

7 Jonathan Last, "The War against Girls," *The Wall Street Journal*, June 18, 2011, C5–6. See also Mara Hvistendahl, *Unnatural Selection: Choosing Boys over Girls and the Consequences of a World Full of Men* (New York: Public Affairs, 2011).

between contraception and abortion. While contraception and abortion are not morally equivalent, they are nonetheless "fruits of the same tree" (EV 13). This is because they both typically flow from a hedonistic mindset "unwilling to accept responsibility in matters of sexuality" (EV 13). This lack of sexual responsibility is precisely the link between contraception and abortion. In defiance of the natural order, couples want to have sex without any procreative consequences, and so they modify their behavior accordingly.

The contraceptive mentality magnifies the temptation to seek out an abortion when contraception fails and this unwanted life is conceived. Some spouses or unmarried couples who contracept will be reluctant to assume responsibility for the new life they have begotten. They have chosen a course of action that aims to preclude that new life, and yet for some reason their choice has been frustrated and the woman finds herself pregnant. The unwanted child is now perceived as an annoyance and even a threat to their future. The result is a strong temptation to resolve this problem by simply visiting the closest abortion clinic. As the Pope explains, "the negative values inherent in the 'contraceptive mentality'... are such that they in fact strengthen this temptation [for abortion] when an unwanted life is conceived" (EV 13).[8]

Thus, in the minds of some couples who contracept, there is a logical transition from contraception to abortion. For those who indulge in casual sex, procreation is almost always regarded as an obstacle to personal fulfillment and unrestrained pleasure. The pursuit of sex for its own sake inevitably induces the subversion of the conjugal act's natural purpose. There is no acknowledgment that a sexual encounter, which makes man and woman "one flesh," is a *moment of special responsibility...the result* of the procreative potential linked to the conjugal act" (LF 12). Similarly, married couples who reject the link between sexuality and procreation can also adopt this same hostility toward life. When they lose sight of new life as a precious gift, they can succumb to the temptation to abort a child, an event that is destined to have a corrosive effect on any marriage.

There is more than sufficient evidence to substantiate the Pope's strong thesis about this connection. People predicted that the use of contraception

8 Rhonheimer, *Ethics of Procreation*, 118–20.

would mean a big drop in the number of abortions, but that has not been the case. Between 1973 and 1989, when contraception use was probably at its peak, there were twenty-one million abortions in America. A study of abortions performed in California revealed that 40 percent of the abortions done in that state were traceable to one reason: failed contraception.[9] Social scientists have also demonstrated how the sexual revolution, abetted by birth control devices, has led to a dramatic increase in both illegitimacy and abortion.[10] Moreover, the methods or technologies for contraception and abortion overlap so they become hard to distinguish. Many contraceptive technologies act in an abortifacient manner. The so-called "morning after pill," for example, is an abortifacient but it is promoted as another form of contraception. It is also just as readily available as contraceptive devices.

Even the courts have conceded that there is a close association between contraception and abortion. Thanks to their obsession with autonomy and egalitarianism, they have enshrined the "rights" to both contraception and abortion in the name of "gender equality." The courts have presumed that for the sake of equality with men, women must be emancipated from the burden of pregnancy. This principle has been a persistent theme in federal abortion jurisprudence. In *Planned Parenthood v. Casey*, for example, the U.S. Supreme Court reaffirmed broad abortion rights. It opined that those rights "could not be repudiated without serious inequity to people who, for two decades of economic and social developments, have organized intimate relationships and made choices that define their views of themselves and their places in society, in reliance on the availability of abortion in the event that contraception should fail."[11] This statement is a stunning acknowledgment that the Pope is absolutely right when he declares that contraception and abortion are fruits of the same tree: the desire to have sex without any procreative consequences.

Some theologians and clerics, who readily acknowledge the sinfulness of abortion, have been hesitant to admit this linkage between abortion

9   This data was provided by Rhomberg, McCaffrey, Riehle, and Wiliken at the 1988 World Conference on Love, Life, and Family, and is cited in Rhonheimer, *Ethics of Procreation*, 122.

10   Mary Eberstadt, *Adam and Eve after the Pill* (San Francisco: Ignatius Press, 2012), 137–38.

11   *Planned Parenthood of Southeastern Pa. v. Casey* 505 U.S. 833 (1992).

and the contraceptive mentality. They contend that the moral evil of abortion committed by a woman at an abortion clinic is far removed from a woman taking the pill in her bedroom to avoid an unwanted pregnancy. However, as the Pope has been at pains to insist, while they certainly differ in moral gravity, both abortion and contraception have the same aim: to prevent a prospective baby from being born. A married couple may have valid reasons for not wanting another baby, but they have wrongly ruled out periodic continence and natural family planning, which respects life along with a woman's natural fertility cycles. Unmarried couples have powerful motives to avoid the procreative consequences of their immoral act. Not only would this event disrupt their lives, but giving birth under these circumstances would be an injustice to this child. In all these cases, contraception represents an attitude of hostility towards life because that new life might interfere with unrestricted sexual activity. Unfortunately, the social acceptability of sterilization, contraception, and abortion is viewed as a "mark of progress and victory of freedom" (EV 17). But exercising absolute power over others, including the unborn, annihilates true freedom. In reality, these medical technologies are the implacable foes of freedom and marriage.

Freedom is secured by conformity to the truth, and so couples can only be free if they respect the truth about the sanctity of life and the procreative purpose of the sexual drive. The optimal way to eradicate the anti-life mentality now embedded in our legal and cultural institutions is to retrieve the traditions of sexual morality and responsible parenthood that were so cavalierly discarded in the 1960s. That tradition acknowledges the unbreakable bond between spousal love, sexuality, and procreation, for this is the way we find conjugal love "in the beginning," before the fall. "It is an illusion to think," declares the Pope, "that we can build a true culture of human life if we do not help the young to accept and experience sexuality and love and the whole of life in their true meaning and in their close interconnection" (EV 97).

Reproductive Technologies and Artificial Procreation

A married couple should avoid the positive exclusion of new life through contraception. On the other hand, they should not be overly preoccupied with the procreative aim of the sexual act so that it becomes a virtual obsession. Sexual union should never be simply a means for procreation. In *Love and Responsibility*, Wojtyła rebuked the philosophy of "rigorism," which claims that sexual relations are not an expression of love but solely a means to ensure the continuation of the human race. This rigorist conception of sexuality follows to some extent the ancient Manichean (or Gnostic) tradition, which degrades the human body and its sexual powers as an evil principle alien to the soul. This perception of the body is still embraced by "spiritualists" who lack the proper balance in their approach to sexual matters (LR 44). Rigorism implicitly condones the couple's using of each other to "produce" a child. Love is purely spiritual, so there is no love involved in conceiving a child, only a couple's pragmatic sexual interaction. Procreation, however, cannot be separated from conjugal love and the mutual self-donation expressed by the sexual act. When this happens, we end up with impersonal breeders instead of loving parents.

The attempt to isolate procreation from spousal love and mutual self-donation is precisely what happens with most forms of artificial procreation. These reproductive technologies, such as in vitro fertilization, surrogacy, and cloning, are proposed as practical solutions to resolve the problem of infertility. Many people, including Catholics, view artificial procreation with complacency, and some enthusiastically endorse these procedures. But there are dangerous implications when the child is coolly viewed as an object of choice or a commodity rather than a gift, a person begotten by the love of his or her parents. Artificial procreation bears a strange resemblance to abortion, since in both cases we find the unsavory conviction that one person can be the possession of another person. As with abortion, so with artificial procreation, "life becomes a mere 'thing,' which man claims as his exclusive property, completely subject to his control and manipulation" (EV 22). The mystery of personal created being and the sexual drive's "existential meaning" is conveniently suppressed. Also, far from being life-affirming, as they are often portrayed, these reproductive technologies can actually open the door for a new breed of threats against life.

The practice of in vitro fertilization (IVF) is especially popular for parents who have a difficult time conceiving a child. The process begins with the collection of eggs from a woman's ovary after she has taken fertility drugs. Those drugs are designed to induce the maturation of a number of eggs at the same time. Semen is collected from the man, usually by means of masturbation. The egg and sperm are united in a petri dish with a chemical solution designed to stimulate fertilization. The fertilized egg or embryo is then transferred into the woman's womb. Sometimes doctors implant several embryos, hoping that one will grow to maturity. But if too many embryos begin to mature inside the womb, there may be need for "selective reduction," a euphemism that describes the termination of the embryo. In most cases both the egg and sperm come from a married couple, while in other cases a third party might donate the eggs or sperm. When this happens, the mother or father of this child will be someone outside the marriage.[12]

Regrettably, artificial reproduction is not just a solution to infertility. Same-sex couples, who believe they have the same right to children as heterosexual couples, must depend on this technology to generate a family. The legalization of same-sex marriage has shifted social mores towards a more widespread endorsement of reproductive technologies as normative and morally equivalent to natural procreation. Natural fatherhood and motherhood lose their privileged status, since they are construed as mere accidents of biology. What matters is the functional roles of motherhood and fatherhood rather than natural kinship. "The eternal mystery of generation…reflected in the woman's motherhood and man's fatherhood" is reduced to a technological process under man's total control (MD 18).[13]

Of course, there are many ethical problems associated with this process of artificial procreation. Common IVF procedures include the production of "spare" embryos, the disposal of unusable embryos, and the selective reduction of embryos implanted in the womb. Yet these practices, along with the freezing or storage of embryos without the definite prospect of transferring them to a mother in a timely manner, fail to respect human life. In these cases, prospective parents and doctors make judgments about the lives of others who are treated as a mere means to an end, in clear violation of the personalistic norm. The well-being and interests of

12 John Haas, "Begotten Not Made: A Catholic View of Reproductive Technology," United States Conference of Catholic Bishops (1998), accessed June 28, 2017, http://www.usccb.org/issues-and-action/human-life-and-dignity/reproductive-technology/begotten-not-made-a-catholic-view-of-reproductive-technology.cfm.

13 Hanby, "Civic Project," 37.

the embryo, who is already a person, are usually disregarded in these life and death decisions.[14]

The major problem with the use of these technologies, often by well-intentioned parents who cannot have children, is that they objectify the newborn child, who can no longer be seen as a gift begotten by the love of his or her parents. Therefore, the child is brought into existence through mechanical means as the "product of conception," which is the label used by pharmaceutical companies. According to John Paul II, this manipulative technology "wants to substitute true paternity and maternity and therefore does harm to parents and child alike."[15] There is nothing wrong with the child herself who is conceived in this way. Obviously, that child should be loved and cared for by her parents. The problem lies with the crude means of his or her conception, which treats that child in a sub-personal way.

These moral deficiencies linked to artificial procreation were clearly elaborated in the Vatican document *Donum Vitae* ("Gift of Life"). This instruction was not written by Pope John Paul II, but it appeared during his papacy in 1987. It was authored by the Congregation of the Doctrine of the Faith and given explicit approval by the Pope. *Donum Vitae* affirms that there is nothing wrong with medical intervention when it helps a couple achieve pregnancy. The problem arises when such intervention becomes a substitute for the marital act itself. In vitro fertilization clearly falls in the latter category. According to this instruction, in vitro fertilization using the wife's ovum and husband's sperm "entrusts the life and identity of the embryo into the power of doctors and biologists and establishes the domination of technology over the origin and destiny of the human person" (DOV 6). Technology replaces the marital act in a way that diminishes the value of spousal love, which is experienced in the language of the body and the union of persons.[16]

Giving in to this technological and cultural imperative may seem prudent in an age where technology is allowed to shape human destiny.

---

14 John Finnis, "C. S. Lewis and Test-Tube Babies," in *Human Rights & Common Good*, ed. John Finnis (Oxford: Oxford University Press, 2011), 273–81.

15 Pope John Paul II, "Address of John Paul II to the Members of the Pontifical Academy for Life" (Rome, February 21, 2004), accessed April 11, 2016, http://w2.vatican.va/content/john-paul-ii/en/speeches/2004/february/documents/hf_jp-ii_spe_20040221_plenary-acad-life.html.

16 Scola, *The Nuptial Mystery*, 130–33. See also Haas, "Begotten Not Made."

Reproductive technologies are welcomed because they appear to expand our freedom by opening up new horizons, especially for infertile couples. However, their use means that the vision of spousal love, with all its Trinitarian resonance, is displaced by a cruder vision of biologism. Sexuality, procreation, and spousal love are essentially tied together. When they are severed, persons are no longer faithful to their given nature as images of God.

As a result, John Paul II has repeatedly insisted that children must be the fruit of marital love and are always to be welcomed and received as a gift. All generation among human creatures "finds its primary model in that generating which in God is completely divine" (MD 8). Just as the Spirit eternally proceeds from the love of the Father and the Son, so children are the fruit of love between husband and wife. In an analogous sense, the child, like the Holy Spirit, "is the personal expression of this self-giving, of this being-love." (DV 10). Procreation, therefore, cannot be detached from spousal love. It must be based on freely given love and total sharing in a way that is "proper to the unity of the two" (MD 8).

"Producing" a child in a test tube, however, bears absolutely no likeness to divine eternal generation, so it is ultimately an affront to that child's dignity, who is not the fruit of spousal love. The problem is particularly severe if the child is not genetically connected to both parents. A child can suffer in many ways when she learns that her mother or father is not her biological parent. Children intuitively understand the importance of natural kinship for the proper development of their own self-identity. As *Donum Vitae* observes, "It is through the secure and recognized relationship to his own parents that the child can discover his identity and achieve his proper human development" (DOV 1). Hence, according to the Pope, it is "gravely illicit" to use these artificial methods of procreation.[17]

We can infer from John Paul II's earlier writings that artificial procreation is not just an affront to the dignity of the child, but to the parents as well. There is something morally offensive when a spouse becomes a

17 Pope John Paul II, "Halt the Production of Human Embryos," May 24, 1996 (unpublished address), accessed October 17, 2016, https://www.ewtn.com/library/PAPALDOC/JP960524.htm. See also Laura Garcia, "Protecting Persons," in *John Paul II's Contribution to Catholic Bioethics*, ed. Christopher Tollefsen (Dordrecht: Springer, 2004), 100–104.

parent by means of the genetic contribution of a third party who intrudes upon this conjugal relationship. Even if that is not the case, the dignity of both parents is diminished through artificial procreation. Their sexual powers are being used to help the cause of procreation (for example, a man's masturbation for semen) in a way that is completely detached from spousal love. Also, it is beneath the dignity of both spouses to allow their genetic material to be harvested by technicians and then used to make a new child. The unnatural production of sperm and egg is a violation of the personalistic norm, because a person's body and its procreative powers are being instrumentalized for the purpose of producing life in a test tube.[18]

There is certainly nothing wrong with a husband and wife who have an ardent desire to bear a child. But a married couple should not become so preoccupied with this goal that their attention is diverted from one another in acts that involve their sexual powers. "*Marriage,*" according to Wojtyła, "*is an institution of love and not only of fertility*" (LR 220). But artificial procreation can temporarily reduce a couple's marriage to an institution of fertility. To focus so intently on becoming a parent that one loses sight of the interpersonal giving and receiving of spousal love does an injustice to both persons in the marital relationship. According to Wojtyła, "Becoming a mother or father is accomplished in virtue of the conjugal act, which itself should be an act of love, an act of uniting persons, and not merely a 'tool' or a 'means' of procreation" (LR 220).

Similar problems also arise with the related technology of gestational or traditional surrogacy. In traditional surrogacy, the surrogate mother has supplied the egg and carries the implanted embryo to full term. In gestational surrogacy, the surrogate mother has not provided the egg and has no biological connection with the fetus that she is carrying. Surrogate mothers are sometimes hired for a fee to carry the child. These paid surrogacy arrangements are handled by brokers who find surrogate mothers for "intended parents."

Surrogacy is morally problematic because it manifests a lack of respect for the special nature of the procreative process and the origin of human life. According to *Donum Vitae*, surrogacy is "contrary to the unity of marriage and to the dignity of the procreation of the human person" (DOV 9).

---

18 Garcia, "Protecting Persons," 100–101.

Unfortunately, surrogacy is on the rise, thanks in part to the legalization of same-sex marriage. Male couples, for example, "use" a woman to bear a child from an implanted embryo containing one of the couple's sperm. The allure of large fees often induces poor women to become paid surrogates. A surrogate mother, however, is typically oblivious of the health risks and cannot anticipate the strength of her bond with the child. Also, none of the parties seems to care what happens when the child is handed over to his parents and is abruptly cut off from that natural maternal bonding. Surrogacy is an unnatural act that violates every child's basic right to be conceived in an act of love by a mother and father, nurtured in the womb, and given birth by his or her own mother.

Surrogacy treats the child as a pawn or commodity who can be bought and sold. However, a child is not a commodity, and so there are endless juridical disputes, along with irresolvable legal ambiguities, about the meaning of parenthood and motherhood. In a famous case in Australia, a couple who hired a surrogate mother to bear their child refused to take the child when it was born with Down's syndrome. This poor child was perceived not as a person but as a damaged product who could be "returned" to the producer. All too often, if the baby produced through artificial procreation is handicapped or becomes seriously ill shortly after birth, the parents become disillusioned and the child becomes a source of dissatisfaction.[19]

In California, a forty-seven-year-old gestational surrogate named Melissa was implanted with three male embryos using the sperm from a single man (C. M.) and an egg from an anonymous donor. C. M. is a fifty-year-old deaf postal worker who lives with his parents. He suddenly decided that he wanted to be a single father, and he hired a broker to make this surrogacy arrangement. Three embryos were implanted to increase the chances that one would survive. In this case, they all survived, and Melissa was soon pregnant with triplets. C. M. is not a wealthy man and didn't bargain for triplets, and so he demanded that at least one of the

19   Arland Nichols, "Why Surrogacy Violates Human Dignity," *Crisis*, April 7, 2015, and Christopher White, "Surrogacy Gives Birth to an Unusual Alliance," *The Wall Street Journal*, September 5, 2014, A11. See also Joseph Cavello, "The Real Costs of the Infertility Industry," *Catholic World Report*, June, 2015, accessed December 18, 2016, http://www.catholicworldreport.com/2015/06/16/the-real-costs-of-the-infertility-industry.

fetuses be aborted. Melissa refused to have an abortion, even though the contract allows C. M. to request a "selective reduction." She offered instead to adopt the unwanted baby, but C. M. would not agree to this alternative. A contentious legal case ensued. Many feminist groups sided with Melissa because they oppose coerced abortion. As the case lingered in the courts it became too late for an abortion. But Melissa filed another lawsuit claiming custody of the triplets; her lawyers argued that as the mother of these triplets she has parental rights. They further maintained that C. M. was not capable of raising triplets. One provocative issue in the case concerns the meaning of motherhood. Is the mother the donor of the egg, or is it Melissa, who bears these children in her womb for nine months? Her lawyers argued that the mother-child bond during pregnancy is preeminent and is not dependent on genetics. However, there is little legal precedent for asserting the parental rights of a gestational surrogate. This unfortunate incident illustrates the profound moral problems associated with surrogacy: technically "producing" a baby using many different parties, and relying on legal contracts crafted in a commercial setting to set the rules for conception, pregnancy, and delivery of that baby.[20]

A number of countries have banned surrogacy completely, while others have forbidden only commercial surrogacy. Commercial surrogacy is illegal in Canada and most of Europe. In the United States, some states, like California, have liberal surrogacy laws that allow for commercial surrogacy with few constraints. Only a handful of states, such as New York and New Jersey, prohibit commercial surrogacy. Others allow it, but with strict restrictions. However, those prohibitions and restrictions are being challenged, and surrogacy laws are slowly but steadily becoming more permissive. Despite the California case of Melissa and C. M., and many others like it, there is an expanding sentiment that gestational surrogacy is essential for those gay and straight couples who cannot build a family without it.[21]

The rise of in vitro fertilization and surrogacy should be no surprise in a world that has turned its back on the Creator and lost "contact with

---

20 Michelle Goldberg, "Is a Surrogate a Mother?," *Slate*, February 15, 2016, accessed, September 1, 2016, http://www.slate.com/articles/double_x/doublex/2016/02/custody_case_over_triplets_in_california_raises_questions_about_surrogacy.html.

21 Cavello, "The Real Costs of the Infertility Industry."

God's wise design" (EV 22). Man is called to have dominion over nature, but these reproductive technologies defy "the fundamental truth about the birth of man in the image of God, according to the laws of nature" (TB 213). They manifest a technological Prometheanism that acknowledges few moral bounds. Dominion over nature does not mean dominance over human life, which belongs to God. God, who creates the human soul and sustains us in existence, is *the sole Lord of this life*" (EV 39). Human life is in the hands of God's power, but also in the loving hands of others "like those of a mother who accepts, nurtures, and takes care of her child" (EV 39). The responsibility of parents is not to assert dominion over life, but to serve life by giving space to the divine creative act. Thus, responsible procreation must acknowledge and heed the Creator's original plan for the transmission of life. What does this mean? Quite simply, children are always to be begotten by a loving mother and father, and they are not to be produced in a laboratory or nurtured to life in a rented womb.[22]

We cannot suppress the use of these reproductive technologies until we retrieve the original meaning of the sexual act, which is unitive and generative, and always an expression of spousal love. Once we recover this view of sexuality, occluded by sin and hubris, people will readily realize that it is unthinkable to conceive a child in any other way than as the fruit of the total mutual self-gift of the conjugal act. Children are a gift from God, and a gift is to be received graciously, not willfully appropriated.

Conclusions

Marriage and family thrive in a "civilization of love," but we have become a "civilization of production and use" (LF 13). Human life is perceived as a commodity, "a mere 'thing,' which man claims as his exclusive property, completely subject to his control and manipulation" (EV 22). As a result, the birth of a child is no longer considered a gratuitous event in the life of a family or a fruit of a married couple's love, but as something completely dependent on the sovereign will of the parents. Safe sex and free love are zealously defended, but they are subversions of love. Even many married couples search in vain for "fairest love" (LF 13). However, the truth and

22 Rhonheimer, *Ethics of Procreation*, 166.

beauty of marital love will be rediscovered only by acknowledging the natural connection between spousal love, sexuality, and procreation. The severance of this connection is baseless, and arguments on its behalf contort common moral sense. This unbreakable linkage finds its theological justification in the Creator's plan for man and woman first presented in Genesis. It also finds moral justification in the nature of spousal love.

Yet this connection has been dissolved in several ways. Many people engage in casual sex that does not express a union of persons open to new life. At the same time, contraceptive intercourse severs the bond between sexuality and procreation by removing the potential for fruitfulness. Those who use contraception sometimes resort to abortion to deal with an unwanted child if the contraceptive technique fails. Although contraception and abortion are not morally equivalent, they are fruit of the same tree that bears the mark of an "anti-birth mentality" (LF 13).

Finally, in the name of reproductive liberty, technologies isolate procreation from spousal love and sexual union. Artificial means of procreation, such as IVF and surrogacy, substitute technology for the marital act open to new life. But the choice to produce a baby in this sub-personal way is an unjust means to a worthy end. Asexual reproduction rejects the truth that "the divine 'we' is the eternal pattern of the human 'we'" (LF 6).

The justification for infertile couples and doctors making these choices is moral autonomy and full reproductive freedom. But John Paul II has always insisted that the moral life is about *theonomy*, our reason's participation in the light of eternal wisdom, which is expressed in the divine law. Man is not so free and independent that he can exercise sovereignty over human life itself. Infertility does not absolve any couple from abiding by God's providential plan. All married couples are called to share in the divine work of creation, but in a manner consistent with the order of nature, which reflects the divine order. The moral law about responsible procreation is an expression of divine wisdom, so when a person submits to the law, he or she lives according to the truth of creation.[23]

---

23 Germain Grisez, "Biology and Christian Ethics," *National Catholic Bioethics Quarterly*, 1 (2001): 33–38. See also Grisez, *Living a Christian Life*, 267.

Epilogue

FATHER WOJTYŁA WAS A DEVOTED PARISH PRIEST, but his parish work lasted for only a few years. After finishing his second doctorate in philosophy at the Jagiellonian University in Krakow, Wojtyła was appointed to the Chair of Ethics at Catholic University of Lublin in 1956. He had concentrated his studies on the work of the great ethicist Max Scheler. By all accounts, Wojtyła was a popular and inspiring teacher and never had trouble filling even the largest of Lublin's lecture halls. Every seat was occupied and latecomers would have to sit on the floor or the windowsills. Students waited expectantly for class to begin, and soon the unfashionable scholar would appear at the podium wearing an ill-fitting and frayed cassock over drab olive pants. His lively lectures engaged the thought of Scheler along with other great philosophers like Plato, Aristotle, and Kant. But he did not neglect the practical side of ethics. Sexual ethics was a recurrent theme.[1]

Wojtyła enjoyed the years he spent at Lublin with its many enticements, including an outstanding group of colleagues. But the arrival of 1958 marked another turning point in the young professor's life. The year had begun with a conference for physicians at the Church of the Felician Sisters in Krakow. Along with his usual teaching duties, Father Wojtyła met weekly with the Polish doctors over the course of several months. He lectured them about their vocation, medical ethics, and even about love and compassion. Some of these talks echoed familiar themes in *Love and Responsibility*. "To love," he said in one presentation, is "to assume responsibility for another person. To see what is his benefit. To be him to the extent that one simply acts somewhat in his name. To understand what is good for him, sometimes better than he himself understands."[2]

---

1 Garry O'Connor, *Universal Father: A Life of John Paul II* (New York: Bloomsbury, 2005), 134–35.

2 Boniecki, *Making of the Pope of the Millennium*, 170.

In addition to a demanding schedule of teaching at Lublin, Wojtyła also gave a day of recollection in Krakow to married couples and another one for the young. Similar mini-retreats were held in June for students at Lublin, along with a pastoral course for the priests of Krakow. As summer progressed, the weary professor looked forward to an August excursion with young friends to the lake region of the Tatras, where cooling breezes brought relief from the summer heat. The trip was a welcome diversion from his intellectual and pastoral work. But in the early morning hours of August 6, as the stars overhead faded into a bluish sky, Wojtyła left the group to meet with Cardinal Wyszynski, the Archbishop of Warsaw. The Cardinal informed him that he had been nominated to serve as auxiliary bishop of Krakow. Would he accept? Wojtyła quickly gave the required "canonical consent," and then returned to kayaking. On September 28, 1958, the feast of St. Wenceslaus, he was consecrated a bishop in Wawel Cathedral. Six years later, in 1964, he became the Archbishop of Krakow.

The Pope later explained the special influence of personalism on his pastoral work as priest and bishop. This philosophy inspired him to safe-guard the personal and distinctive qualities of each relationship, since "every person is a chapter to himself" (RW 66). One of Bishop Wojtyła's favorite duties was pastoral visits, which took place each year in spring and fall. In one of his memoirs, he regrets not being able to visit all of Krakow's 300 parishes in his 20 years as bishop. But he admits that this was probably because his visits were too long. Almost every one of his visitations included a special gathering in the church for all married couples. Mass was celebrated and each couple received Bishop Wojtyła's blessing. The homily, of course, was dedicated to the topic of marriage. He was especially exhilarated at the sight of a big family: "I always felt moved when I encountered large families and expectant mothers, and I wanted to express my respect for motherhood and fatherhood" (RW 76).

This extraordinary pastoral sensitivity for married couples and fam-ilies has been quite evident throughout Wojtyła's ministry to the people of God. It has also given birth to many of the works we have considered here that disclose the profound enigma of love and marriage. Perhaps the greatest threat to marriage originates in the "crisis of meaning" that plagues modern society (FR 81). People now assume that they have the power to reinvent the meaning of sexuality and marriage and to reconceive the nature of motherhood and fatherhood. Those who surrender to the forces of secular culture no longer concede that marriage is naturally oriented to procreation and the education of children. The confusion is compounded by the rejection of our "human nature as a 'given reality'" along with the obfuscation of sexuality's creative powers (MI 12). As a result, we don't know who we are anymore. In the words of philosopher Elizabeth Anscombe, few appreciate "the mystical value" of the human person.[3]

However, we cannot attain "the core of the moral truth" about sexuality and marriage without the "anthropological truth" (TB 638). Thus, the Pope sought to restore the proper anthropological foundation for marriage, which must be centered on *personhood, gift, and communion*. These three principles pervade John Paul II's discussions of love, marriage, and family. The embodied person, gifted with self-possession and self-governance, is a social being. He was not made to be "alone" or to be self-sufficient, and therefore he needs a "helper." These two words from Genesis (2:18) capture "how fundamental and constitutive the relationship and the communion of persons is for man" (TB 182). This communion or "unity of the two" is created through mutual self-donation, which generates a lasting bond. When human life is devoid of this generosity, there can only be self-dissipation rather than fulfillment. Self-donation requires *freedom from* egoism and self-centered desires and *freedom for* life as a gift for the other. Communion with other persons, and ultimately with God Himself, is the source of human fulfillment and perfection. "To be human," explains the Pope, "means to be called to interpersonal communion" (MD 7).

Arguably, the Pope's greatest contribution to modern discourse about marriage is his affirmation of the body, designed by the Creator with its "generative" and "spousal" meaning. The body is not sub-personal, but belongs to our personal reality and subjectivity. The body is a vital part of that gift of self that forms communion. The human body "in its masculinity and femininity is oriented from within to the communion of persons" (TB 652). Sexual difference and fertility, therefore, are never in opposition to freedom, as something to be controlled or suppressed.

3 Elizabeth Anscombe, "Murder and the Morality of Euthanasia," in *Human Life, Action and Ethics,* eds. Mary Geach and Luke Gormally (Exeter, UK: Imprint Academic, 2005), 260.

Rather, they are a means for man and woman to live life together freely and fruitfully in the manner of a gift.

Self-giving is not incidental to human perfection. Inscribed in every person is the "law of the gift," which reflects the expansive generosity of being itself. Interpersonal self-sharing and receiving is the only way to create an "authentically personal union" that will fulfill our longing for truth, goodness, and happiness (LR 288). Self-donation originates in more basic forms of love, which always affirm the other person for his or her own sake. Love implies a "striving" for the good of the other, and a "uniting of persons" (LR 78). In *Love and Responsibility*, Bishop Wojtyła concentrates on the special character of spousal love, an exclusive, mutual belonging whereby a man and woman dedicate themselves fully to each other. Every type of love involves reaching beyond ourselves in order to concentrate our attention on the other person, but none are as far-reaching as spousal love.

Unlike friendship or parental love, spousal love has a sexual nature, since a man and woman give themselves totally (body and soul) to each other in accordance with the fruitful nature of their spousal bodies. The body is the means and sign of this unbreakable union of persons, which is deeper and stronger than sensuality or emotion. Recreational or contraceptive sex undermines spousal love because it transforms the human subject into a sexual object. When the conjugal act is "deprived of its inner truth…it ceases to be an act of love" (TB 633).

Unless a person chooses to dedicate him or herself to God, the vocation to spousal love is lived out within the institution of marriage. Marriage is not just a social institution or a legal contract. Nor is marriage something external to the person superimposed from without. On the contrary, marriage proceeds from "the interiority of spousal love" and the need to give ourselves totally to another person (LR 293). Marriage is a covenant, a communion of love, sealed by the sacramental bond and confirmed by the language of the body. From the logic of spousal love and the Gospel, it follows that marriage is defined by three fundamental properties: real and total unity, absolute fidelity, and fruitfulness. As a result, marital union must always be heterosexual, monogamous, indissoluble, and open to life.

Total union requires sexual complementarity, and this means that marriage can only be between a man and a woman. The truth about marriage hinges on the words of the creation account: "Man and woman He created

them" (Gn 1:27). Only a man and a woman, who are the same and yet
sexually different, can be a total gift for each other in a way that creates a
fruitful communion of persons. Indissolubility is an interior requirement
of this total interpersonal giving and receiving of spousal love. Marriage
epitomizes unconditional self-giving, and a gift is always permanent. God
Himself wills indissoluble marriage as "a fruit, a sign, and a requirement of
absolutely faithful love" that reflects Christ's love for His Church (FC 20).
Exclusivity, which is reinforced by the bodily nature of spousal love, is also
at the heart of the marriage vocation. It is only possible to give one's whole
self to one other chosen person. Finally, only a potentially fruitful union
can be a union of persons in which a man and a woman relate to each other
as husband and wife and fulfill the purpose of marriage. The marital act
must be unitive and procreative, and it cannot be one without the other.
Conjugal intercourse is a free and total gift of persons only if there is no
interference with its "full meaning" and "procreative finality" (LR 294).

It is not easy to live up to these requirements, but married couples
have at their disposal the sacramental graces that accompany the married
state. Marriage is the sacred sacrament of creation, but also the sacrament
of redemption instituted by Christ to assist the man of concupiscence,
heavily burdened by the heritage of original sin. Despite that heritage,
marriage remains the "platform" for the realization of God's eternal plans.

This fruitful marital union implies that marriage is a vocation to parenthood and achieves even greater fulfillment as a family. The family is a
community of persons where children must be valued for their own sake
and formed into mature persons who can become a gift for others. In order
to fulfill this role, the family requires sovereign power that is grounded in
"the strength of the family bond" and its exclusive "communal character"
(PC 342). Like marriage, the family is a natural reality where the child
first discovers his or her personal identity. While other institutions can
socialize children, the family is indispensable for "personalization," helping children grow into wise, generous, and morally responsible persons.
The family is also a domestic church: it is a "saved" community but also
a "saving" community, called to spread the Gospel.

The family is "organically linked" to the "civilization of love," a culture
that promotes interpersonal self-giving and receiving (LF 13). But the
family is threatened by forces contrary to a culture of love. Contraception,

abortion, and artificial procreation are the inevitable result of a false sense of freedom that assumes the authority to break the intrinsic connection between spousal love, sexuality, and procreation. When marriage as a "communion of life and love" is misunderstood, there is a refusal to see the child as a gratuitous event, the gift of spousal love. That communion of persons is naturally open to new life, through which it attains greater fulfillment and perfection. However, modern culture suppresses the categories of communion and gift and exalts human freedom instead. Priority is given to the sovereign will of the parents, who impede the transmission of life through contraception. If the child is conceived anyway, there is recourse to abortion. An authentic marital communion naturally resists the intrusion represented by donors and surrogates. But in modern society, if a couple cannot give birth but want a baby, there is recourse to artificial procreation. However, the truth about conjugal union and personhood requires both openness to life and conception of a child only through the conjugal act.[4]

Any attempt to apprehend the nature of love and marriage inevitably brings us to the edge of mystery. The Pope of the Family's meditations certainly cannot fully unveil the great nuptial mystery that plays such a dynamic role in the entire drama of the human condition. But they provide a discerning account of the provident Creator's plan for man and woman as it was conceived "from the beginning."

---

4 Scola, *Nuptial Mystery*, 170.

Further Reading

WORKS BY KAROL WOJTYŁA

Love and Responsibility. Translated by Grzegorz Ignatik. Boston: Pauline Books
& Media, 2013.
Person and Community: Selected Essays. Translated by Theresa Sandok. New York:
Peter Lang, 1993.
The Jeweler's Shop. Translated by Boleslaw Taborski. San Francisco: Ignatius
Press, 1992.
Radiation of Fatherhood. In *The Collected Plays and Writings on Theater.* Translated
by Boleslaw Taborski. Berkeley: University of California Press, 1987.
Sign of Contradiction. New York: Seabury Press, 1979.
The Acting Person. Translated by A. Potocki. Dordrecht, The Netherlands: D.
Reidel Publishing, 1979.
"The Anthropological Vision of *Humanae Vitae.*" Translated by William May.
Lateranum 44 (1978): 123–45. http://www.christendom-awake.org/pages/may/
anthrop-visionjpII.htm.

WORKS BY JOHN PAUL II

Man and Woman He Created Them: A Theology of the Body. Translated by Michael
Waldstein. Boston: Pauline Books & Media, 2006.
Memory and Identity: Conversations at the Dawn of a Millennium. New York:
Rizzoli International Publishers, 2005.
Rise, Let Us Be On Our Way. New York: Warner Books, 2004.
Fides et Ratio. Boston: Pauline Books & Media, 1998.
Gift and Mystery. New York: Doubleday, 1997.
Evangelium Vitae. Boston: Pauline Books & Media, 1995.
Letter to Women. Vatican City: Libreria Editrice Vaticana, 1995. https://w2.vatican.
va/content/john-paul-ii/en/letters/1995/documents/hf_jp-ii_let_29061995_
women.html.
Crossing the Threshold of Hope. New York: Alfred A. Knopf, 1994.
Letter to Families. Boston: Pauline Books & Media, 1994.
Veritatis Splendor. Boston: Pauline Books & Media, 1993.
Mulieris Dignitatem. Boston: Pauline Books & Media, 1988.

Dominum et Vivificantem. Boston: Pauline Books & Media, 1986.
Familiaris Consortio. Boston: Pauline Books & Media, 1981.
Redemptor Hominis. Boston: Pauline Books & Media, 1979.

VATICAN DOCUMENTS

Pope Leo XIII. *Arcanum Divinae Sapientiae*. *Acta Apostolica Sedis* 12 (1879): 385–404.
Pope Pius XI. *Casti Connubii*. *Acta Apostolica Sedis* 22 (1930): 539–92.
Pope Paul VI. *Humanae Vitae*. *Acta Apostolica Sedis* 60 (1968): 481–503.
Congregation for the Doctrine of the Faith. *Donum Vitae*. *Acta Apostolica Sedis* 80 (1988): 88–116.

GENERAL WORKS

Allegri, Renzo. *John Paul II: A Life of Grace*. Cincinnati: Servant Books, 2005.
Anderson, Carl and José Granados. *Called to Love: Approaching John Paul II's Theology of the Body*. New York: Random House, 2009.
Aquinas, Thomas. *Summa Contra Gentiles*. Translated by James Anderson. Notre Dame: University of Notre Dame Press, 1975.
—. *Summa Theologiae*. 5 vols. New York: Benziger Bros., 1948.
Boniecki, Adam. *Making of the Pope of the Millennium: Kalendarium of the Life of Karol Wojtyła*. Stockbridge, MA: Marian Press, 2000.
Budziszewski, J. *On the Meaning of Sex*. Wilmington, DE: ISI Books, 2012.
Clarke, W. Norris. *The Creative Retrieval of St. Thomas Aquinas*. New York: Fordham University Press, 2009.
—. "The Integration of Person and Being in Twentieth-Century Thomism." *Communio* 31 (2004): 434–44.
—. *Explorations in Metaphysics*. Notre Dame: University of Notre Dame Press, 1994.
—. *Person and Being*. Milwaukee: Marquette University Press, 1993.
—. *The Universe as Journey*. New York: Fordham University Press, 1988.
Crawford, David. "Gay Marriage, Public Reason, and the Common Good." *Communio* 41 (2014): 380–404.
Deely, Brooke Williams, ed. *John Paul II Speaks on Women*. Washington, DC: Catholic University of America Press, 2015.
Dziwisz, Stanisław. *A Life with Karol*. New York: Doubleday, 2007.
Eberstadt, Mary. *Adam and Eve after the Pill*. San Francisco: Ignatius Press, 2012.
Finnis, John. *Human Rights and Common Good*. Oxford: Oxford University Press, 2011.
—. "On Retranslating *Humanae Vitae*." In *Religion and Public Reasons*, edited by John Finnis, 344–67. Oxford: Oxford University Press, 2011.
—. *Intention and Identity*. Oxford: Oxford University Press, 2011.
—. "Marriage: A Basic and Exigent Good." *The Monist* 91 (2008): 396–414.
—. *Historical Consciousness*. Toronto: University of Toronto Press, 1990.

Geach, Mary and Luke Gormally eds. *Faith in a Hard Ground: Essays on Religion, Philosophy, and Ethics by G. E. M. Anscombe*. Exeter, UK: Imprint Academic, 2008.

—. *Human Life, Action and Ethics*. Exeter, UK: Imprint Academic, 2005.

George, Robert. "Gnostic Liberalism." *First Things*. December, 2016: 33–38.

Girgis, Sherif, Ryan Anderson, and Robert George. *What is Marriage? Man and Woman: A Defense*. New York: Encounter Books, 2012.

Gneuhs, George, ed. *The Legacy of Pope John Paul II*. New York: Crossroad, 2000.

Grisez, Germain. *Living a Christian Life*. Quincy, IL: Franciscan Press, 1993.

Grygiel, Stanisław. *Discovering the Human Person: In Conversation with John Paul II*. Grand Rapids, MI: Eerdmans, 2014.

Hanby, Michael. "A More Perfect Absolutism." *First Things*. October, 2016: 25–31.

Healy, Nicholas. "The Merciful Gift of Indissolubility and the Question of Pastoral Care for Civilly Divorced and Remarried Catholics," *Communio* 41 (2014): 306–30.

Hebblethwaite, Peter. *Paul VI: The First Modern Pope*. New York: Paulist Press, 1993.

Hogan, Richard and John LeVoir. *Covenant of Love*. San Francisco: Ignatius Press, 1992.

Hütter, Reinhard. "The Virtue of Chastity and the Scourge of Pornography." *The Thomist* 77 (2013): 1–39.

Jonas, Hans. *Philosophical Essays: From Ancient Creed to Technological Man*. New York: Atropos Press, 2010.

Kengor, Paul. *Takedown: How the Left Has Sabotaged Family and Marriage*. Washington, DC: WND Books, 2015.

Kupczak, Jarosław. *Gift and Communion: John Paul II's Theology of the Body*. Washington, DC: Catholic University of America Press, 2014.

Lee, Patrick. "Marriage, Procreation and Same-Sex Unions." *The Monist* 91 (2008): 427–35.

Lee, Patrick and Robert George. *Conjugal Union: What Marriage Is and Why It Matters*. New York: Cambridge University Press, 2014.

Lemmons, Mary, ed. *Woman as Prophet in the Home and the World*. Lanham, MD: Lexington Books, 2017.

Lopez, Antonio. "Marriage's Indissolubility: An Untenable Promise?" *Communio* 41 (2014): 269–305.

Maritain, Jacques. *Creative Intuition in Art and Poetry*. New York: Meridian, 1955.

May, William. "The Mission of Fatherhood." *Josephinum: Journal of Theology* 9 (2002): 42–55.

McDermott, John, ed. *John Paul II on the Body*. Philadelphia: St. Joseph's University Press, 2007.

McInerny, Ralph. *What Went Wrong with Vatican II*. Manchester, NH: Sophia Institute Press, 1998.

Meroni Fabrizio. "Pastoral Care of Marriage: Affirming the Unity of Mercy and

Truth," *Communio* 41 (2014): 438–61.

Nietzsche, Friedrich. *Also Sprach Zarathustra*. Stuttgart, Germany: Philip Reclam, 1951.

Noonan, John. *Contraception*. New York: New American Library, 1965.

O'Connor, Garry. *Universal Father: A Life of John Paul II*. New York: Bloomsbury, 2005.

Ouellet, Cardinal Marc. *Mystery and Sacrament of Love*. Translated by Michelle Borras. Cambridge, UK: Eerdmans, 2015.

Patterson, Colin and Conor Sweeney, eds. *God and Eros*. Eugene, OR: Wipf and Stock, 2015.

Petri, Thomas. *Aquinas and the Theology of the Body*. Washington, DC: Catholic University of America Press, 2016.

Piderit, John. *Sexual Morality: A Natural Law Approach to Intimate Relationships*. New York: Oxford University Press, 2012.

Pieper, Josef. *Faith, Hope, and Love*. San Francisco: Ignatius Press, 1997.

Pruss, Alexander. *One Body: An Essay in Christian Sexual Ethics*. Notre Dame: University of Notre Dame Press, 2013.

Rędzioch, Włodzimierz. *Stories about St. John Paul II*. San Francisco: Ignatius Press, 2015.

Reilly, Robert. *Making Gay Okay: How Rationalizing Homosexual Behavior is Changing Everything*. San Francisco: Ignatius Press, 2014.

Rhonheimer, Martin. *Ethics of Procreation and the Defense of Human Life*. Washington, DC: Catholic University of America Press, 2010.

Rocchetta, Carlo. *Il Sacramento Della Coppia*. Bologna: EDB, 1996.

Schindler, David. *Ordering Love*. Grand Rapids, MI: Eerdmans, 2011.

Schu, Walter. *The Splendor of Love: John Paul II's Vision for Marriage and Family*. Cheshire, CT: New Hope Publications, 2002.

Scola, Angelo. *The Nuptial Mystery*. Translated by Michelle Borras. Grand Rapids, MI: Eerdmans, 2005.

Scruton, Roger. *On Human Nature*. Princeton: Princeton University Press, 2017.

Seifert, Josef. *True Love*. South Bend, IN: St. Augustine's Press, 2015.

Shivanandan, Mary. *Crossing the Threshold of Love*. Washington, DC: Catholic University of America Press, 1999.

Smith, Janet. "The Krakow Document." *Nova et Vetera* 10 (2012): 361–81.

—, ed. *Why Humanae Vitae Was Right: A Reader*. San Francisco: Ignatius Press, 1993.

Spaemann, Robert. *Persons*. Translated by O. O'Donovan. Oxford: Oxford University Press, 2006.

Spinello, Richard. *Understanding Love and Responsibility*. Boston: Pauline Books & Media, 2014.

—. *The Encyclicals of John Paul II: An Introduction and Commentary*. Lanham, MD: Rowman & Littlefield, 2012.

—. *The Genius of John Paul II: The Great Pope's Moral Wisdom*. Lanham, MD:

Sheed & Ward, 2007.

Stein, Edith. *Essays on Woman*. Translated by Freda Oben. Washington, DC: ICS Publications, 1996.

Tanner, Norman, ed. *Decrees of the Ecumenical Councils*. 2 vols. London: Sheed & Ward, 1990.

Tollefsen, Christopher, ed. *John Paul II's Contribution to Catholic Bioethics*. Dordrecht, The Netherlands: Springer, 2004.

Topping, Ryan. *Rebuilding Catholic Culture*. Manchester, NH: Sophia Institute Press, 2012.

Voegelin, Eric. *Science, Politics and Gnosticism*. Wilmington, DE: ISI Books, 2004.

von Hildebrand, Dietrich. *Marriage: The Mystery of Faithful Love*. Manchester, NH: Sophia Press, 1997.

—. *The Nature of Love*. Translated by John Crosby. South Bend, IN: St. Augustine's Press, 2009.

Weigel, George. *Witness to Hope*. New York: Harper Collins, 1999.

West, Christopher. *The Theology of the Body Explained*. Boston: Pauline Books & Media, 2003.

Yenor, Scott. *Family Politics*. Waco, TX: Baylor University Press, 2011.

Zimmerman, Carle. *Family and Civilization*. Wilmington, DE: ISI Books, 2008.

ABOUT THE AUTHOR

Richard Spinello is a Professor of the Practice at Boston College and a member of the adjunct faculty at St. John's Seminary in Boston. He is the author of *The Genius of John Paul II: The Great Pope's Moral Wisdom*; *The Encyclicals of John Paul II: An Introduction and Commentary*; and *Understanding* Love and Responsibility: *A Companion to Karol Wojtyła's Classic Work* — along with numerous other books and articles on ethical theory and applied ethics.